NAVWEPS 01-245FCB-501

Flight Handbook

NAVY MODELS
F3H-2, -2M
AIRCRAFT

THIS PUBLICATION IS INCOMPLETE WITHOUT CONFIDENTIAL
SUPPLEMENT NAVWEPS 01-245FCB-501A

©2009 Periscope Film LLC
All Rights Reserved
ISBN #978-1-935327-73-8   1-935327-73-9

PUBLISHED BY DIRECTION OF
THE CHIEF OF THE BUREAU OF NAVAL WEAPONS

NAVWEPS 01-245FCB-501

Flight Handbook

NAVY MODELS
F3H-2, -2M
AIRCRAFT

THIS PUBLICATION IS INCOMPLETE WITHOUT CONFIDENTIAL
SUPPLEMENT NAVWEPS 01-245FCB-501A

THIS PUBLICATION SUPERSEDES NAVWEPS 01-245FCB-501
DATED 15 JUNE 1960 REVISED 15 DECEMBER 1960

PUBLISHED BY DIRECTION OF
THE CHIEF OF THE BUREAU OF NAVAL WEAPONS

1 May 1961

NAVWEPS 01-245FCB-501

Reproduction for non-military use of the information or illustrations contained in this publication is not permitted without specific approval of the issuing service (BuWeps or AMC). The policy for use of Classified Publications is established for the Air Force in AFR 205-1 and for the Navy in Navy Regulations, Article 1509.

LIST OF REVISED PAGES ISSUED
INSERT LATEST REVISED PAGES. DESTROY SUPERSEDED PAGES.

NOTE: The portion of the text affected by the current revision is indicated by a vertical line in the outer margins of the page.

Page No.	Date of Latest Revision	Page No.	Date of Latest Revision	Page No.	Date of Latest Revision

* The asterisk indicates pages revised, added or deleted by the current revision.

ADDITIONAL COPIES OF THIS PUBLICATION MAY BE OBTAINED AS FOLLOWS:

USAF ACTIVITIES. - In accordance with Technical Order No. 00-5-2.
NAVY ACTIVITIES. - Submit request to nearest supply point listed below, using form NavWeps-140; NAS, Alameda, Calif.; ASD, Orote, Guam; NAS, Jacksonville, Fla.; NAS, Norfolk, Va.; NASD, Pearl City, Oahu; NASD, Philadelphia, Pa.; NAS, San Diego, Calif.; NAS, Seattle, Wash.
For listing of available material and details of distribution see Naval Aeronautics Publications Index NavWeps 00-500.

NAVWEPS 01-245FCB-501

TABLE OF CONTENTS

SECTION

I DESCRIPTION 1

II NORMAL PROCEDURES 49

III EMERENCY PROCEDURES 67

IV AUXILIARY EQUIPMENT 91

V OPERATING LIMITATIONS 117
(Refer to NAVWEPS 01-245FCB-501A)

VI FLIGHT CHARACTERISTICS 119

VII SYSTEMS OPERATION 121

VIII CREW DUTIES (NOT APPLICABLE) ... 130

IX ALL WEATHER OPERATION 131

APPENDIX I OPERATING DATA CHARTS 137
(Refer to NAVWEPS 01-245FCB-501A)

INDEX 139

NAVWEPS 01-245FCB-501

Welcome Aboard!

This handbook with publication NAVWEPS 01-245FCB-501A comprise the Flight Handbook. The manufacturer and the NAVY have presented this information in a form best suited to your use. The descriptions, flight characteristics, techniques and procedures herein enable you to fly this airplane in most efficient and safe manner. All information is based on engineering and service data, plus observations by experienced pilots. Use this handbook for a ready reference. Study the handbook and you study the airplane.

This handbook is subject to revisions and should be kept current throughout the life of the airplane.

This handbook is divided into nine sections and an appendix as follows:

Section I, DESCRIPTION - a detailed description and discussion of the airplane and systems (including emergency equipment that is not part of auxiliary equipment) which are essential for flight.

Section II, NORMAL PROCEDURES - operational instruction sequence from approach to airplane to leaving plane after flight.

Section III, EMERGENCY PROCEDURES - concise procedures for any emergency (except those connected with auxiliary equipment) that could reasonably be expected to be encountered.

Section IV, DESCRIPTION AND OPERATION OF AUXILIARY EQUIPMENT - a description of, and procedure for operating both under normal and emergency conditions, all equipment not essential for flying the airplane. A portion of this section is contained in publication NAVWEPS 01-245FCB-501A.

Section V, OPERATING LIMITATIONS - all operating limitations and restrictions that must be observed during flight. This section is contained in publication NAVWEPS 01-245FCB-501A.

Section VI, FLIGHT CHARACTERISTICS - general flight characteristics both advantageous and dangerous peculiar to the airplane as based on flight tests. This section is contained in publication NAVWEPS 01-245FCB-501A.

Section VII, SYSTEM OPERATION - additional information on special characteristics and factors pertaining to airplane systems under various conditions.

Section VIII, CREW DUTIES - this section is not applicable to single-place aircraft.

Section IX, ALL WEATHER OPERATION - procedures and techniques for proper operation under instrument flight and extreme weather conditions.

Appendix I, OPERATING DATA - operating date for preflight and in-flight planning is presented in publication NAVWEPS 01-245FCB-501A.

HOW TO GET COPIES If you want to be sure of getting your manuals on time, order them as early as possible. Early ordering will assure that enough copies are printed to cover your requirements. Order your publications using form NAVWEPS-140, refer to Flight Manual "A" page to obtain address of nearest supply point. Make sure to establish some system that will rapidly get the manuals, interim revisions, and pocket check list to the flight crews once they are received in your squadron.

Interim revisions are issued as a praid means of promulgating operating limitations, restrictions and other vital operating instructions for specific model aircraft pending incorporation of such instructions into the Flight Manual by Regular Revision. Interim Revisions are identified as to which Flight Manual they are written against by using the same number as the Flight Manual along with the model of aircraft affected. Interim Revisions written against a Flight Manual will start with number one, and will be assigned consecutively in order of issue throughout the life of the Flight Manual. It is important that you remain aware of the status of all Interim Revisions. The interim revision summary in the front of the Flight Manual list the Interim Revisions that have been cancelled or have been incorporated in the Flight Manual.

POCKET CHECK LIST A pocket check list has been published to provide, in abbreviated form, essential information for flight crews engaged in the operation of the aircraft. The pocket check list (NAVWEPS 01-245FCB-1B) is not distributed automatically with the Flight Manual, and therefore, should be ordered as a separate publication. The check list is printed on cardboard stock with tab pages, and is designed to be fastened to the pilots need pad.

WARNING, CAUTIONS, AND NOTES For your information, the following definitions apply to the "Warnings", "Cautions", and "Notes" found throughout the manual:

WARNING

Operating procedures, practices, etc., which will result in personal injury or loss of life if not carefully followed.

Operating procedures, practices, etc., which if not strictly observed will result in damage to equipment.

Note

An operating procedure, condition, etc., which it is essential to emphasize.

REVISION SYMBOL

Revised text is indicated by a black vertical line in the outer margin opposite the Revised text.

NAVWEPS 01-245FCB-501

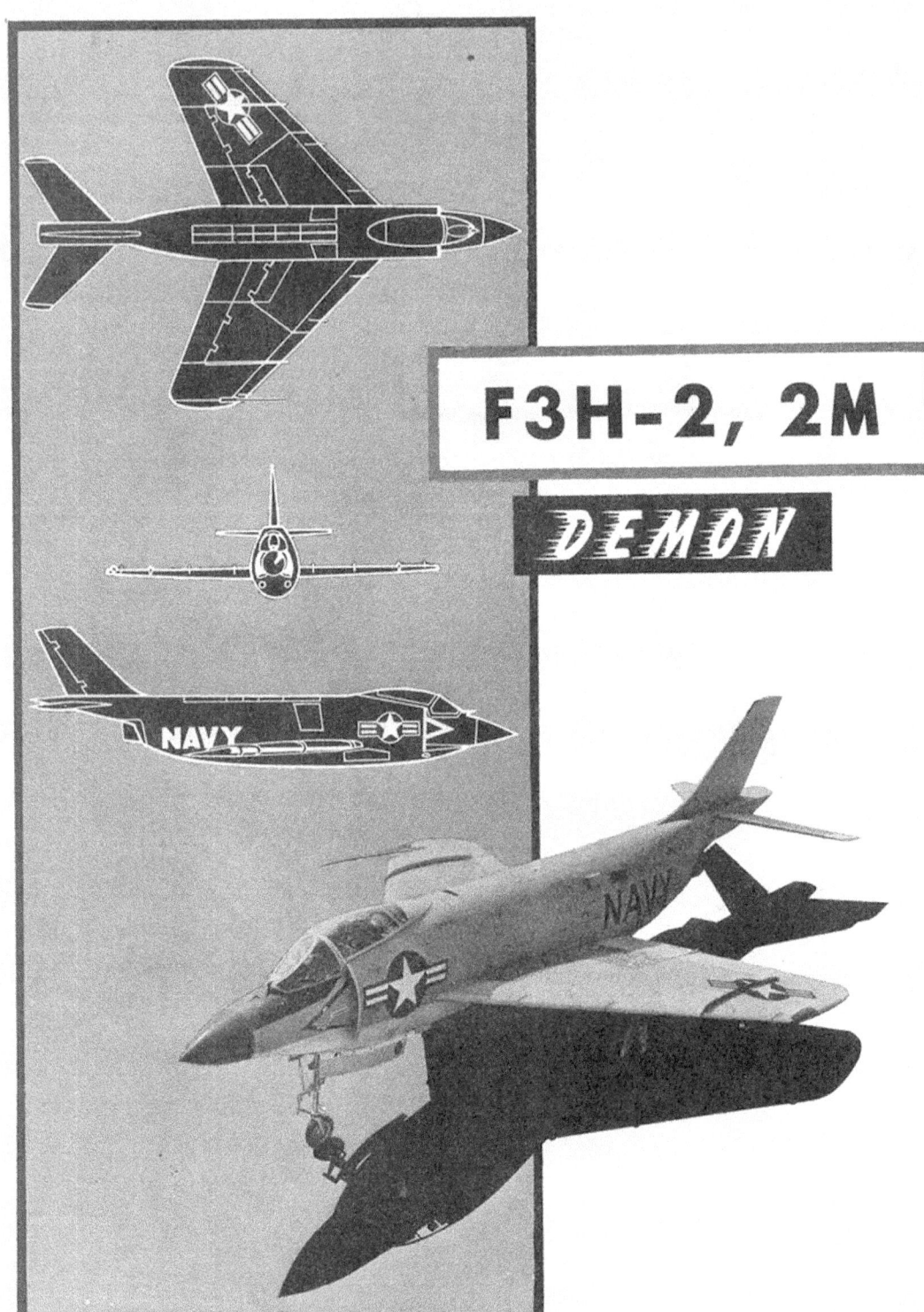

F3H-2, 2M
DEMON

Section I DESCRIPTION

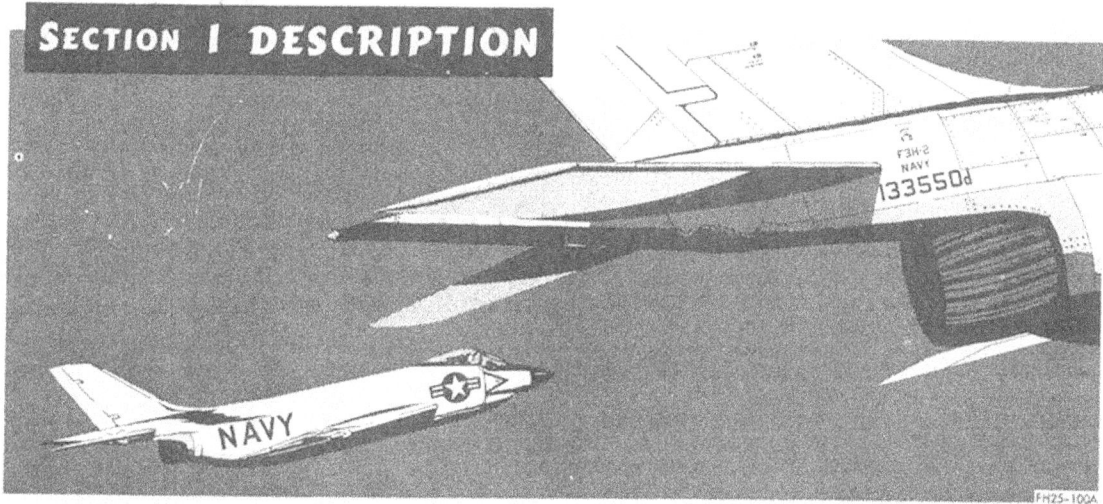

AIRPLANE

The McDonnell F3H-2 and F3H-2M are single place, all weather fighters. Principal recognition features are slightly canted "needle" nose appearance, with sweptback wing and empennage. The cockpit is located well forward of the wing leading edge and in line with the engine air inlet duct which appears to encircle the fuselage. The airplane is powered by an axial flow, turbojet engine with afterburner. Added to its fighter design are the latest in electronic equipment to accurately accomplish its mission. As fighters, they have all the requisites for rapid maneuvering and yet the stability needed for their fire control systems. Typical of all Navy fighter aircraft, the F3H-2 and F3H-2M are designed for land or carrier based operation; incorporating catapult provisions, arresting gear and folding wing panels.

AIRPLANE DIMENSIONS

Overall dimensions of the airplane are as follows:

Wing Span	(Wings Spread)	35' 4"
	(Wings Folded)	25' 4"
Length		58' 11 1/2"
Height -	To Top of Tail	14' 9 1/2"

ARMAMENT

Four fixed, forward firing, MK 12, 20 MM cannons with provisions for external stores. Upon incorporation of ASC No. 169 the two upper cannons will be removed.

ENGINE

The airplane is powered by an Allison Model J71-A-2 axial flow, turbojet engine equipped with a high altitude afterburner. The sea level standard day thrust ratings are 10,000 pounds military power, and 14,500 pounds maximum (with afterburner) power. The complete power plant basically consists of a double entry air inlet duct incorporating an integrally cast lubricating oil reservoir, variable air inlet guide vanes and an hourglass shaped accessory case mounted between the inlet duct entries, a 16 stage compressor, 10 annular through-flow combustion chambers, three stage turbine and an afterburner, with an iris type variable area exhaust nozzle. A pneumatic type starter, driven by air from an external Auxiliary Power Unit, is used to crank the engine rotor during starting. The engine rotor is supported by five bearings. The engine oil system is a dry-sump type used only for lubricating purposes and is completely contained on the engine. A hydraulic oil system, also completely contained on the engine, is used to actuate the variable air inlet guide vanes and the exhaust nozzle. The exhaust nozzle area is hydromechanically controlled by the throttle up to and including full military power, unless turbine outlet temperature exceeds red line. In this event the engine temperature control amplifier electronically controls the nozzle to effect a drop in temperature. When conditions causing overtemperature are no longer present, nozzle control returns to hydromechanical. During afterburner operation the nozzle is completely controlled by the amplifier to maintain maximum thrust and red line temperature. An automatic eighth stage acceleration bleed system provides air unloading of the compressor resulting in smoother rpm transition through the compressor surge tendency range. Air bled from the compressor air discharge section provides a means for ground cooling of the engine accessories, cockpit pressurization and air-conditioning, and also the air source for aircraft pneumatic system operation.

ENGINE FUEL CONTROL SYSTEM

The schematic on sheet 2 of figure 1-7 shows the flow of fuel through the engine fuel system from the point of entry into the engine from the aircraft fuel system. Only the engine fuel system is discussed in the following paragraphs. The Afterburner Fuel System is discussed separately in this section.

1

GENERAL ARRANGEMENT

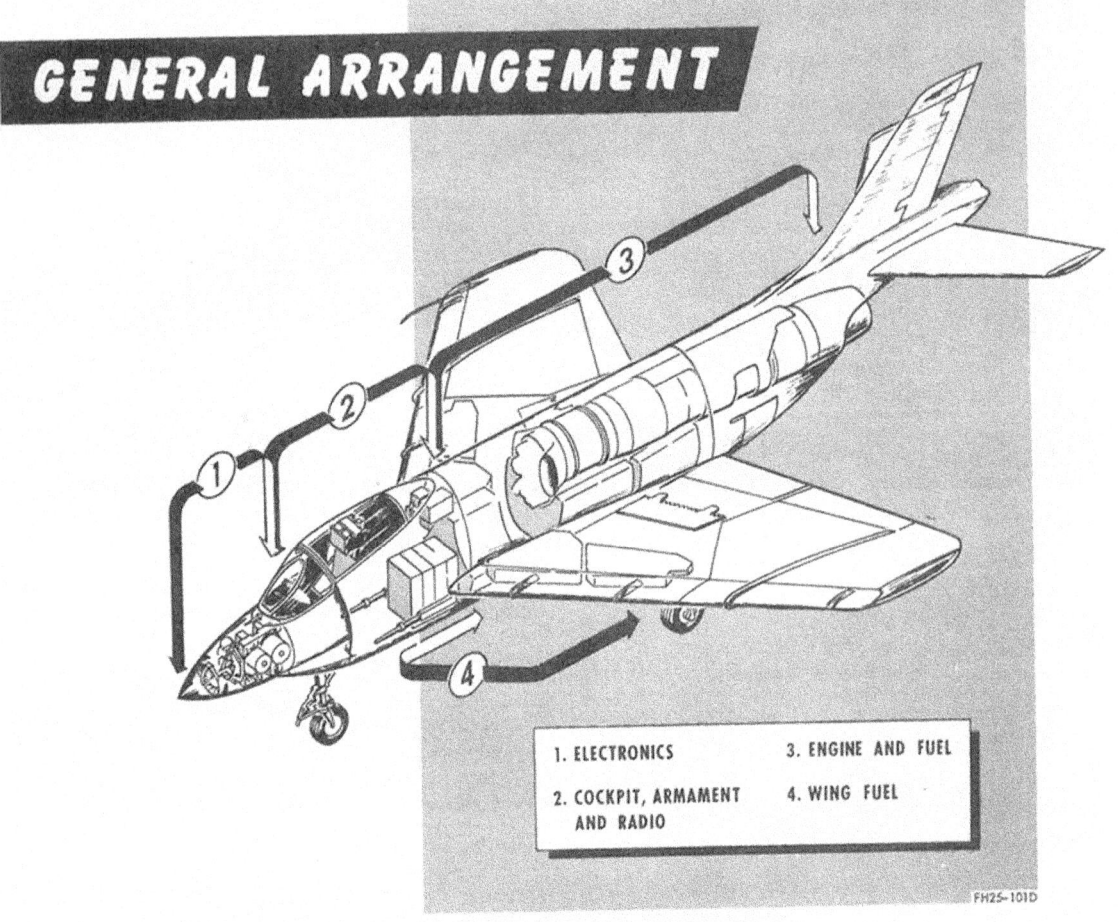

Figure 1-1. General Arrangement

Fuel Pump

Two separate, identical, engine-driven fuel pumps operate in parallel to supply fuel to the fuel regulator under increased pressure. Fuel flow from the aircraft center feed tank is split to enter each pump separately. Each pump has a centrifugal pumping element ahead of, and in series with, the positive displacement gear pumping element. The centrifugal element maintains a head of fuel pressure on the gear element but provides very little pressure increase. Thus a centrifugal element failure will not hinder main pumping element operation. Suitable shear sections are provided in the coaxial drive shaft such that the gear element could continue to function if the centrifugal element sheared. If the main element becomes inoperative, the boost section does also. Suitable check valves prevent loss of fuel through the failed pump. There are no pressure regulators provided. Pump discharge pressure and flow depends upon changes in engine demands due to variations in throttle setting, rpm and inlet air pressure and temperature.

Fuel Pump Failure Warning Light

Each fuel pump has an outlet port check valve which is held open by pump discharge pressure. Should either pump discharge pressure fall below a preset minimum, the check valve spring closes and actuates the pump failure switch. The fuel pump failure warning light on the inboard engine control panel on the left console will show ENG EMERG PUMP (see figure 1-19, this section).

Note

During engine starting the warning light will glow until engine rpm reaches approximately 34 to 42 percent.

Fuel Filter

A filter, mounted on brackets extending out from the right hand side of the accessories case, assures a clean fuel supply from the fuel pumps to the fuel regulator.

MAIN DIFFERENCES TABLE

ITEM	F3H-2	F3H-2M
SPOILERS	Yes	Some Airplanes ★
RADAR	AN/APG-51C	AN/APQ-51A
TACAN	Yes	Provisions Only
MISSILE CAPABILITY	SIDEWINDER, SPARROW III,	SIDEWINDER SPARROW I
SELECTIVE IDENTIFICATION FEATURE	Yes	Some Airplanes ★

★ THIS SYMBOL DENOTES AN ITEM WHICH INVOLVES AN EFFECTIVITY. CONSULT THE APPLICABLE TEXT FOR COMPLETE COVERAGE.

Figure 1-2. Main Differences Table

Fuel Regulator

The fuel regulator is an engine-driven hydromechanical unit which establishes a fuel flow to the engine fuel nozzles which results in the rpm selected by the pilot. The throttle is the primary control of the metering orifice. However, the amount of fuel metered is automatically altered by devices within the regulator which sense changes in inlet air pressure and temperature and rpm. The net result is an rpm selected by the pilot and held within 1% regardless of varying ambient and operating conditions. Fuel in excess of engine requirements is by-passed back to the gear pumping elements of both fuel pumps. The fuel regulator also provides correct fuel flow for engine starting, acceleration, and maintains a minimum fuel flow during deceleration to prevent "flame-out". Sea level idle rpm is varied automatically with changes in ambient air temperature 64 +1, -0 percent rpm at -10 degrees Fahrenheit to 68.3 +1, -0 percent rpm at 120 degrees Fahrenheit. A cutoff valve is closed to shut off fuel to the engine fuel nozzles when the throttle is placed in the OFF position. Effective F3H-2 airplanes 137013i and subsequent and F3H-2M airplanes 137041i thru 137095k, a fuel enrichment solenoid valve is utilized to furnish additional fuel to the engine during emergency afterburner modulation at speeds below 86 percent rpm. The purpose of the enrichment is to permit throttle retardation down to idle and acceleration from idle without stagnation or stall. The enrichment is automatic, in response to rpm. The P2-P4 solenoid valve is energized open below 86 percent rpm and de-energized close above 86 percent rpm.

Flowmeter Transmitter

The fuel flowmeter transmitter is mounted on the left side of the engine compressor section and measures the rate of flow from the fuel regulator to the fuel nozzles and engine. No afterburner fuel flows through the transmitter. The transmitter translates fuel flow into an electrical signal to the fuel flow indicator to give the pilot the engine fuel consumption reading in pounds per hour. The transmitter is powered from the primary a-c bus.

Heat Exchangers

Fuel metered from the fuel regulator and flowing through the flowmeter passes straight through the cored passages of the heat exchanger and then to the fuel nozzles and engine. The fuel serves as the coolant for lubricating and hydraulic oils which flow across the cores in the two separate sections within the heat exchanger body which is located on the lower portion of the compressor section.

Drip Valve and Fuel Dump Tank

The drip valve is mounted on the fuel discharge side of the heat exchanger. The function of this valve is to drain fuel remaining between the fuel regulator cutoff valve and the fuel nozzles when the engine is shut down. During normal engine starting when the ignition switch is depressed, the drip valve solenoid is energized closed by electrical power from the utility d-c bus and no fuel flows to the dump tank. After engine light-off and the ignition switch is released, the drip valve is de-energized but remains held closed by fuel pressure. When the engine is shut down and fuel pressure in the fuel manifold drops to a predetermined point, the valve springs open and the remaining fuel is drained into the dump tank. The dump tank is located above the arresting hook well and has a capacity adequate for three shutdowns. The manual drain valve located near the fuselage fuel tanks vent mast, just below the left speed brake, is utilized to drain the tank. Any fuel present in the tank after take-off is siphoned overboard through the fiberglas drain mast located just below the right-hand speed brake.

Manifold Fill Valve and Manifold Pressure Switch

During engine start when the ignition switch is depressed, d-c power from the utility d-c bus passes through a closed pressure actuated switch (manifold pressure switch) to energize a solenoid actuated switch which completes the circuit to the manifold fill valve, energizing the valve open. Part of the engine-driven fuel pump's discharge is then by-passed around the metering portions of the fuel regulator and routed directly through the fuel regulator cutoff valve, flowmeter transmitter, heat exchanger, fuel manifold and fuel nozzles. This results in "quick-filling" of the fuel manifold which aids in obtaining efficient starts. When fuel pressure in the fuel manifold rises to a predetermined amount, the pressure actuated switch is opened, de-energizing the solenoid operated switch which de-energizes the manifold fill valve closed. All of the fuel

Section I
NAVWEPS 01-245FCB-501

BLOCK LETTERS

143433n BuAer SERIAL NUMBER
n BLOCK DESIGNATION LETTER

F3H-2
NAVY
143433n

BLOCK d (4)
F3H-2 133549d thru 133568d
F3H-2 133570d thru 133578d
F3H-2M 133569d *

BLOCK e (5)
F3H-2 133579e thru 133603e
F3H-2M 133623e thru 133627e

BLOCK f (6)
F3H-2 133604f thru 133622f
F3H-2M 133628f thru 133638f

BLOCK g (7)
F3H-2 136966g thru 136982g
F3H-2M 137033g thru 137040g

BLOCK h (8)
F3H-2 136983h thru 137012h *

BLOCK i (9)
F3H-2 137013i thru 137020i
F3H-2M 137041i thru 137062i

BLOCK j (10)
F3H-2 137021j thru 137030j
F3H-2M 137063j thru 137082j

BLOCK k (11)
F3H-2 137031k and 137032k
F3H-2M 137083k thru 137095k

BLOCK m (12)
F3H-2 143403m thru 143432m

BLOCK n (13)
F3H-2 143433n thru 143462n

BLOCK o (14)
F3H-2 143463o thru 143492o

BLOCK p (15)
F3H-2 145202p thru 145231p

BLOCK q (16)
F3H-2 145232q thru 145261q

BLOCK r (17)
F3H-2 145262r thru 145291r

BLOCK s (18)
F3H-2 145292s thru 145306s
F3H-2 146328s thru 146339s

BLOCK t (19)
F3H-2 146709t thru 146740t

*DENOTES PROTOTYPE

FH25-103E

Figure 1-3. Block Letters

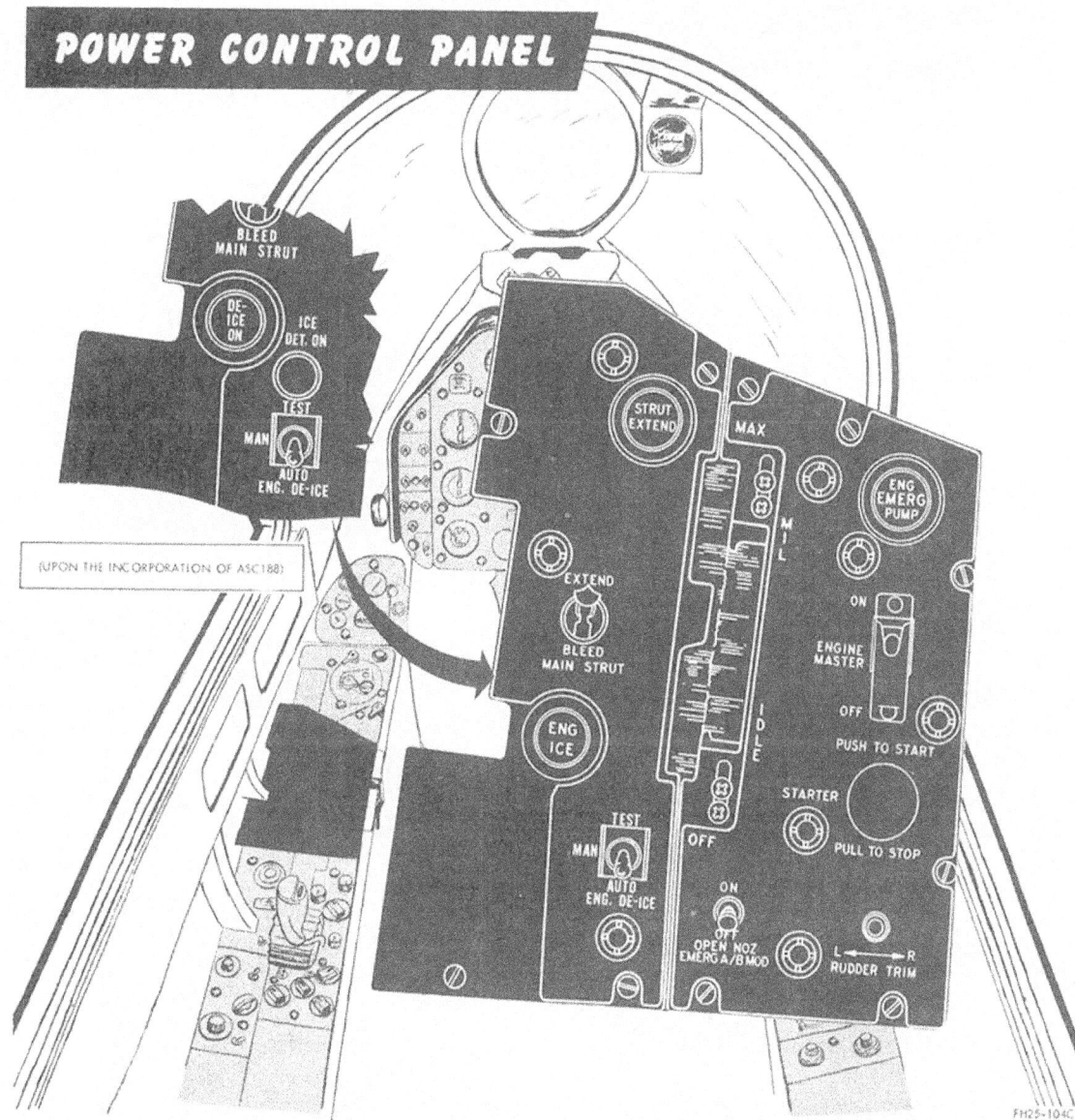

Figure 1-4. Power Control Panel

pump's discharge then enters the fuel regulator. Releasing the ignition switch prior to actuation of the pressure switch also de-energizes the manifold fill valve closed.

Fuel Nozzles

A duplex type fuel nozzle in each inner combustion chamber liner sprays metered fuel from the fuel regulator into the compressor discharge air entering the combustion chamber. The fuel-air mixture is ignited by the spark plugs in number 4 and 8 chambers during starting after which the burning is self-sustaining.

ENGINE MASTER SWITCH

The guarded, two-position engine master switch is located on the inboard engine control panel. In the ON position the switch supplies power to the engine control circuits, opens the engine fuel inlet shutoff valve, and starts the fuel boost and transfer system. In the OFF position it closes the air bleed and shutoff valve on the starting auxiliary power unit, in addition to stopping power to the items mentioned above. Electrical power sources of the equipment controlled by this switch are discussed in the various paragraphs describing the equipment.

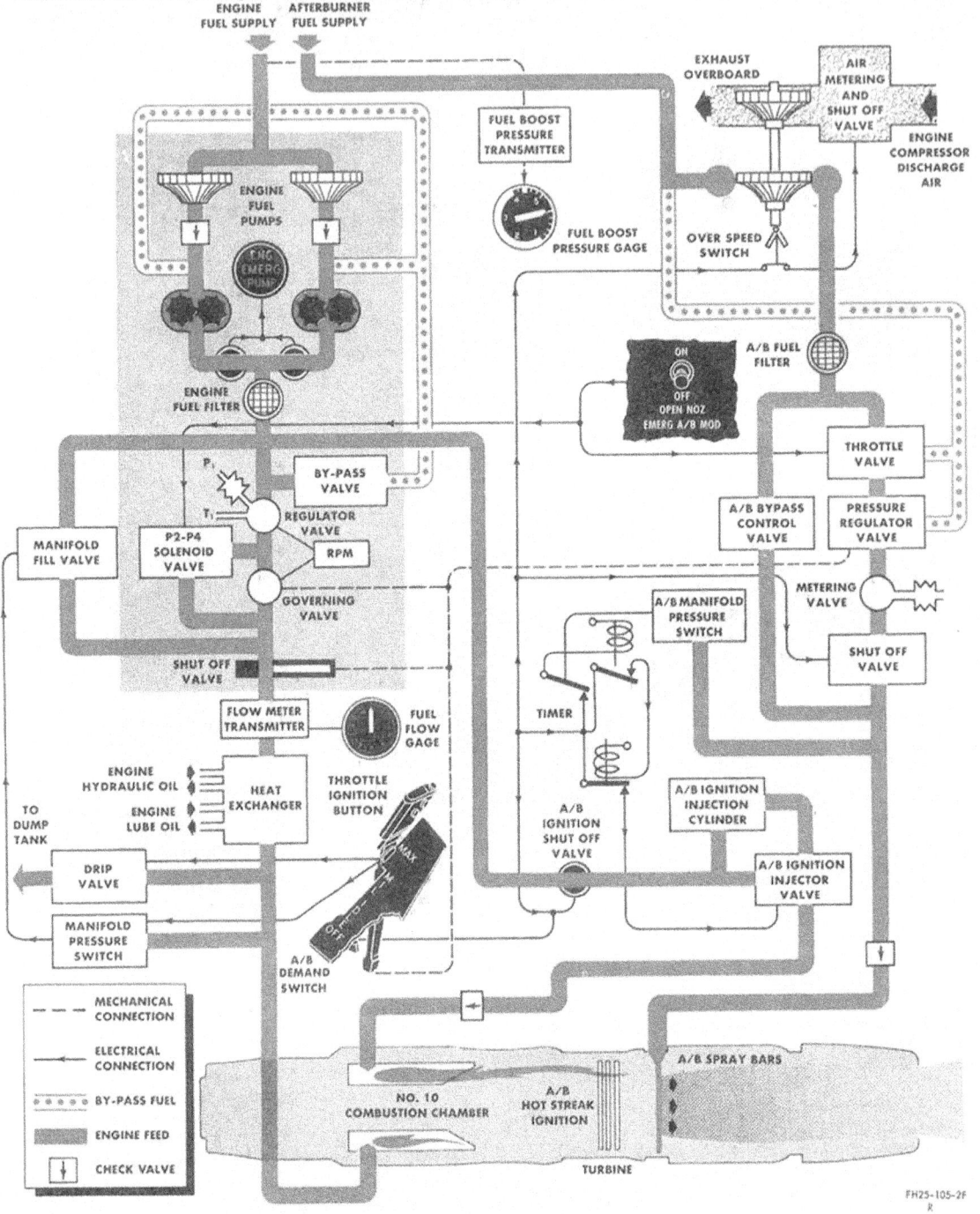

Figure 1-5. Engine Fuel System

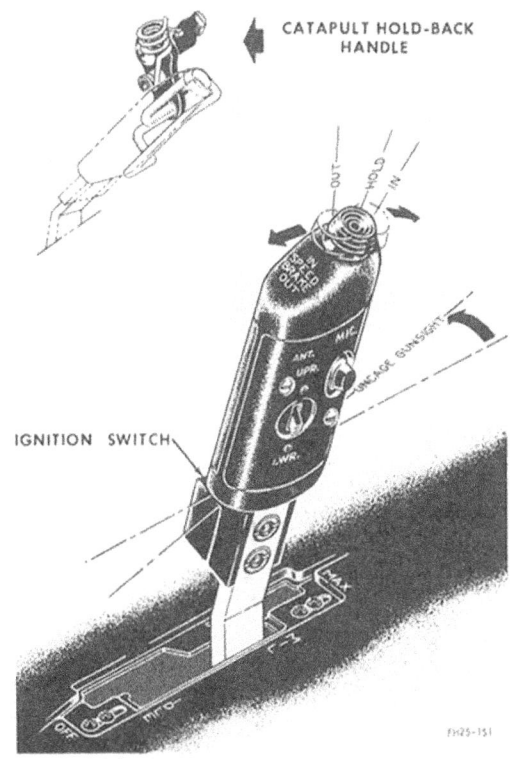

Figure 1-6. Throttle

THROTTLE

The throttle is located in the left cockpit console. It travels in a brush sealed cutout formed by the inboard and outboard engine control panels. It is connected to the engine fuel regulator control arm through a push-pull rod and bell crank system. The engine fuel regulator control arm is connected to the afterburner fuel regulator control arm. Therefore, the throttle establishes desired engine power, and also modulates afterburner power from 100 percent (full MAX) down to 50 percent (subject to alterations as mentioned in paragraphs Engine Fuel Regulator and Afterburner Fuel Regulator). Advancing the throttle from OFF to IDLE opens the cutoff valve in the fuel regulator, permitting fuel to flow to the engine fuel nozzles. Engine thrust increases almost proportionally with advancement of throttle from IDLE to MIL, with full Military power (100 percent thrust and rpm and red line temperature) established with the throttle against the MIL stop. Moving the throttle laterally away from the MIL detent actuates the afterburner demand switch to initiate the afterburner light-off cycle. The throttle cutout detents prevent inadvertent movement into OFF or MAX positions. The throttle lever is not laterally spring-loaded, but is maintained in the military range slot and maximum range slot by a ball and seat arrangement which "pops in"

when the throttle is placed in either slot. The throttle grip houses the speed brake, communications antennas, microphone and ignition switches. The gun sight gyro switch is incorporated within the grip and is operated by rotating the grip counterclockwise to uncage and clockwise to cage the gyro. A friction lock lever located to the right of the throttle permits individual preference in setting throttle movement friction to suit operational requirements. Advancing the lever increases friction.

Engine Fuel Shutoffs

Fuel may be shut off from the engine by electrical or mechanical means. Fuel is electrically shut off by the motor driven engine fuel inlet shutoff valve when the engine master switch is placed in the OFF position. On F3H-2 airplanes, 133549d thru 133580e, power is supplied by the primary d-c bus. On F3H-2 airplanes 133581e and subsequent and F3H-2M airplanes 133623e thru 137095k, power is supplied by the utility bus. On all airplanes fuel is mechanically shut off by placing throttle in the off position. This action closes the cutoff valve in the fuel pressure line.

Catapult Hold-back Handle

A handle secured to the cockpit structure and located above the MIL throttle detent may be hinged down to line up with the throttle grip. The grip and hold-back handle may then be held together during catapulting to prevent inadvertently throttling back. The hold-back handle is designed to permit gripping with the throttle when throttle is in MIL or MAX position.

INLET FUEL PRESSURE GAGE

The inlet fuel pressure indicator is mounted on the pedestal panel. The indicator dial is calibrated from 0 to 5 with readings multiplied by 10. A pressure transmitter mounted on the engine measures pressure in the aircraft fuel system as it enters the engine fuel pump. This signal is transmitted via a-c circuits to the indicator. In some airplanes, this instrument is labeled fuel boost pressure.

FULL FUEL INDICATOR

The fuel flow indicator, mounted on the main instrument panel, provides a continuous indication of the rate of fuel flow out of the fuel regulator to the fuel distributor and engine. This flow is measured by an a-c transmitter mounted on the engine. Flow to the afterburner is not measured. The rate of fuel flow is shown in 1000 pounds per hour by a pointer moving over a scale calibrated from 0 to 24.

TACHOMETER

The electric tachometer system is composed of the tachometer indicator on the main instrument panel and a tachometer generator driven by the engine. The system is completely self-contained in that it requires no external source of power. The indicator dial is calibrated from 0 to 100; the equivalent 100 percent engine speed being 6175 rpm. The indicator includes two pointers, a large one operating on the 0 to 100 scale and a small one operating on a separate scale calibrated from 0 to 10.

TURBINE OUTLET TEMPERATURE GAGE

The turbine outlet temperature indicator, mounted on the main instrument panel, is calibrated in degrees of temperature centigrade. The scale range is 0 to 1000 degrees. The system indicates the temperature of the exhaust gas as it leaves the turbine unit during engine operation. Twelve thermocouples are installed on the engine just aft of the turbine outlet. These thermocouples are connected in parallel and provide a signal voltage to the cockpit indicator. Temperature limitations are indicated by markings placed on the instrument glass. These markings vary according to the characteristics of the particular engine being used.

NOZZLE POSITION AND THRUST INDICATOR

The thrust indicator (figure 1-17) is used to determine that the engine thrust output on the ground with MIL power setting is acceptable for take-off. This is accomplished by comparing turbine outlet pressure with ambient air pressure, and conveying resulting data to the indicator. The indicator is mounted on the right side of the main instrument panel and also incorporates the nozzle position indicator. The thrust indicator scale is calibrated in thousands of pounds of military thrust, and ranges from 0 to 12. The nozzle position scale ranges from OPEN to CLOSED with the scale indexed in quarters. Electrical power is supplied from the primary a-c bus.

VARIABLE AREA EXHAUST NOZZLE

The engine hydraulic oil system functions to operate the variable inlet guide vanes and the variable area exhaust nozzle. A change in exhaust nozzle area affects engine exhaust gas temperature, pressure, velocity and therefore thrust. In general, as nozzle area decreases, thrust increases. Below approximately 85% rpm, the nozzle is held wide open by the exhaust nozzle override valve which ports hydraulic pressure to the "open" side of the nozzle actuators. This aids in obtaining rapid, surge free accelerations through the critical rpm range. Above 85% rpm, the engine-driven speed switch opens to de-energize the override valve. Hydraulic pressure to begin closing the nozzle is then varied by the servo-valve actuator in direct response to throttle movement. At full MIL throttle position and 100% rpm, the nozzle is closed to its minimum area, which (at ambient temperature of 59°F) results in 100% thrust and maximum allowable stabilized temperature (red line). Aircraft having J71 engines serial number 800111 and up, or lower serial numbers with Allison SCB-J-124 incorporated, utilize a "high step" cam in the nozzle actuator. This actuator in effect overcloses the exhaust nozzle, allowing a more rapid increase in turbine outlet temperature and consequently a more rapid increase in thrust. This substantially lowers the time spent on catapult, and eliminates any possibility of exhaust temperature (and thrust) drop during climb. On engines with this high lift cam, exhaust overtemperature (up to 750°) can be expected while operating in or near the military power setting if the a-c power system has failed or has not been turned on. Ambient temperatures below 59°F permit some increase in thrust. Ambient temperatures above 59°F result in a decrease in thrust while maintaining maximum temperature by increasing nozzle opening area. This is due to action of the engine temperature control amplifier which is an overtemperature protection device. Thus, when red line temperature is exceeded, the amplifier senses overtemperature through connection to the temperature measuring thermocouples and sends an electronic signal to the exhaust nozzle servo-valve actuator. The actuator ports hydraulic pressure to open the nozzle and decrease the temperature. Amplifier control of the nozzle overrides the servo-valve actuator until overtemperature conditions are no longer present. The actuator then regains controls in response to throttle position. When normal afterburning is initiated, the resulting momentary drop in rpm causes the nozzle to automatically open fully to prevent overtemperature and permit rpm to recover. When rpm recovers, the nozzle automatically returns to normal stabilized afterburning scheduling which is controlled by combined amplifier and servo-valve actuator action to maintain rated afterburner thrust. Upon the incorporation of ASC 174, a barometric pressure switch is installed in the afterburner ignition circuit. At altitudes of 20,000 to 25,000 feet and above, the exhaust nozzle will be energized to the full open position immediately upon actuation of the afterburner ignition timer instead of being opened by a drop in engine rpm. This will reduce the possibility of an engine flameout under high altitude low airspeed conditions by relieving the initial afterburner back pressure. The unit will have no effect on the operation of the exhaust nozzle at altitudes below 20,000 feet. When the afterburner is shut down or should it flameout, the nozzle automatically closes to the military area to prevent engine overspeed and shuts off the afterburner fuel system by actuating a nozzle two-position switch through a follow-up cable attached to the nozzle. In event of an a-c power failure to the amplifier during afterburning, the nozzle is positioned and held in the wide open position. This permits retention of afterburning, but at some loss of thrust. (Refer to Engine Temperature Control Amplifier Failure, Section III.) The nozzle is also held in the open position during operation of the emergency modulation system (refer to Operation of Afterburner Emergency Modulation System, Section III).

ENGINE DUCTING SYSTEM

The engine is supplied with air through two inlet air ducts running along the insides of the fuselage with the openings on either side and below the cockpit. The ducting leads back to two removable duct sections which join the aircraft ducting to the split inlet duct on the engine by strap and seal attachment. The airplane's static attitude eliminates the danger to ground personnel of being drawn into the inlet air ducts and reduces the amount of foreign matter entry into the engine.

Engine Inlet Duct Water Removal System

Effective F3H-2 airplanes 145232q and subsequent, and in all F3H airplanes in which F3H ASC 143 have been incorporated, the engine air inlet ducts have been modified to facilitate removal of excess water which enters the engine during flight through rainfall. This effectively increases the airplane's all-weather capability by decreasing the amount of water ingested during operation through precipitation. The majority of the water which exists in the duct at any time takes the form of a film which collects on the walls of the duct. Removal of this water film is accomplished by means of scuppers which collect the water and dump it overboard through drain tubes. These scuppers resemble splitter plates which are used for removal of boundary layer air; they line the inlet duct just forward of the engine. Since duct pressure is less than ambient pressure at low airspeeds a jet pump is used to assist in the ejection of collected water under low speed flight conditions. The jet pump is operated in conjunction with an anti-reverse valve which closes to prevent reverse flow through the drain tubes. Actuation of the pitot heat switch opens a valve in the compressor bleed line; this air flows around the duct scupper through tubes to act as an anti-icing measure and then flows to its exit, where it contributes the jet pump action. A thermostatic overtemperature protection feature closes the compressor bleed line when duct temperature tends to exceed its safe operating level.

ENGINE COOLING SYSTEM

The engine compartment is divided into fore and aft sections by the engine fire shield, for cooling purposes. The forward compartment is cooled in flight by ram air entering through a duct immediately behind the cockpit canopy. This cooling air exits overboard through the left-right acceleration bleed ducts and the left-right compressor seal leakage ducts. Aft engine compartment cooling air enters behind the fire shield through the left/right blister ducts. This air is forced to exit between the exhaust nozzle shroud and exhaust nozzle by a seal around the exhaust nozzle, and in so doing helps cool the shroud actuating linkages. The flow of engine exhaust gas out the exhaust nozzle creates a "pumping" action which aids in drawing out aft engine compartment cooling air. A pair of small blister ducts on each side of the aft fuselage directs ram air to cool the exhaust nozzle actuators. This air also exits with aft engine compartment cooling air. During taxi and static ground operation, the lack of ram air entry into the forward engine compartment is overcome by opening a jet air pump shutoff valve. This valve is energized from the secondary d-c bus when the landing gear is down. This permits air from the engine compressor to flow into the forward engine compartment air entry duct. Inside the duct, air passes through a jet pump which, through a venturi action, sets up a suction or pumping action to draw outside air into the forward engine compartment.

AFTERBURNER COOLING SYSTEM

When afterburning is initiated, an afterburner cooling air shutoff valve is pneumatically opened by compressor discharge air from the air metering and shutoff valve to cool the variable area exhaust nozzle shroud and exhaust nozzle linkages, and the afterburner combustion chamber liner. Cooling air is cut off when afterburning is discontinued and the air metering and shutoff valve is de-energized closed by retarding the throttle from the maximum range.

ENGINE ACCESSORIES COOLING

In flight the a-c and d-c generators are cooled by ram air entering the duct aft of the cockpit canopy. Air flows into the plenum chamber from which it is directed through lines to cool the a-c and d-c generators and transformer-rectifier. During ground and static operation when ram air is not sufficiently available for cooling, a jet air pump shutoff valve is energized open from the secondary d-c bus when the landing gear is down. This allows air bled from the engine compressor to enter the jet air pump which, through a venturi action, sets up a suction or pumping to draw outside air into the plenum chamber. When the landing gear is retracted, the jet air pump shutoff valve closes and the above mentioned accessories are cooled by ram air.

IGNITION SYSTEM

The ignition system consists of an ignition button, two low voltage, high energy ignition units on the engine, two spark plugs in No. 4 and 8 combustion chambers, and the necessary wiring. The ignition unit provides an intermittent low voltage but very hot spark which facilitates ground starting and air starting at high altitudes.

Ignition Buttons

The ignition switch is a spring-loaded, push button type switch located on the lower forward face of the throttle grip (see figure 1-6). Depressing the ignition button causes the spark plugs to discharge, igniting the fuel-air mixture as the throttle is moved from OFF to IDLE during engine start. The ignition switch also actuates the drip valve (refer to Drip Valve and Fuel Dump Tank) and the engine fuel manifold quick-fill system (refer to Manifold Fill Valve).

Note

- Maximum continuous ignition per starting cycle is based on cycles of 2 minutes on, 3 minutes off, 2 minutes on and 23 minutes off. Refer to Section II, Starting Procedures.

- The spark plugs will fire only while the ignition button is depressed.

Effective F3H-2 airplanes 133549d thru 133622f and F3H-2M airplanes 133623e thru 133638f, power is supplied to the ignition switch and ignition units from the utility d-c bus which is energized at all times either directly by the battery or (when external or generator power is supplied) by the primary d-c bus. Effective F3H-2 airplanes 136966g and subsequent and F3H-2M airplanes 137033g thru 137095k the engine master switch must also be ON to energize the ignition system.

STARTING SYSTEM

The starting system is pneumatic and consists of a cockpit starter switch, and an external A.P.U. to provide a compressed air source to an air-driven starter. Pilot control is over the A.P.U. air bleed and shutoff valve which is electrically connected to the airplane by a separate electric line and controls airflow to the engine starter.

Engine Start Button

The starter button is located on the inboard engine control panel in the cockpit. The switch is powered from the utility d-c bus. With the A.P.U. air and electrical lines connected to the airplane through door 33, and A.P.U. operating, pressing the starter button energizes the A.P.U. air bleed and shutoff valve open. Air flows to the starter turbine and engine cranking is initiated. The starter button may be released since it is held "on" by a holding solenoid. At approximately 36 to 40% rpm, during a normal start, the engine rotor should be turning at a self-sustaining speed so that the starter button automatically kicks up to close the A.P.U. air valve, stopping air to the starter.

AFTERBURNER FUEL SYSTEM

Air Metering and Shutoff Valve

The air metering and shutoff valve controls air bled from compressor discharge section of the engine to operate the air driven afterburner fuel pump. When afterburning is initiated, the valve pilot is energized open from the utility d-c bus to start afterburner pump operation. The amount of air permitted to the afterburner fuel pump is pneumatically controlled by the valve in response to compressor discharge pressure.

Afterburner Fuel Pump

The afterburner fuel pump supplies fuel to the afterburner fuel system. It is an air turbine driven centrifugal type operated by engine compressor discharge air which is controlled by the air metering and shutoff valve. Thus, pump output is controlled in response to compressor discharge pressure to approach metered fuel requirements. An overspeed switch in the pump is actuated to de-energize the air metering and shutoff valve closed in event of pump overspeed. Should the overspeed switch fail, the pump turbine is designed to stretch and seize to prevent pump disintegration.

Afterburner Fuel Strainer

A strainer assures a clean fuel supply to the afterburner fuel regulator and ignition valve from the afterburner fuel pump.

Throttle Valve

The throttle valve is a separate unit attached to the inlet of the afterburner fuel regulator. This valve automatically restricts afterburner fuel pump discharge to the fuel regulator during first stage of afterburner initiation, and at altitude when pump discharge pressure has decreased due to fuel boiling. The restricting action thus keeps a pressure head on the pump to prevent pump cavitation. When pump discharge pressure is within normal limits the valve presents a minimum flow restriction to afterburner fuel regulator.

Afterburner Fuel Control

The afterburner fuel control governs flow to the afterburner fuel manifold and spray bars in response to engine compressor discharge pressure and throttle position. Afterburning may be initiated by moving the throttle outboard from MIL to MAX position (past the 94° point). Afterburner light off should be initiated by moving throttle directly outboard from MIL detent until light off is obtained and then immediately moving throttle to the full afterburner (MAX) position. This is known as a modulated light. Refer to Afterburner Light Off, Section V, Confidential Supplement for altitude and airspeed restrictions. Normal afterburner power may be modulated to 50 percent of the available afterburner thrust under emergency conditions (i.e., on an NACA standard day at sea level thrust can be modulated from 14,500 pounds to 12,000 pounds). At 94° throttle, the shutoff valve pilot is electrically opened from the utility d-c bus allowing the valve to be opened by fuel which then flows to the afterburner spray bars. Retarding the throttle to 93° or less, de-energizes the shutoff valve pilot stopping fuel flow to the afterburner.

Afterburner Fuel Spray Bars

Fuel metered by the afterburner fuel regulator is admitted into the afterburner ahead of the flame holder through the fuel nozzles or spray bars.

AFTERBURNER IGNITION SYSTEM

Normal afterburning may be initiated if engine rpm is 98 percent or above by placing the throttle into the outboard MAX position and advancing to full MAX, or by a modulated light (see Afterburner Fuel Control above and refer to Afterburner Light Off, Section V, Confidential Supplement for altitude and airspeed restrictions). This closes the afterburner demand switch (refer to Throttle Control) which permits the afterburner fuel control shutoff valve to open allowing fuel to be discharged into the afterburner (refer to Afterburner Fuel and Air Systems). Simultaneously, the demand switch initiates the "hot-streak" ignition system by energizing the ignition shutoff valve open and energizing the injector valve to such a position as to charge the injector cylinder with fuel pressure from the discharge side of the engine fuel filter. When afterburner manifold fuel pressure rises to a predetermined point, the afterburner manifold pressure switch is actuated to begin energizing a timer relay. After a delay of one second (to insure that adequate fuel is discharging into afterburner) the timer relay is energized to break the circuit to the injector valve. The injector valve is then positioned so that fuel pressure actuates the injector cylinder. This results in a single "shot" of fuel discharged into No. 10 combustion chamber where it is ignited to form a "hot-streak" traveling through the turbine to ignite the afterburner. When rpm drops due to afterburner ignition, the speed sensing control de-energizes the ignition shutoff valve closed. In case of an unsuccessful light-off, the ignition timer will de-energize the ignition shutoff valve closed. Upon incorporation of ASC 174, a barometric pressure switch installed in the ignition timer circuit will position the exhaust nozzle to full open simultaneously with the actuation of the ignition timer at altitudes of 20,000 to 25,000 feet and above. The ignition shutoff valve remains open during emergency afterburner modulation (refer to Emergency Afterburner Modulation System). Should the "light-off" fail, the throttle must be retarded to MIL and again advanced to MAX to "recycle" the system. The afterburner ignition system is designed to operate normally even if the exhaust nozzle should fail in the wide open position. This feature provides afterburner thrust during a nozzle open failure. Without this safety factor, it would be difficult to sustain flight since the engine alone would possibly not be able to furnish adequate thrust with the exhaust nozzle open, should the inlet guide vanes also fail to open. A flight test has shown that on a standard day a clean airplane will maintain an altitude from 6,000 to 10,000 feet, dependent upon gross weight, if the exhaust nozzle fails in the open position. Normal modulation is possible in the MAX range from 110° to 93° on throttle quadrant.

Afterburner Emergency Modulation System

An afterburner emergency modulation system is provided as an emergency feature only. With a failure of the engine hydraulic system the exhaust nozzle will go to the open position. With an open nozzle full Military power is not sufficient to maintain flight in the landing configuration. The emergency afterburner modulation system permits light-off of the afterburner in the military sector of the quadrant and allows modulation to the landing power range. This is accomplished by bypassing additional fuel around the afterburner fuel control to supplement the normal metered fuel. The additional fuel prevents a lean mixture "blowout" when throttling back to an engine speed below 100% rpm. The by-pass fuel valve is controlled by the open nozzle emergency afterburner modulation switch on the power control panel. This system permits afterburner emergency modulation within the range of IDLE to full MAX power. This is made possible by the automatic energizing of a fuel enrichment solenoid valve on the engine fuel control which provides additional fuel below 86 percent rpm. The valve automatically closes above 86 percent.

AFTERBURNER EMERGENCY MODULATION SWITCH. The two-position afterburner emergency modulation switch, marked Open Noz Emerg A/B Mod, is located just aft of the throttle. When this switch is placed in the ON position, the afterburner demand switch is electrically by-passed, the afterburner control fuel by-pass valve is energized open, the acceleration bleed valves are de-energized open, the inlet guide vanes are de-energized closed, and the exhaust nozzle override valve is energized causing the exhaust nozzle to open (if the nozzle is not fully open). Refer to Operation of Afterburner Emergency Modulation System in Section III. In addition to the above, this switch permits the fuel enrichment solenoid valve to operate below 86 percent rpm as explained in Afterburner Emergency Modulation System, this section.

OIL SYSTEM

The dry sump, full scavenging oil system is completely contained on the engine. Its purpose is to provide lubrication to rotor bearings and engine accessories, and furnish a supply of oil to operate the constant speed transmission for a-c and d-c generator drive. Oil is supplied from a reservoir which is integrally cast between the split inlet air ducts as part of the forward frame. From the reservoir, the oil flows to a gear-type pump from which it then passes under increased pressure to the a-c and d-c generators constant speed drive, and to the accessories drive case. The two flow paths meet and are then routed directly to the No. 1 compressor rotor bearing and the heat exchanger. The heat exchanger is by-passed if the oil thermostatic or pressure valve dictate that no cooling is necessary. Otherwise, oil flows through the heat exchanger where it is cooled by engine fuel before passing on to lubricate the remaining four rotor bearings. Three scavenger pumps return oil to the reservoir through a diffuser horn which reduces aeration. Refer to servicing diagram this section for oil system capacity, grade and servicing instructions.

HYDRAULIC OIL SYSTEM

The integral, closed, hydraulic oil system is completely contained on the engine. Its purpose is to actuate the variable exhaust nozzle and the variable inlet guide vanes. The hydraulic tank is located between the inlet air ducts. Hydraulic oil is drawn from the tank by a hydraulic pump which delivers through a relief valve and filters to the inlet guide vanes, pilot valve, servo-valve actuator (exhaust nozzle actuators control), exhaust nozzle actuators override valve and exhaust nozzle actuators. Below 85 percent rpm the inlet guide vanes pilot valve is de-energized and the vanes moved to an angle which offers resistance to air flowing to the engine compressor. The result is an "unlocked" compressor, permitting rapid acceleration through the compressor surge and stall rpm range. Above 85 percent rpm the vanes pilot valve is energized by actuation of an engine speed sensing switch from utility d-c bus. The vanes are then rotated to offer minimum air resistance and the compressor is "loaded" for normal operation. A power failure to the vanes pilot valve permits the vanes to be moved to "unload" the compressor below 85 percent rpm by the action of a precision spring on each of the three vane hydraulic actuators. Thus stall and surge protection remains in effect.

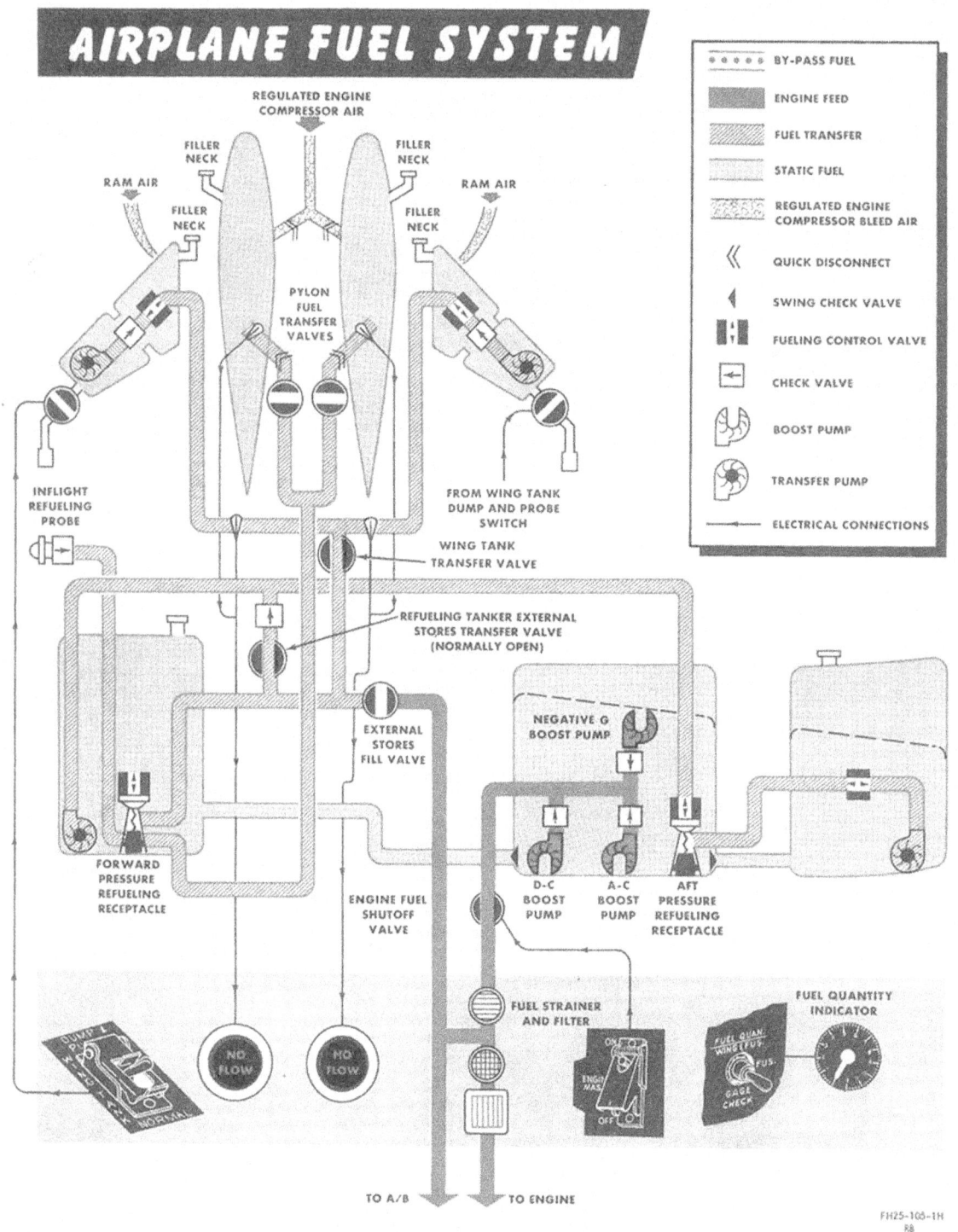

Figure 1-7. Airplane Fuel System

Above 85 percent rpm, ram airflow will tend to overcome the springs to force the vanes to move to a partial compressor "load" position. Below 85 percent rpm the exhaust nozzle override valve is energized from the utility d-c bus to port hydraulic pressure to both sides of the four nozzle actuators pistons. The head sides having more area than the rod sides causes the nozzle to be moved to and held in the wide open position. This permits burst acceleration through the critical compressor stall and surge rpm range. Above 85 percent rpm the override valve is de-energized by the engine speed sensing switch. Hydraulic pressure on the head side of the nozzle actuators piston is then controlled by the servo valve actuator in response to throttle position. Exhaust nozzle area can then be controlled. The hydraulic oil returns to the reservoir via the heat exchanger. A pressure and thermostatic controlled bypass valve on the heat exchanger determines whether the oil will pass through the heat exchanger to be cooled by engine fuel or by-passed directly to the reservoir. (See Servicing Diagram, figure 1-24, for hydraulic oil specification.)

ACCELERATION BLEED VALVES

Four pneumatically operated acceleration bleed valves, controlled by a solenoid operated pilot valve bleed air from the eighth stage of the engine compressor section in order to avoid compressor surge and stall. The operation is automatic, being triggered by the engine speed sensing control, hereafter referred to as speed switch. A two-step speed switch, which allows the acceleration bleed valves to open at an average 92 percent rpm, provides compressor surge and stall protection below that setting. Above 92 percent rpm the bleed valves are again closed by the pilot valve, which is energized by the utility d-c bus. Loss of d-c power will cause the acceleration bleed valves to open automatically, providing compressor surge and stall protection. However, approximately 10 percent loss in power may be expected.

AIRPLANE FUEL SYSTEM

The airplane fuel system (see figure 1-7) contains seven tanks, three interconnected self-sealing tanks in the fuselage and two interconnected bladder type tanks in each inner wing section. Provisions are made for two droppable type external tanks, an in-flight refueling installation and a refueling tanker external store (see figure 1-24 Servicing Diagram, for fuel specifications and quantities). A positive fuel transfer system is provided to transfer wing and external tank fuel to the fuselage tanks, and forward and aft fuselage tank fuel to the center engine feed tank. Also, gravity fuel transfer is provided from the forward and aft fuselage tanks to the center fuselage tank via flap check valve interconnectors. The wing tanks may be fueled through a gravity filler provided on top of each wing, the fuselage tanks through gravity fillers on the forward and aft fuselage tanks from the right side of the fuselage and the external tanks through filler ports in the top forward end of each tank. The system may be pressure fueled from a single point, through pressure fueling unit at the bottom of the forward fuselage tank, at the rate of approximately 160 gallons per minute; the fueling time will be reduced approximately 50% when using the pressure fueling and defueling unit at the bottom of the center fuselage tank in conjunction with the forward cell unit. The fuel system is provided with an automatic dual shutoff system which, through the action of dual float pilot valves in each internal tank, shuts off pressure fueling when a predetermined tank level is reached, leaving adequate expansion space. The two tanks in each inner wing section have independent venting systems and are maintained under pressure in flight to prevent fuel boiling and provide a pressure source for dumping and purging. The fuselage tanks are vented independently from the wing tanks, being dually vented due to the horseshoe shape of the center and aft fuselage tanks. All internal tanks have capacitor type fuel gaging units which provide a quantity reading in pounds.

FUEL BOOST SYSTEM

Fuel is supplied to the engine by two a-c powered boost pumps (one a negative "g" type at the top of the tank) and a d-c power boost pump in the center fuselage tank. All are of the submerged-centrifugal type. The negative "g" pump assumes pumping duty during inverted flight and other negative "g" maneuvers. The boost pumps become operative when the engine master switch is ON, if external a-c and d-c is applied. Without external power, the boost pumps will not operate until the engine attains idle rpm and generators are operative. In the event of either a-c or d-c failure, the remaining energized pump will supply the engine with fuel adequate for engine and afterburner operation.

Note

Power to the d-c boost pump is supplied by the primary d-c bus, however, the boost pump control is supplied by the d-c monitored d-c bus. Since the boost pump control energizes the boost pump power circuit, loss of the d-c generator will render the d-c boost pump inoperative.

FUEL QUANTITY DATA TABLE

	CAPACITY (PRESSURE FUELING) U.S. GALLONS	USABLE FUEL (PRESSURE FUELING)	CAPACITY (GRAVITY FUELING) U.S. GALLONS	USABLE FUEL (GRAVITY FUELING)
FWD FUS TANK	368	APPROX 15 GALLONS IS UNUSABLE	356	APPROX 15 GALLONS IS UNUSABLE
CTR FUS TANK	500		502	
AFT FUS TANK	340		342	
WING TANKS	282		306	
TOTAL	1490		1506	
EXT FUEL	564		564	
TOTAL	2054		2070	

Figure 1-8. Fuel Quantity Data Table

Section I   NAVWEPS 01-245FCB-501

FUEL TRANSFER SYSTEM

Fuel Transfer Selector Switch

The fuel transfer selector switch is a seven-position rotary type switch located on the fuel control panel on the left console. The switch selects operation of either the wing or fuselage transfer pumps, which are powered from the a-c monitored a-c bus. The REFUEL positions (AIR and GND) are used for refueling only, these positions cannot be selected until the selector knob is pulled up. Selecting the GND REFUEL position opens the wing and pylon fuel transfer valves, which receives its power from the utility bus, allowing wing and external tanks to be filled while pressure fueling through the underside of the forward fuselage tank. The AIR REFUEL position opens the wing and pylon transfer valves and extends the in-flight refueling probe to permit refueling all tanks. When placed in WING TRANSFER position, in flight, the motor-operated wing transfer valve opens and a submerged centrifugal a-c powered transfer pump in each outer wing tank delivers fuel to fuselage tanks. The wing vent valves are closed during transfer. Crossfeed is prevented through fueling valves which are also electrically closed at the time. Wing transfer pumps will continue to operate until the selector switch is moved from the WING TRANSFER position or the wing tank switch is placed in DUMP & PURGE, in which case the wing transfer pumps will stop and the fuselage transfer pumps start. In the FUS position, the wing transfer pumps stop, wing and pylon transfer valve closes, wing fueling valves open, aft fuselage tank fueling valve closes (to prevent CG transfer beyond 36% M.A.C. in event of aft tank transfer pump failure) and the wing vent valves are controlled by the wing tank pressure switches. At the same time a submerged centrifugal pump in the forward and aft fuselage tanks begins to operate, delivering fuel to the center engine feed tank. The pumps will continue to operate until the selector switch is placed in the WING TRANSFER position. In the BOTH PYLON TRANSFER position, the wing transfer pumps stop, the wing transfer valve closes, the pylon transfer valve opens and air under pressure displaces fuel from both external tanks to the fuselage tanks. In the LEFT PYLON TRANSFER position, the switch performs the same function as in the BOTH PYLON TRANSFER position, however, only fuel from the left pylon is transferred.

CAUTION

- The minimum airspeed for wing fuel transfer is 250 knots IAS. This limitation is imposed due to the possibility of wing tank collapse if transfer occurs at a lower airspeed.

- No provisions are made for automatic transfer pump shutoff. Immediately upon completion of wing tank transfer the FUS TRANSFER position should be selected to eliminate the possibility of burning up the wing transfer pumps.

Figure 1-9. Fuel Control Panel

Note

- Effective F3H-2 airplanes 136983h and subsequent and F3H-2M airplanes 137041i thru 137095k, wing fuel cannot be transferred when the landing gear is extended. An interlock is incorporated in the landing gear uplock switches to prevent possible collapse of the wing fuel tanks during the landing configuration.

- In F3H-2 airplanes 143463o and subsequent, the landing gear interlock feature has been changed from the landing gear uplock switches to the landing gear control handle. This is to permit wing fuel transfer in the event the landing gear cannot be retracted. The landing gear control handle must be in the UP position during the transfer operation.

Emergency Fuel Transfer

In the event of forward and aft fuselage tank transfer pump failure, fuel is still admitted to the center tank through gravity interconnectors. There is no such provision for the wing tanks. However, limited transfer will occur due to the pressure maintained in the wing tanks if wing transfer is selected.

No Flow Warning Lights

Two no flow warning lights are mounted on the pedestal panel and will illuminate when the wing or pylon fuel transfer has decreased to 3.0 gallons per minute or less. Lights will go out when FUS position is selected on the fuel transfer selector switch (see figure 1-19, this section).

VENT SYSTEM

Wing Tank Vent System

The wing tanks are vented to atmospheric pressure when the airplane is on the ground and electrical power is off. In flight, ram air enters the tanks through a pick-up on the underside of the wing near the leading edge and then through a pressure regulator which closes when tank pressure reaches approximately 5 psi. When pressure exceeds approximately 5.5 psi, a pressure switch opens the vent valve allowing excessive pressure to bleed off through the emergency dump line. Wing tanks, therefore, are maintained under 5.5 psi pressure to prevent fuel boiling and to provide a means for dumping fuel and purging tanks.

Fuselage Tank Vent System

Refer to Fuselage Tank Vent and Pressurization System, this section.

FUSELAGE TANK VENT AND PRESSURIZATION SYSTEM

Separate climb and dive vent systems are used on the fuselage tanks to maintain internal tank pressures close to atmospheric pressure during the climbing and diving maneuvers. Special valves installed in the dive vent line fittings at the tanks prevent fuel spillage during catapulting or climb. Due to their peculiar "horseshoe" shape, the two aft tanks are dually vented, having two sets of climb and dive vent lines. The forward tank is singly vented in the conventional manner. All vent lines run fore and aft atop the tanks. Tank ventilation and pressurization are both accomplished through the scoop-shaped vent mast, just below the left speed brake, which maintains the tanks at a slightly positive pressure. No attempt is made to regulate the internal tank pressure.

WING TANK PRESSURIZATION SYSTEM

In flight, the wing tanks are maintained under a 5.5 psi pressure by action of the pressure regulator, pressure switch and solenoid vent valve in each wing. This pressure is used to dump wing fuel in any emergency. On all F3H-2M airplanes and F3H-2 airplanes 143462n and previous, while the landing gear is down, the wing tank vent valve remains open so that pressure built up by ram air is retained. When the landing gear is retracted, the right landing gear uplock switch is closed allowing the vent valve to close and pressure to build up to 5.5 psi, thereafter being maintained by action of the pressure switch controlling the vent valve. Effective F3H-2 airplanes 143463o and up, the landing gear vent valve interlock feature is changed from the landing gear uplock switches to the landing gear control handle. In the event that the landing gear cannot be extended, the tanks may be vented by placing the landing gear control handle in the DOWN position. This will reduce the fire and explosion hazard created by pressurized tanks.

EXTERNAL TANKS PRESSURIZATION SYSTEM

The external tanks are pressurized continuously when the landing gear is retracted, except during in-flight refueling. Air bled from the engine compressor (see figure 4-1) passes through a pressure regulator which closes when external tank pressure reaches approximately 12 psi. A pressure relief valve in each fuselage pylon opens if tank pressure exceeds 14 psi to bleed off excess pressure. When the gear is extended, or the fuel selector switch is in AIR REFUEL position, the relief valves open and vent the external tanks to ambient pressure. A vacuum relief valve and a pressure relief valve, located on top of the forward section of each tank, provide tank venting in the event of failure of pressure relief valves or pressure regulator.

WING TANK DUMP AND PURGE SWITCH

Should it become necessary to dump wing fuel during wing fuel transfer, placing the snap-guarded, two-position wing tank switch on the fuel control panel of the left console in DUMP & PURGE position will cause the wing tank transfer pumps to stop, the fuselage tank transfer pumps to start, the wing transfer valve to close, the wing vent valve to close, and the motor-operated dump valve to open, allowing the fuel to be dumped and the tanks purged out the emergency dump line at the wing fold trailing edge. This time required to dump and purge the tanks is dependent upon airspeed; higher airspeed yields faster dumping and lower airspeed gives slower dumping. If the wing tank switch is placed in DUMP & PURGE during fuselage tank transfer, the vent valve closes and the dump valve opens to allow the fuel to be expelled. The position of the landing gear control handle or the landing gear itself will not prevent the wing vent valve from closing and permitting pressure build-up for dumping when the wing tank switch is placed in DUMP & PURGE position. Therefore, wing fuel may be dumped at any time the DUMP & PURGE position is selected, regardless of the position of the landing gear or the landing gear control handle.

CAUTION

- Wing fuel will be dumped ON THE DECK when wing tank switch is placed in DUMP & PURGE position and external d-c power is applied.

- If DUMP & PURGE position has been selected the pilot must return the switch to the NORMAL position, as there is a possibility of collapsing wing tanks while in the landing configuration due to insufficient ram air pressure at low airspeeds.

Note

Selecting DUMP and PURGE position will close wing fuel shutoff valves. If an emergency exists, this will allow air refueling without fuel entering the wing tanks.

Section I

NAVWEPS 01-245FCB-501

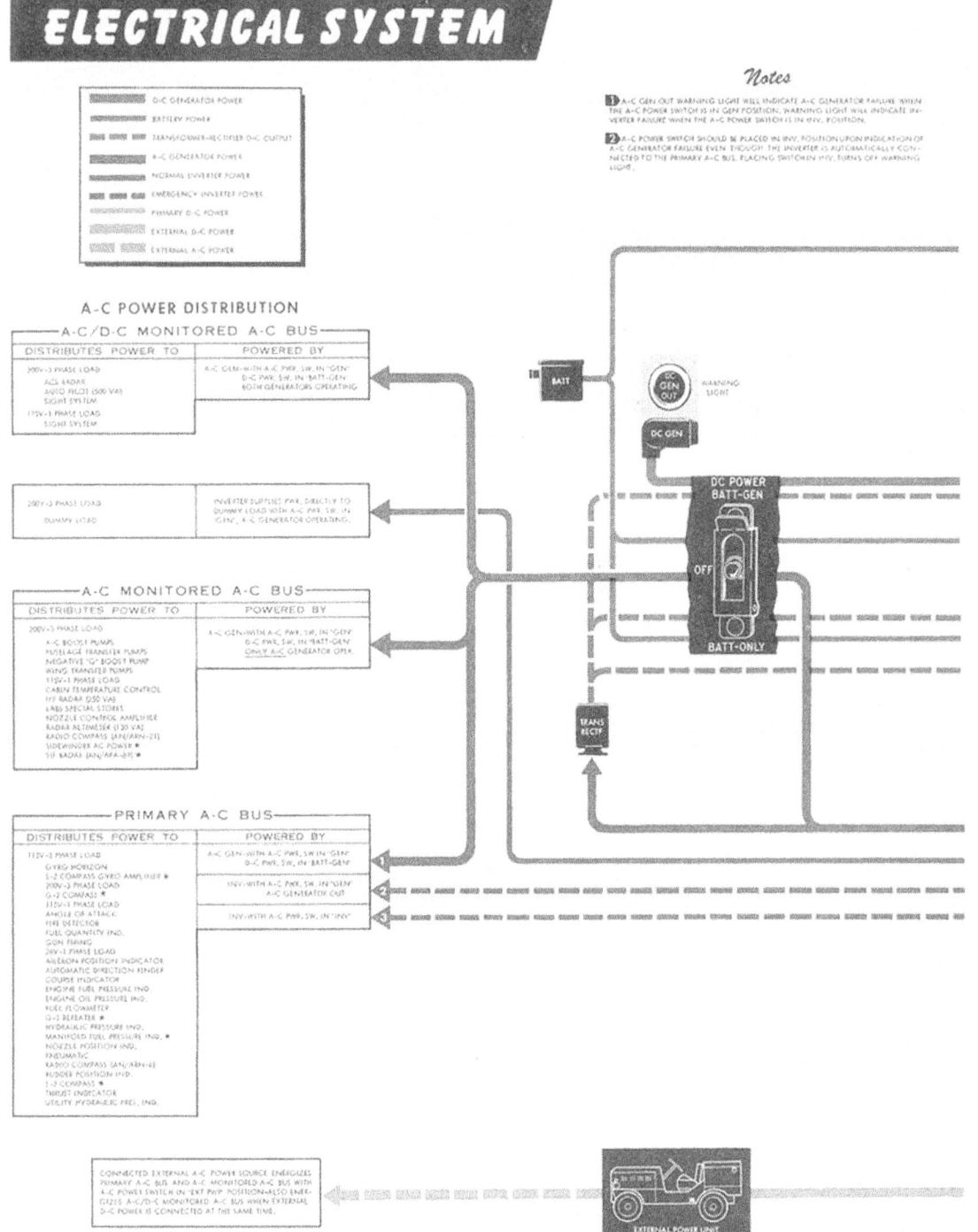

Figure 1-10. Electrical System Schematic (Sheet 1)

NAVWEPS 01-245FCB-501 — Section I

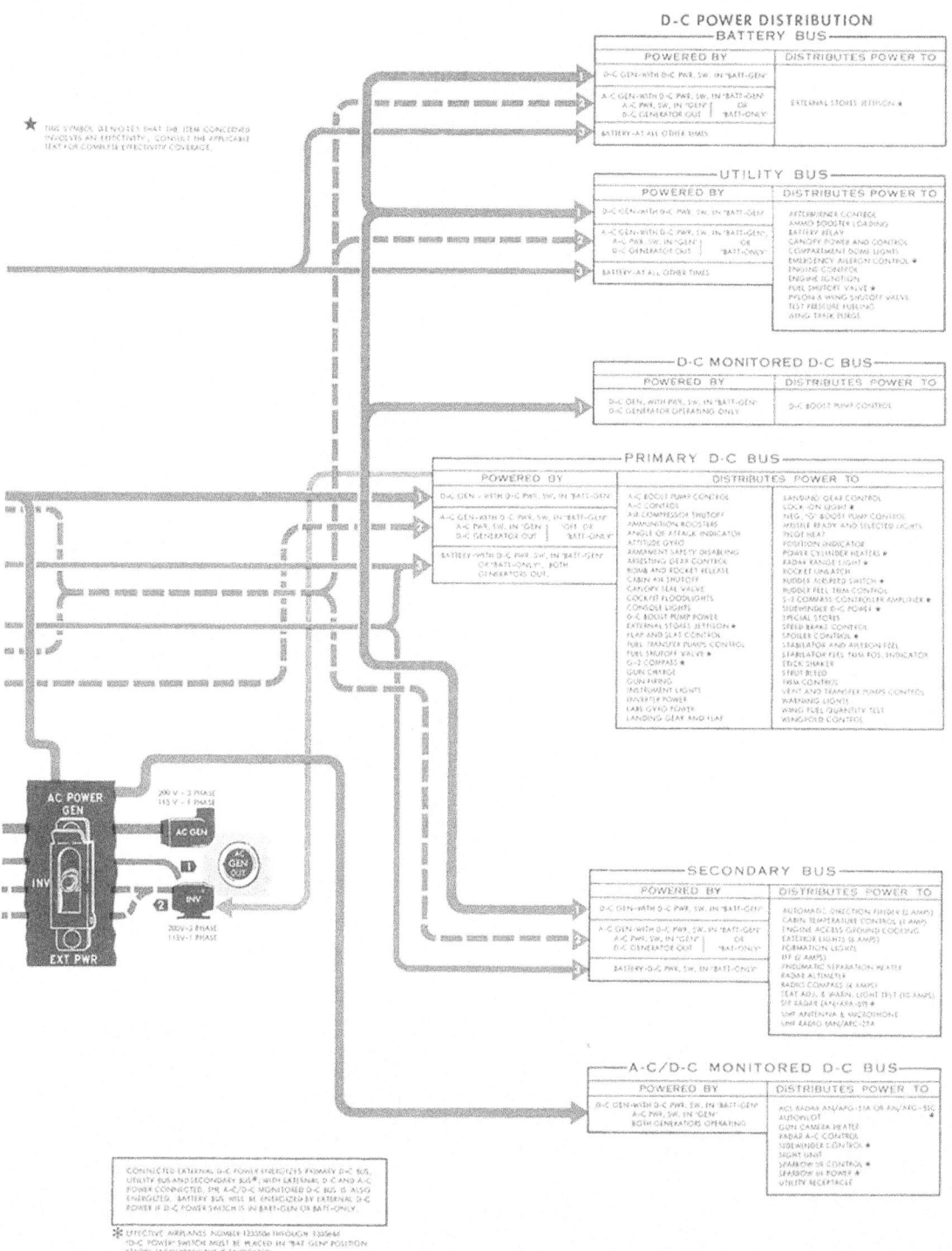

Figure 1-10. Electrical System Schematic (Sheet 2)

FUEL QUANTITY INDICATING SYSTEM

The fuel quantity indicating system, electrically powered by the a-c bus, is of the capacitor type and provides a reading, in pounds, of total internal fuel. Cockpit components of the system include the indicator, a fuel quan check switch and a fuel low warning light.

Fuel Quantity Gage

The fuel quantity indicator is mounted on the main instrument panel and registers, by means of tank capacitors, total fuel aboard the aircraft. The indicator dial is calibrated from 0 to 12 with reading being multiplied by 1000.

Fuel Quantity Check Switch

The fuel quantity check switch is a three-position momentary contact switch, located on the lower right side of the main instrument panel. The switch makes it possible to determine the amount of fuel in both wings, the fuselage or total amount (internally) available. Placing the switch to the WING and FUS position gives a reading of wing plus fuselage tanks; with the switch in the FUS position a reading of fuselage only is given. If wing tanks are full, approximately four seconds are required to register total measured fuel. Placing the switch to GAGE CHECK causes a deflection of the pointer on the fuel quantity indicator. When the switch is released, the pointer should return to its original position ± 25 pounds. The fuel quantity check switch is normally retained in the FUS position.

Fuel Low Warning Light

The fuel low warning light is mounted on the right console subpanel (see figure 1-19). A thermistor type sensing unit located on the center fuselage tank fuel quantity probe activates the low level warning light when the fuel level of the center fuselage tank drops to 1500 pounds. This unit operates independently of the fuel quantity indicating system and receives electrical power from the primary d-c bus.

ELECTRICAL POWER SUPPLY SYSTEM

Electrical energy in the airplane is supplied through a 28 volt d-c system and a 200 volt, a-c three-phase system. The d-c system furnishes power to operate control valves in the hydraulic and pneumatic systems, d-c voltage to the electronic systems, and power to solenoid and d-c motor-operated mechanism. The electrical system is powered by one 28 volt, 300 ampere engine-driven d-c generator, a 24 volt, 36 ampere hour battery, and one engine-driven 15,000 volt-ampere a-c generator. Both the a-c and d-c generators are geared to an engine-operated constant speed transmission arranged to give constant speed generator operation at engine speed of idling or above. The d-c generator comes on the line at 10-15% rpm or 28-30% rpm depending upon which type of constant speed drive is used. The a-c and d-c power supply systems are interconnected through the transformer-rectifier unit and through the inverter. The a-c system supplies a portion of the d-c system with rectified a-c power through the transformer-rectifier unit upon d-c generator failure and the d-c system operates the inverter to supply a portion of the a-c system upon a-c generator failure.

D-C ELECTRICAL POWER

The d-c power supply system consists primarily of a 24-volt battery and a 300 ampere engine-driven generator. The output voltage of the generator is maintained at 28 volts automatically by the voltage regulator. Normally the generator supplies the d-c system and keeps the battery charged. The battery is held in reverse to supply power when generator output is low or in emergency upon failure of both a-c and d-c generator. A reverse current relay automatically connects the generator to the d-c distribution system when the generator reaches normal voltage and disconnects the generator when voltage falls below normal. In addition, the reverse current relay initiates action in the circuits that causes the a-c system to furnish power to the d-c system through the transformer-rectifier unit. Power is distributed to the individual circuits by means of six buses. (See figure 1-10.) The primary bus distributes power to circuits essential to flight, the secondary bus distributes power to circuits needed during normal flight and the a-c/d-c monitored bus distributes power to the circuits necessary to maintain a tactical airplane. See figure 1-10 for the conditions under which the various buses are energized. The utility bus will be energized at all times if there is a battery in the airplane, thus the circuits connected to the utility bus will be energized at all times regardless of the position of the d-c power switch.

D-C Power Switch

The d-c power switch is mounted on the right console sub-instrument panel. It has three positions, BATT-GEN, OFF and BATT-ONLY. The switch exercises control over the d-c generator and buses as shown on figure 1-10. BATT-GEN is the normal position of the switch. In the event that both generators become inoperative, the utility and both primary buses will remain energized by the battery without changing the position of the d-c power switch. The secondary bus may then be energized in addition to the above mentioned buses, if necessary by placing the switch in BATT-ONLY position. The switch is provided with a safety guard to prevent possible discharge of the battery through accidental switching to BATT-ONLY position. The switch may be placed in BATT-ONLY position by lifting the guard and moving the switch to its down position.

Note

In the event that the d-c power switch has been placed in the OFF position it may be necessary to momentarily switch to the INV or EXT position on the a-c power switch to reconnect the d-c generator to the bus system.

Circuit Breakers

The d-c circuits are protected by magnetic type circuit breakers. The circuit breakers in essential circuits are located on panels above the right and left consoles and are accessible during flight. The majority of the remaining circuit breakers are located on the panels in the equipment compartment and are inaccessible during flight.

D-C Generator Warning Light

A generator warning light marked D-C GEN OUT is located on the right console sub-instrument panel. (See figure 1-19, this section.) When generator is inoperative, the warning light will be energized and remain so unless output of the generator returns to normal. Application of external power will extinguish the warning light. The d-c power switch must be in the BATT or BATT GEN position to illuminate the warning light without external power.

D-C External Power Receptacle

The d-c external power receptacle is located in the leading edge of the right wing near the center fuselage and is accessible through door No. 77. An external power source capable of delivering 30 volts at a minimum of 300 ampere should be used. An AN2551 cable used with the power supply equipment mates with the airplane d-c external power receptacle.

A-C ELECTRICAL POWER

An a-c generator and inverter supplies a-c power to the airplane. The generator is driven by a constant speed engine drive. The generator is rated at 15,000 volt-ampere, 200/115 volts three-phase, 400 cycles. The inverter is rated at 200/115 volts three-phase, 400 cycle. The inverter becomes operative upon placing the d-c power switch in either the BATT GEN or BATT-ONLY position connecting the inverter to the primary d-c power system. During normal operation the inverter powers a dummy load. In the event of a-c generator failure the inverter power automatically energizes the primary a-c loads. Upon failure of the a-c generator the a-c power switch should be placed in the INV position, the a-c gen out warning will be extinguished but will light again in the event of inverter failure. An automatic a-c system control unit is provided to cut out the generator in event of a-c system malfunction. If an overvoltage condition exists, the a-c generator will not cut back in unless the a-c power switch is recycled (moved from the GEN position and then back again). The a-c generator will provide the d-c bus system, with the exception of the a-c/d-c monitored buses, with d-c power through a transformer-rectifier, in the event of d-c generator failure. The d-c power supplied by the a-c system is automatically supplied upon d-c generator failure, providing the a-c generator is operating properly. The a-c power system and distribution of a-c power is shown on figure 1-10. Power from the a-c system is divided into the following loads:

primary loads
a-c monitored loads
a-c/d-c monitored loads

The primary load consists of those systems essential to the flight of the airplane. The a-c monitored load consists of those systems necessary to maintain safe flight. The a-c/d-c monitored load consists of the systems necessary in maintaining a tactical airplane.

A-C Power Switch

The a-c power switch is installed on the sub-instrument panel located at the forward end of the right console. The a-c power switch is a three-position toggle switch with GEN, INV and EXT PWR position. A guard is provided to eliminate accidental movement of the switch position. The switch is used for selection of the a-c power source and to connect the a-c gen out warning light to the a-c generator circuit or the inverter circuit. The switch is normally left in the GEN position. Upon failure of the a-c generator the a-c gen out warning light will light and the switch should be placed in the INV position. This position will allow the a-c gen out warning light to illuminate in the event of inverter failure. The EXT position is used only for ground operation.

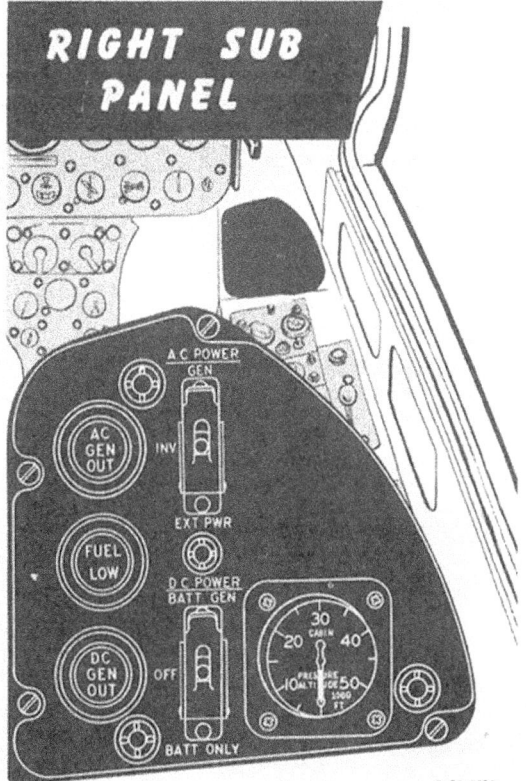

Figure 1-11. Right Sub Panel

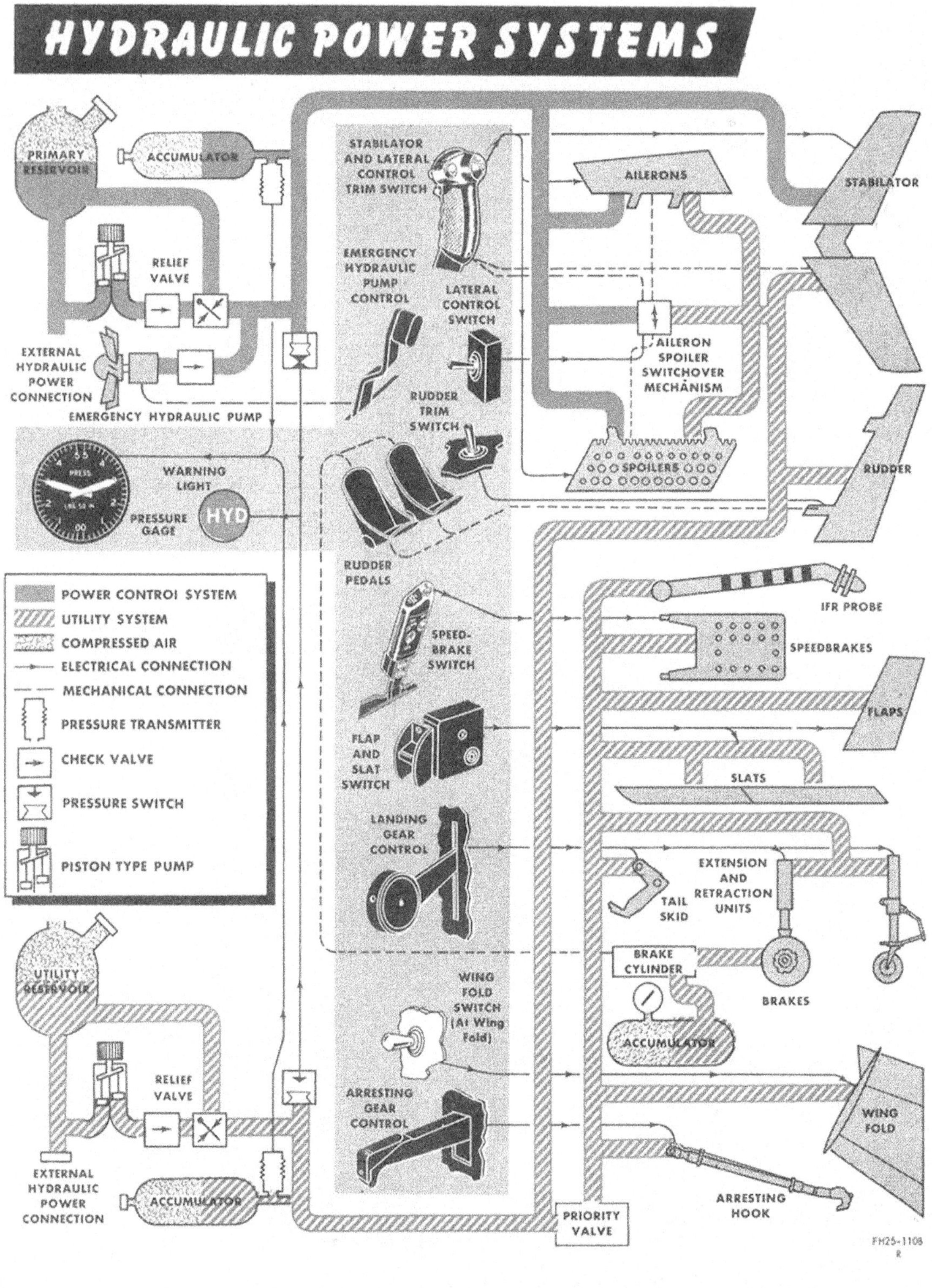

Section I

NAVWEPS 01-245FCB-501

HYDRAULIC POWER SYSTEMS

Figure 1-12. Hydraulic Power System Schematic

A-C Generator Warning Light

The a-c gen out warning light is installed on the sub-instrument panel located at the forward end of the right console. (See figure 1-19, this section.) The warning light will glow in the event of a-c generator failure with the a-c power switch in GEN position. The light will go off when the a-c power switch is placed in the INV position provided the inverter is operating normally. In the event of inverter power failure, the warning light will glow providing the a-c power switch is in the INV position. The light may be dimmed when the instrument lights are on. Testing of the light may be accomplished by placing the warning lights and fire test switch, located on the main instrument panel, momentarily in the TEST WARN. LTS. position.

A-C External Power Receptacle

An external a-c power receptacle is located near the leading edge of the right wing, close to the fuselage, and is accessible through the same door as the external d-c power receptacle. A "Y" connected, 15,000 volt-ampere external a-c power source capable of delivering 200/115 volt, three-phase, 400 cycle power should be used. An AN3430 plug and cable assembly should be used to connect the power source to the mating receptacle. Phase A of the power source should be connected to pin A of the plug, phase B to pin B, phase C to pin C, and neutral to pin N. Pins E and F of the plug are connected together. The a-c power switch must be placed in the EXT position when using external power.

HYDRAULIC POWER SUPPLY SYSTEM

Two 3000 psi hydraulic systems are used in the F3H airplane; the power control hydraulic system and the utility hydraulic system. These systems are discussed in detail below.

POWER CONTROL SYSTEM

The power control hydraulic system supplies hydraulic pressure for actuation of the following systems:

    Ailerons
    Spoilers
    Stabilator

A variable delivery engine-driven pump mounted on the engine accessory drive receives its fluid from the pressurized 1.5 gallon power control system reservoir. Pressure from the pump flows through a relief valve which opens to return at pressures exceeding 3450 psi. Downstream from the relief valve, a piston type accumulator, precharged to 500 psi air pressure, is located to supply an auxiliary volume of fluid when system demand exceeds pump output and also to serve as a pressure surge absorption chamber. A pressure transmitter for the cockpit remote reading hydraulic pressure gage is also located in the main pressure manifold from the pump.

UTILITY SYSTEM

The utility hydraulic system supplies hydraulic pressure for actuating the following items:

    Landing Gear
    Arresting Gear
    Tail Skid
    Wheel Brakes
    Flaps & Slats
    Speed Brakes
    Wing Fold and Wing Fold Pin Pull
    Air Compressor
    Ailerons
    Spoilers
    Stabilator
    Rudder and Rudder Feel
    In-Flight Refueling Probe

A 2.8 gallon pressurized reservoir supplies fluid to the utility systems engine-driven pump mounted on the engine accessory drive. Function of the utility systems pump, reservoir, relief valve, accumulator, (precharged to 1000 psi) and pressure transmitter is identical with those in the power control system.

Note

Although the utility and power control hydraulic systems are independent systems, a pressure line from the power control system is ducted to a pressure operated shutoff valve in the utility system. This valve closes in the event of a pressure loss in the power control hydraulic system. The valve begins to close when power control system pressure drops to 600 psi, and is completely closed when pressure reaches 150 psi. The closing of this valve blocks utility system pressure to all units in the utility system except the aileron tandem power control cylinders, the dual stabilator power cylinder, and the spoiler actuating cylinders.

Hydraulic Pressure Gage

The hydraulic pressure indicating system consists of a dual scale indicator and two transmitters, one for power control hydraulic pressure and the other for utility control hydraulic pressure. The indicator is mounted on the pedestal panel while the two transmitters are located in the engine accessories compartment. The left hand scale on the indicator registers pressure in the power control hydraulic system while the right hand scale registers utility control hydraulic pressure. Both scales are identical, having a range of 0 to 5000 pounds with the calibration being 0 to 5 and the reading being multiplied by 1000. Both systems normally will have a pressure range of 2750 to 3150 pounds while the aircraft is on the ground and hydraulically operated equipment is not functioning. Electrical power for the dual indicator is supplied from the primary a-c bus. A hydraulic warning light located on the main panel glows when pressure in either system drops to 1500 psi. (See figure 1-19, this section.) The light ceases to glow when pressure exceeds 1750 psi in both systems. The light is operated by switches in the power and utility control pressure lines.

EMERGENCY HYDRAULIC POWER

FH25-152

The power control hydraulic system contains an emergency pump which is used to supply hydraulic power to the power control system in event of failure of the power control system's engine-driven pump. The emergency hydraulic pump is attached to a pneumatically actuated door which is raised and lowered by means of the emerg hyd pump handle on the left console. When the door is lowered into the airstream, a small turbine drives the pump. To operate the emergency hydraulic pump, perform the following:

1. Pull emerg hyd pump handle full aft to lower pump.
2. Push handle full forward to raise pump.

Note

The emergency hydraulic pump handle requires slightly less force during the first part of its travel than during the latter. The handle must be pulled to its ABSOLUTE LIMIT in order to effect emergency pump extension.

PNEUMATIC POWER SUPPLY SYSTEM

The 3000 psi pneumatic system enables actuation of the following systems:

    Gun Feed
    Gun Charge
    Gun Bay Louvers
    Emergency Canopy Operation
    Emergency Landing Gear Extension
    Emergency Hydraulic Pump Door
    Emergency Slat Extension

Air supplied from the engine compressors for maintenance of a constant inlet pressure at any altitude is compressed to 3000 psi by the hydraulically operated air compressor, and maintains the air bottles at 3000 psi.

A solenoid operated shutoff valve in the hydraulic line to the compressor motor is controlled by a pneumatic pressure switch cutting hydraulic flow to compressor when air pressure is 3000 ± 100 psi and opening the hydraulic line when air pressure drops to 2800 ± 50 psi. The air compressor discharges into a manifold which contains the air drying equipment, a pressure switch and a pressure transmitter for the cockpit gage. The system normally will have a range of 2650-3200 psi after preflight recharging of the system. A branch isolated from the system during operation by a shuttle valve contains an air charging fitting and a system gage for ground charging of the system at preflight. The manifold then branches to each of the pneumatic operated units. The branch systems are isolated from return flow to the manifold by air check valves. Reverse flow into the compressor is prevented during ground charging by the shuttle valve in the manifold between compressor and charging valve.

PNEUMATIC PRESSURE GAGE

The pneumatic pressure gage is mounted on the pedestal panel and operates in conjunction with the pneumatic pressure transmitter which is located in the engine accessories compartment. The indicator has a range of 0 to 5000 pounds with calibrations of 0 to 50 and readings multiplied by 100. Normal system pressure ranges from 2650 to 3200 pounds.

FLIGHT CONTROL SYSTEM

Primary flight controls consist of ailerons, spoilers, rudder and stabilator, the stabilator being a one-piece movable horizontal tail. All surfaces are actuated by irreversible hydraulic power control cylinders. Artificial feel systems provide the pilot with simulated stick and pedal forces due to the lack of aerodynamic "feed back" forces from the power cylinders. All feel systems have trim actuators which are controlled by the pilot. Cockpit indicators show position of stabilator feel trim, aileron and rudder position. Viscous dampers are used in the stabilator and rudder systems. Secondary controls are leading edge slats, trailing edge flaps and fuselage mounted speed brakes. Refer to Flight Controls, Section VII.

LATERAL CONTROL SYSTEM

To reduce high speed aerodynamic loading of the outer wing panels, and to increase roll rate, a spoiler system is utilized in conjunction with the ailerons. The lateral control system consists of the aileron control system, the spoiler control system, and a hydromechanical shift mechanism for control selection.

Aileron Control

The aileron control system is identical to that used in conventional airplanes except for a shift mechanism incorporated as a part of the normal push rod linkage. During normal and low speed operations the aileron control system operates exactly the same as the conventional system.

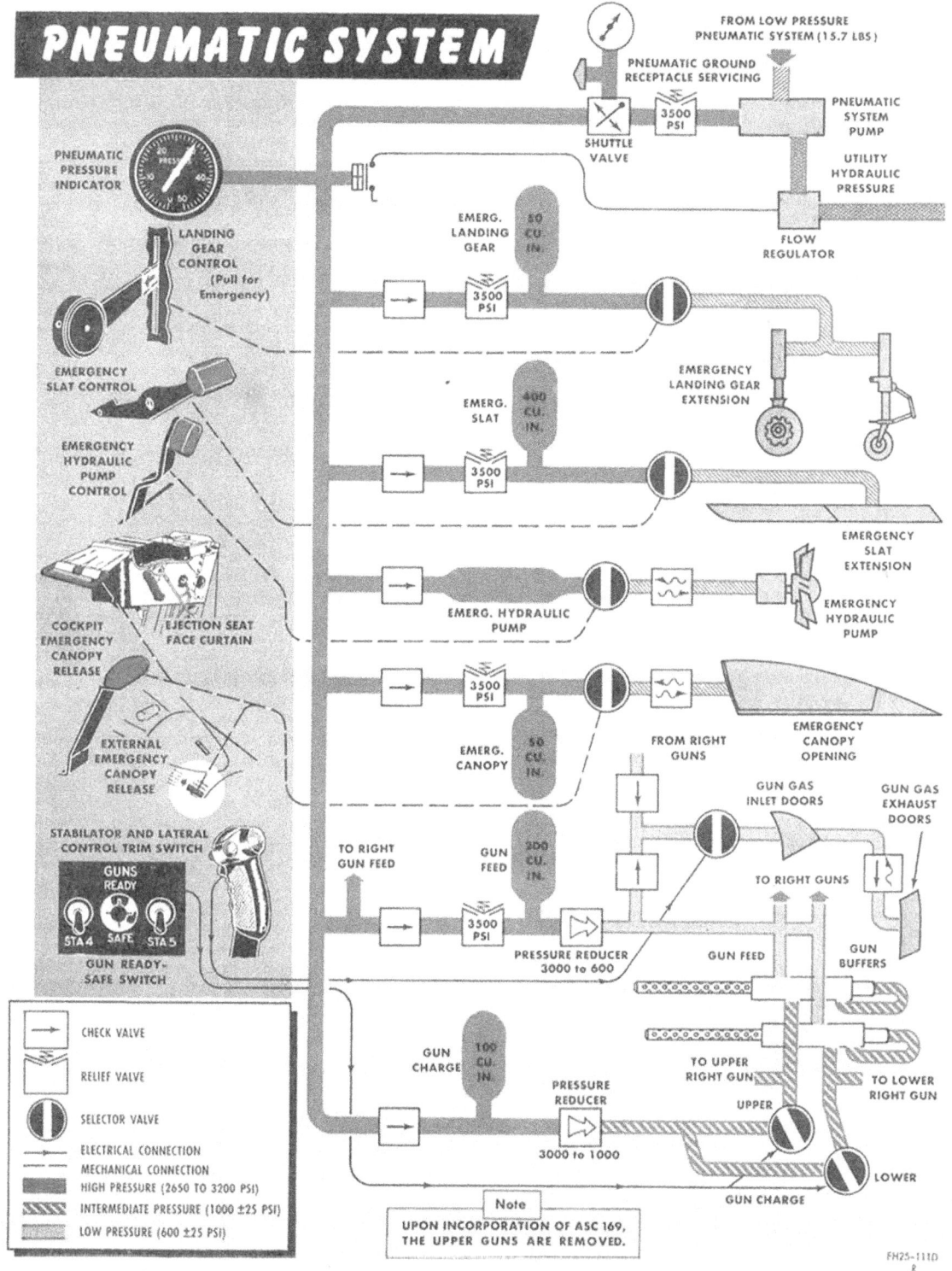

Figure 1-13. Pneumatic System

Spoiler Control

The spoiler control system contains the stick, push rods, aileron-spoiler shift mechanism, airspeed switch, lateral control switch, servo valves and dual actuating cylinders. At predetermined airspeeds (see figure 6-2, Section VI) an airspeed switch, acting on a hydraulic selector valve, causes power control system hydraulic pressure to be directed to the shift mechanism which transfers push rod movements from the aileron actuators to the spoiler actuators. While the spoilers are operating the ailerons remain in the neutral position. Aileron control is again resumed at an airspeed approximately 15 knots slower than the spoiler cut-in airspeed. The time required to complete the shift from one condition to the other is from 1.6 to 2.2 seconds.

Note

Different static pressure sources are used in the system. One source is used for the airspeed switch and another for the airspeed indicator. For this reason, cockpit airspeed indications and actual switch-over airspeeds will vary with altitude. (See figure 6-2, Section VI NAVWEPS 01-245FCB-501A.)

Each spoiler utilizes two actuators, the inboard one being controlled by power control system pressure, and the outboard one being controlled by utility system pressure. Thus, should one system fail, the spoilers will still function at reduced power. The shift mechanism is spring-loaded to the aileron condition and a restrictor is placed in the hydraulic lines. Thus, in the event of power control failure, after a time interval of approximately 5 minutes, system pressure will bleed off enough to allow spring pressure to regain the aileron control condition. Electrical failure locks hydraulic fluid in the shift mechanism, if that is the control condition at the time of failure, and pilot must use the lateral control switch to regain the aileron condition.

Note

• No provisions are made for autopilot control of the spoilers. However, when engaged the autopilot continues to deflect the ailerons even though they are neutralized during spoiler operation. Since autopilot aileron correction will oppose spoiler movement, there is a possibility of control reversal, and a definite reduction in control effectiveness. It is recommended, therefore, that the autopilot be disengaged above spoiler switchover airspeeds (see figure 6-2, Section VI, NAVWEPS 01-245FCB-501A).

• Approximately 5/8 of the normal control stick throw is necessary for full spoiler deflection.

Lateral Control Switch

A guarded, three-position switch, marked EMERG. SPOILERS, AUTO, and EMERG. AILERON is located on the inboard, left-hand side of the glare shield. This switch serves a threefold purpose. In the EMERG. AILERON position the switch transfers lateral control of the aircraft back to the ailerons in the event of electrical power failure. In the AUTO position the lateral control system functions normally, the spoilers being actuated by the airspeed switch at predetermined airspeeds. A guarded switch is provided, which automatically centers the switch toggle when closed. The guard must be lifted in order to move the switch out of the AUTO position. The EMERG. SPOILER position has been provided for ground test of the spoilers as well as in-flight selection in the event of airspeed switch failure. This position by-passes the airspeed switch allowing the spoilers to be operated on the ground. A manually dimmable light located above the switch illuminates when the switch is in any position other than AUTO. Electrical power to the EMERG. SPOILER position of the lateral control switch is supplied by the primary d-c bus, power to the EMERG. AILERON position is from the utility d-c bus, and the AUTO position is open, receiving power via the airspeed switch, which is supplied by the primary d-c bus.

Lateral Control Switch Warning Light

A warning light is located immediately above the lateral control switch (see figure 1-19, this section). This light will illuminate when the switch is in any other position than AUTO. Electrical power to this light is provided by the utility d-c bus. This light is dimmed manually by rotating the reflector clockwise.

Lateral Control Feel and Trim

The use of irreversible power cylinders in the aileron control system results in the absence of any aerodynamic forces being present at the control stick. An artificial feel system, consisting of a double-acting spring cartridge, is directly connected to the push rod system and thereby produces simulated forces at the control stick, which are constant at all airspeeds and proportional to stick deflection. An electrical actuator moves the spring cartridge to give aileron trim in the range of 12° up and 9° down. The actuator is controlled from the trim switch which is located on the stick grip. (See figure 1-14.) Due to the placement of the artificial feel system components within the lateral control system, simulated forces at the control stick are produced in both aileron and spoiler control systems.

Aileron Position Indicator

The aileron position indicator, located on the left-hand subpanel, indicates to the pilot aileron position. The indicator receives electrical signals via a transmitter which is powered from the primary a-c bus.

Note

As the aileron position transmitter is linked directly to the ailerons, the aileron position indicator functions only when the aileron control system is in operation.

STABILATOR SYSTEM

The stabilator system contains the stick, push-pull rods, dual power control cylinder, damper, and the stabilator. The stabilator is a single unit horizontal tail which is actuated by an irreversible dual power control actuator. Hydraulic pressure to the actuator is supplied by both the power control and utility hydraulic systems. Normal operation is from both systems, however, if one system should malfunction, the actuator will operate on the other system with reduced performance. A stabilator feel system is used to produce simulated aerodynamic forces at the control stick. Autopilot control in the stabilator system is operated by a servo which is directly coupled to the stabilator push rod system. Autopilot operation of the stabilator will move the control stick fore and aft. Refer to Autopilot, Section IV.

Stabilator Feel and Trim

The stabilator feel system is an arrangement basically consisting of a spring and ram air bellows appropriately connected to the variable bell crank so as to provide opposing forces. When the airplane is trimmed for a given stabilator position, the moment about the variable bell crank is zero, providing zero longitudinal stick force. Any change of speed will vary the air pressure on the bellows and give a different trimmed position to the control stick. The spring and air pressures act upon a variable bell crank which is operated by an electric actuator. Operation of this actuator changes the moment arms of the two forces, thereby allowing different positions of trim providing feel forces proportional to speed and stick deflection. An indicator in the cockpit gives the pilot a constant reference to stabilator feel trim position. The feel trim actuator is controlled by the trim switch on the control stick or by the autopilot. A viscous damper is used in the stabilator feel system linkage to increase feel forces with abrupt control stick movement. A system of spring cartridge is incorporated in the control linkage which enables the pilot to override the feel system in the event of a malfunction. A "bob" weight is used on the control stick to produce desirable "g" forces during maneuvering flight.

Stabilator Trim Indicator

The stab. trim indicator is located on the left-hand subpanel. It is directly controlled by a transmitter which is integral with the stabilator feel trim actuator.

RUDDER CONTROL SYSTEM

Standard type rudder pedals in the cockpit are linked by a push rod system to the servo valve in the rudder power control cylinder. The power control cylinder is of the irreversible type which means that the aerodynamic forces on the rudder will not be felt by the pilot at the rudder pedals. An artificial feel system is employed to simulate these forces, thereby giving the pilot "feel" at the rudder pedals. Two viscous dampers are coupled directly to the rudder to prevent vibration. In the absence of hydraulic pressure to the power control cylinder, an internal by-pass valve opens to allow fluid to pass from one side of the piston to the other. Thus the cylinder acts as another "link" in the rudder system and the rudder can be moved by pilot effort. Autopilot operation of the rudder is by a linear type actuator installed in the push rod system. Operation of this actuator does not move the rudder pedals. For autopilot information, refer to Section IV.

Rudder Feel and Trim

An artificial feel system is employed to simulate the forces acting on the rudder. The system consists essentially of a spring cartridge, a trim actuator, and a hydraulic cylinder. The spring cartridge supplies constant feel forces at speeds below 225 knots. At speeds over 225 knots, the airspeed switch actuates hydraulic pressure to the cylinder in the feel system. Pressure in this cylinder requires greater pilot effort to move the rudder pedals. An electric trim actuator is connected to one end of the spring cartridge. Trimming of the rudder system is accomplished by operation of this actuator which lengthens or shortens the coupling between the feel system and the rudder push rod system. The actuator is controlled electrically from the cockpit.

Rudder Trim Switch

The rudder trim switch is located on the left console aft and slightly outboard of the throttle, with an arrow indicating NOSE L and NOSE R. This switch controls the trim actuator in the rudder feel system which trims the airplane directionally.

Rudder Pedals

The rudder pedals are conventional type suspended units which are coupled to the rudder push rod system by individual screw jacks. The screw jacks provide adjustment of the rudder pedals for pilot comfort and are adjusted simultaneously by turning a crank on the pedestal. The pedals are also coupled to the brake master cylinders so that toe pressure on the pedal will apply the brakes. The master cylinders deboost utility system pressure to the required braking pressure. The left rudder pedal has a hook to accommodate the surface controls lock.

Rudder Trim Indicator

The rudder trim indicator is located on the left-hand subpanel adjacent to the stabilator feel trim indicator. The indicator is controlled by a transmitter which is mechanically coupled to the rudder. This indicator operates from the primary a-c bus.

CONTROL STICK

The control stick is mounted in a yoke which permits both left to right and fore and aft motion. The control

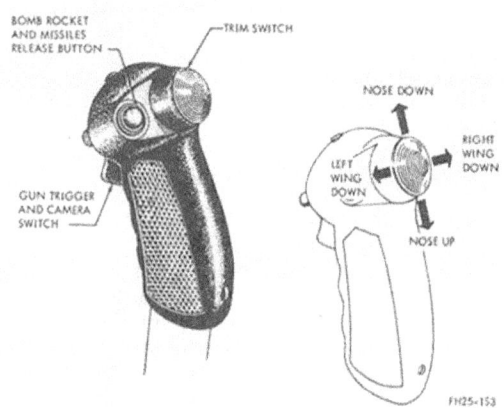

Figure 1-14. Control Stick Grip

grip is a quick removable assembly containing three switches, a two-position trigger switch for gun firing and gun camera actuator, a bomb, rocket and missiles firing switch and a trim switch which operates both the aileron feel trim and the stabilator feel trim actuators. A "bob" weight is attached to the control stick to give desired stick forces during maneuvering flight.

Stall Warning Vibrator

A stall warning vibrator is attached to the control stick to warn the pilot of approaching stall conditions. The vibrator consists of an electric motor which drives an eccentric weight. Rotation of the weight causes the control stick to vibrate, warning the pilot of an impending stall. A sufficient margin exists to allow the pilot to return to proper flight attitude by normal reaction to the warning. The vibrator is electrically connected to a preset switch in the angle-of-attack indicator. When the indicator reads 19.5 units the switch closes the circuit, setting the vibrator in motion. The vibrator is also connected to the right landing gear scissors switch to prevent vibrator operation while the airplane is on the ground. On F3H-2 aircraft 133549d through 133622f inclusive, upon the incorporation of ASC 170, the stall warning vibrator is actuated when the angle of attack indicated is 20.0 units or greater.

WING FLAPS AND SLATS

Leading edge slats are incorporated in both the inner and outer wing panels and trailing edge flaps are mounted on the inboard wing panels. Flaps and slats may be selectively controlled by the flap and slats switch. A flap position indicator and a slats warning light are located in the cockpit on the left-hand subpanel.

Flap and Slat Switch

A three-position flap and slat control switch is incorporated. The switch is located outboard of the throttle on the left console and is marked FLAP SLATS RETRACT, SLATS EXTEND FLAPS STOP, and FLAP SLATS EXTEND. Actuating the switch will allow simultaneous travel of the flaps and slats with the exception of the center, SLATS EXTEND FLAPS STOP position. This position allows the extension of slats without flaps and intermediate flap settings. Power is supplied to the switch from the primary d-c bus.

Emergency Slat Extension

Emergency extension of the slats is accomplished through the high pressure pneumatic system. The slats are lowered pneumatically, during a utility hydraulic failure, by pushing down the emerg. slat handle above the aft section of the left console. The air bottle contains air sufficient for one extension of the slats.

CAUTION

Do not attempt to retract the slats hydraulically after extending pneumatically unless the procedure outlined in Section VII has been followed before extension, and is followed during retraction. Failure to follow this procedure may result in loss of the hydraulic system.

Flap Position Indicator

The flap position indicator is combined with the landing gear indicator into a single unit located on the left-hand subpanel. Indication is constant from full up to full down positions. The indicator is controlled by a transmitter located in the right inboard wing panel and mechanically coupled to the flaps.

Figure 1-15. Flap and Slats Switch

Slats Warning Light

An indicator light, located near the aileron trim indicator on the left-hand subpanel (see figure 1-16, this section), is illuminated at any time the slats are not in the position indicated by the flap and slats switch. The light is connected to the warning light test relays to check light for operating condition; it is also connected to the warning light dimming system. Pilot should make visual check to assure slat position.

SPEED BRAKES

The hydraulically operated speed brakes are sections of the aft fuselage skin which are hinged on the forward side permitting the brakes to open outward and forward. Speed brakes are controlled from a switch on the throttle grip and may be positioned at any point in their travel. Hydraulic restrictors prevent speed brakes from "banging" shut. Due to the construction of the selector valve, the speed brakes will not close following a hydraulic pressure failure unless the speed brake circuit breaker on the left circuit breaker panel is pulled. This opens a solenoid by-pass valve allowing fluid to pass from one side of the piston to the other. Air loads will then close the brakes. A light on the console forward of the oxygen regulator indicates speed brakes out.

SPEED BRAKE SWITCH

The speed brake switch, located on the throttle grip, has two positions, IN and OUT. Only the OUT position is momentary (see figure 1-6). Placing the switch in OUT position will operate speed brakes toward the extended position, and positioning switch to IN will close speed brakes flush with the fuselage. Releasing the switch to return to the neutral position will retain speed brakes in any desired position. The switch operates a solenoid valve which hydraulically "locks" when electrical supply to it is shut off. Safety switches are located in the aft fuselage just aft of speed brakes which can be switched to either NORMAL or SAFE position.

Note

Speed brake safety switches should be checked for NORMAL position prior to flight. If either switch is in SAFE position, speed brakes will be inoperative.

Speed Brakes Out Light

An indicator light is located on the oxygen panel to indicate when either or both the speed brakes are not fully closed (see figure 1-19, this section). When brakes are partially open, light is illuminated.

LANDING GEAR SYSTEM

The airplane is equipped with fully retractable tricycle landing gear which are completely covered by flush doors when retracted. The gear is electrically controlled and hydraulically actuated from the utility hydraulic system. Electrical power is supplied from the primary d-c bus. During normal operation, the tail skid is extended and retracted with the landing gear. Accidental retraction of the gear, when the airplane is on the ground is prevented by safety switches on each main gear torque scissors.

MAIN GEAR

Each main gear is hydraulically retracted and extended. The gear is locked down by a spring-loaded overcenter lock link assembly which prevents folding of the side brace. The main gears retract inboard and are enclosed by fairing doors that are flush with the underside of wing. The gear is locked up by a hydraulically actuated mechanism which also controls operation of the inboard door so that it cannot close until the gear is up and locked. All main gear doors remain open when the gear is extended. The main gear shock struts can be pneumatically extended to provide additional deck clearance for external stores. An external source of clean dry compressed air is used to extend the struts. Strut bleed valves are electrically operated by a switch on the left console. Operating the valves bleeds extension air and returns the struts to the normal condition.

NOSE GEAR

The nose gear is hydraulically retracted and extended. As the nose gear retracts, the strut is mechanically compressed. It automatically returns to its fully extended position when the gear is let down. The gear is locked in both the up and down position by spring-loaded overcenter lock links. The lock links are automatically released by the actuating cylinder at the beginning of the retraction or extension cycle. The nose gear retracts aft into the fuselage and is covered by mechanically operated doors that close flush with the underside of the fuselage. The nose gear is equipped with a shimmy damper and is steered by differential braking of the main gear wheels.

LANDING GEAR HANDLE

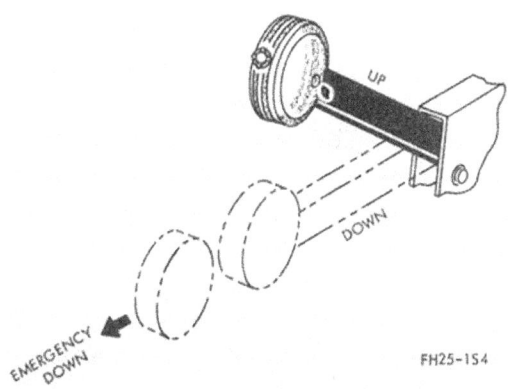

FH25-154

Operation of the landing gear is controlled by a handle at the left side of the main instrument panel. The handle has a wheel-shaped knob for ease of identification. Placing the handle in the up or down position actuates a switch, which energizes the hydraulic control valve to operate the gear. Switches in the gun charging armament safety and landing gear position indicator circuits are also actuated by the control. A red warning light is located in the landing gear control handle knob. This light comes on whenever the control handle is moved to retract or extend the gear and it remains on until the gear completes its cycle. Pulling the landing gear control handle full aft operates the landing gear emergency system.

Emergency Landing Gear Control

Emergency extension of the landing gear is accomplished pneumatically. Pulling the landing gear control handle full aft operates an air valve which directs 3000 psi compressed air to extend the nose gear, open the main gear inboard doors, and unlock the main gear uplocks, permitting the main gear to free fall. A 50 cu. in. air bottle provides sufficient compressed air to extend the gear in the event of a hydraulic system failure.

Note

The tail skid will not extend by the emergency method. The pilot should attempt to keep the tail from touching down during landing after emergency extension.

CAUTION

Do not attempt to retract gear after the emergency extension system is used, unless the procedure outlined in Section VII is followed before and during the emergency extension. The utility hydraulic reservoir may be destroyed by high pressure air if incorrect procedures are used.

LANDING GEAR POSITION INDICATORS

The landing gear position indicator and flap position indicator are combined in a single instrument that is mounted on the left-hand subpanel. The unit contains four elements, three of which are used for landing gear position indication. The indicator operates in conjunction with position switches on the landing gear. The position of the landing gear wheels is indicated by drum dials viewed through cutouts in the front scale plate of the instrument.

MAIN STRUT CATAPULT EXTENSION

The main strut switch, located on the left console outboard of the throttle, is a two-position, lever lock toggle switch. Since the strut extension operation is entirely a ground servicing operation and only utilized for special missions, the switch is normally retained in the

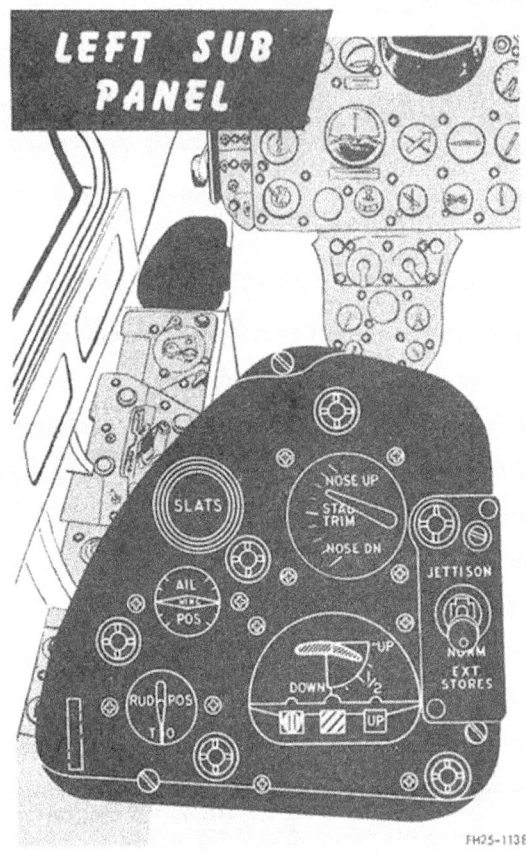

Figure 1-16. Left Sub Panel

EXTEND position. When conditions no longer warrant extended struts, the pilot can bleed off extension air and return the struts to a normal condition by placing the main strut switch to the BLEED position. Electrical power is supplied from the primary d-c bus.

Note

The main strut switch does not provide a means for the pilot to extend the landing gear struts. This operation is accomplished by ground crew only.

Strut Extend Warning Light

A red warning light, marked STRUT EXTEND, is located on the left console just forward of the main strut switch. The light illuminates when the landing gear control handle is in the down position and the struts are extended. It may be desirable to land with the struts extended (refer to F3H-2 Special Stores Handbook, NAVWEPS 01-245FCB-513). Electrical power is supplied from the primary d-c bus.

WHEEL BRAKE SYSTEM

The main landing gear wheels are equipped with hydraulically operated dual disc-type brakes. The brakes are individually actuated by power boosted master brake cylinders, operated by toe pressure on the rudder-brake pedals. The power boost is provided by pressure from the utility hydraulic system. A 25 cu. in. accumulator contains sufficient pressurized fluid for several brake applications in the event of a utility hydraulic system failure.

Note

Violent or forceful application of the brakes may "bottom out" the master brake cylinders. This action is evidenced to the pilot by a sudden relaxing of the pedal effort required; MAXIMUM BRAKE FORCE IS BEING APPLIED in this condition. Forceful application of the brakes should be avoided, as the brakes are very powerful and may be locked quite easily.

ARRESTING GEAR

The arresting gear consists of a conventional arresting hook and mechanism to pneumatically extend and hydraulically retract it into the lower aft fuselage. The hook is actuated by two combination shock absorbing, actuating cylinders. A mechanical latch secures the hook in the retracted position.

ARRESTING GEAR CONTROL

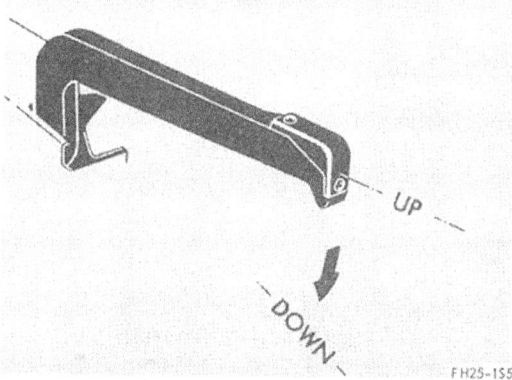

The arresting gear is controlled by a handle located at the right of the main instrument panel. When the control handle is pushed down, the latch is released and the hook is extended by gravity and compressed air in the cylinders. Placing the arresting gear handle in the up position actuates a switch which energizes a solenoid valve which directs hydraulic pressure to the cylinders to raise the arresting hook. A red warning light inside the control handle will come on when the control handle is placed in the down position and will remain on until the arresting gear is fully extended. Warning light will not illuminate again until system is recycled. Electrical power is supplied from the primary d-c bus.

APPROACH LIGHT SYSTEM

An approach light system, with red-amber-green indications, is used to show the Landing Signal Officer the attitude of the airplane on approach to arrested landings. A unit with three individual colored lights is utilized. This unit operates in conjunction with the angle-of-attack system. The approach light relays, acting on signals from the angle-of-attack system will illuminate the applicable colored light. The arresting gear by-pass switch is located on the right cockpit sill. The switch has two positions; FIELD and CARRIER. When in the CARRIER position, the approach lights will be:

1. Off when the gear is up, regardless of hook position.
2. On (flashing) when the gear is down and the hook is up.
3. On (steady) when the gear and hook are extended.

In the FIELD position, the approach lights are off with the gear up and on with the gear extended, regardless of arresting hook position. Adjacent to the approach light switch is a rheostat, provided for dimming the approach indexer.

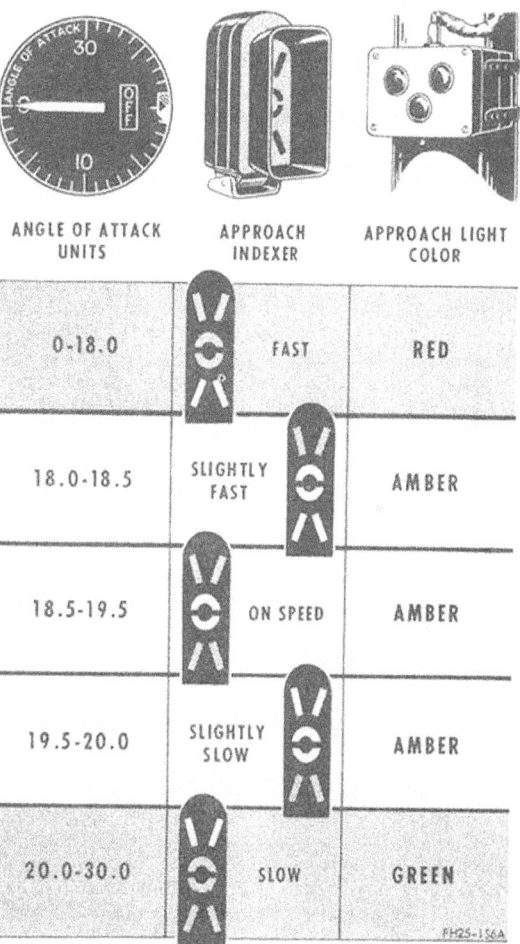

Section I

The angle of attack indicator range with the applicable indications for both the approach indexer and the approach light system are shown in the preceeding chart. All systems are automatically energized when the landing gear is extended and locked. The approach lights will dim when the exterior lights master switch is turned on. The stall warning vibrator is energized when the angle-of-attack indicated is 19.5 units or greater. On F3H-2 airplanes 133549d thru 133622f, the stall warning vibrator is actuated when the angle-of-attack indicated is 20.0 units or greater. Electrical power to the approach light system is provided by the exterior lights circuit (secondary d-c bus).

APPROACH INDEXER

The approach indexer is mounted directly over the fire warning light on the main instrument panel. This unit is coupled to the approach light system in such a manner that the pilot receives a cockpit indication of the approach light signals seen by the L.S.O. In operation, slots cut in the face of the indexer will glow, the sequence of illumination provides the indication of approach attitude. The indexer with its indications is illustrated below.

PITOT-STATIC SYSTEM

A conventional pitot-static system is used in the airplane, with a single pitot tube located in the base of the cockpit windshield structure. F3H airplanes have static sources at fuselage station 460.0 and a wing boom, located near the tip of the right wing. The MK 86 computer, angle-of-attack compensator, autopilot altitude controller and the rudder airspeed switch are supplied with static pressure by the wing source under all flight conditions. The airspeed indicator receives its static pressure from the fuselage station 460.0 source at all times. Below 225 knots IAS, the altimeter and rate-of-climb indicator receive static pressure from the fuselage station 460.0 source. Above 225 knots IAS, a solenoid valve switches these instruments to the wing boom static source, in order to achieve more accurate instrument readings. A separate independent static vent located on the left side of the fuselage at station 170.0 is provided for the spoiler system airspeed switch.

INSTRUMENTS

The instruments utilized in the aircraft are conventional in design and operation. All of the instruments except the stand-by compass, position indicators (gear, flaps and trim) and the cabin pressure altimeter are mounted on the main instrument and pedestal panels. The stand-by compass is mounted directly above the main panel and has a separate means of illumination. The position indicators are on the left subpanel. The cabin pressure altimeter is on the right subpanel. A discussion of all flight instruments except those associated with systems which are discussed in detail elsewhere in this book is set out below.

ALTIMETER

All F3H-2M and F3H-2 airplanes 146339s and previous prior to incorporation of ASC 141 are equipped with conventional triple pointer barometric altimeters. These instruments have a small pointer indicating 10,000 feet, an intermediate pointer indicating 1,000 feet, and a large pointer indicating 100 feet. The instruments are provided with a window in which the field barometric pressure may be read and adjusted by means of a rotary knob below the instrument face. F3H-2 aircraft 146709t and subsequent and those in which ASC 141 has been incorporated utilize a counter-pointer altimeter. This instrument has only one pointer, which indicates hundreds of feet. Altitude to the nearest thousand is read from a counter which indicates consecutive thousands of feet from 1 upward. Field barometric pressure is read and adjusted in the same manner as in the previous instrument. Both altimeters utilize pressure from the pitot-static system.

Note

Upon incorporation of ASC 141A, all counter-pointer altimeters will be removed for modification. While undergoing this modification, a three-pointer instrument will be re-installed.

RATE-OF-CLIMB INDICATOR

Rate of climb or dive up to 6,000 feet per minute may be read from this instrument. Climb or dive in the first 1,000 feet is divided into hundreds and from 1,000 to 6,000 the indication is in 500 feet per minute increments. Static pressure from the pitot-static system is used to operate the instrument.

AIRSPEED AND MACH INDICATOR

The combination airspeed and Mach indicator shows airspeed readings at low speeds and includes Mach number readings at high speeds. Both readings are provided by a single pointer moving over a fixed airspeed scale, graduated from 0 to 650 knots, and a rotatable Mach number scale, graduated from Mach .5 to Mach 2.2. A movable "bug" is included as a landing speed reference and can be positioned by the knob on the face of the instrument. The same knob can position another "bug" on the Mach number scale for a maximum indicated airspeed reference. The airspeed indicator pointer and the Mach number scale are synchronized so that a proper relationship between the two is assured throughout all altitude changes. Thus at sea level and under standard conditions, the pointer will indicate Mach 1 at approximately 660 knots. Under the same conditions but at 50,000 feet, if the same true airspeed is maintained, the pointer will indicate approximately 292 knots and a Mach number of 1.15.

TURN-AND-SLIP INDICATOR

A conventional turn-and-slip indicator is powered by the low pressure pneumatic system. This instrument uses a standard (jet) 4 minute - one needle width turn.

ATTITUDE INDICATOR

The five inch attitude indicator contains a two-tone spherical presentation with the conventional fixed airplane and moving horizon. The miniature airplane is mounted permanently on the inside surface of the bezel glass. Changes in pitch indications are accomplished by rotating the pitch indicator trim knob located at the lower right hand corner. Clockwise rotation of the knob produces a dive indication to a maximum of 15° dive, and counterclockwise rotation produces a climb indication to a maximum of 10° climb. Pitch indication may be trimmed to indicate zero pitch within ± 1/2 of the horizon line width. The spherical background is painted two-tone with a prominent horizontal line separating the upper light tone representing "sky" and the lower dark representing "earth". Horizontal pitch graduations appear every five degrees within the limits of ± 85° with the words CLIMB and DIVE appearing at their respective 45° pitch points. The attitude indicator functions as a repeater unit. The indicator gimbals are servo driven by signals received from the vertical gyro and control unit. The indicator system utilizes both a-c and d-c power simultaneous for its operation. Both sources of power are derived from the aircraft electrical system. Upon initial application of power to the VGI system, a time delay of approximately 2 minutes ± 30 seconds is required for the attitude gyro to erect fully. A "power off" warning flag located at approximately 11 o'clock is designed to disappear at the end of the delay period. The "power off" flag will appear to show the loss of either or both a-c and d-c power to the indicator system. On normal inverter change-over the "power off" flag will appear only for that period of time in which a-c power is lost.

Note

- The pilot should not rely upon the indicator when the "power off" flag is visible.

- A loss of either a-c or d-c power will cut off all power to the system. This is due to the placement of interlock relays in the indicator wiring.

If a-c power is lost for a period in excess of five minutes, pull and reset the vertical gyro d-c circuit breaker when a-c power is again obtained. The system will then undergo a normal recycling.

Note

During a recycle period in flight, the airplane should be flying a constant heading.

When the "power off" flag disappears after momentary power loss or system recycle during flight, the accuracy of the indicator should be checked against the basic flight instrument. No manual caging device is needed on the indicator, as the gyro is maintained at vertical by virtue of an electrolytic leveling switch, sensitive to the earth's gravity. The indicator has complete freedom through 360° about the roll axis and effective freedom of 360° about the pitch axis, making use of stop for the inner gimbal near the 90° dive and climb positions to prevent the gyro from entering the gimbal lock position. The action of controlled precession near the 90° pitch points is momentary and must not be confused with tumbling or upsetting of the gyro. Upon completion of this precession, the gyro will be completely operative. Precessional errors appearing on the indicator resulting from centrifugal forces encountered in flight are approximately one degree for level turns. Precessional errors due to aerobatic maneuvers are approximately five degrees. Indicators exhibiting errors in excess of the above should be checked for a malfunction.

ANGLE-OF-ATTACK INDICATOR

The angle-of-attack indicator reflects the position of the aircraft relative to its line of flight. This is accomplished by means of a probe protruding through the fuselage skin just aft of the cockpit on the right side. This probe rotates in direct relationship to any change in the angle-of-attack and transmits a signal to the indicator via an amplifier. The indicator, with a scale range of 0 to 30 units, converts this signal into a reading of the angle of attack. The system receives power from the primary a-c bus and a power off flag appears when the a-c power is disconnected.

Note

The difference between the indicated and actual angle of attack are shown in figures 6-7 and 6-8, Section VI of the classified supplement to this handbook, publication NAVWEPS 01-245FCB-501A.

ACCELEROMETER

An accelerometer, with three indicating hands, registers and records positive and negative "g" loads. One hand moves in the direction of the "g" load being applied while the other two, one for positive "g" loads and one for negative "g" loads, follow the indicating pointer to its maximum travel. The recording pointers remain at the respective maximum travel positions, thus providing a record of maximum acceleration encountered. Depressing the push-to-reset knob, at the lower left corner of the instrument allows the recording pointers to return to normal (1 "g") position.

Note

Accelerometer may read as much as 1/2 "g" low; possibly lower if the pull-in rate is high.

Section I NAVWEPS 01-245FCB-501

MAIN INSTRUMENT PANEL

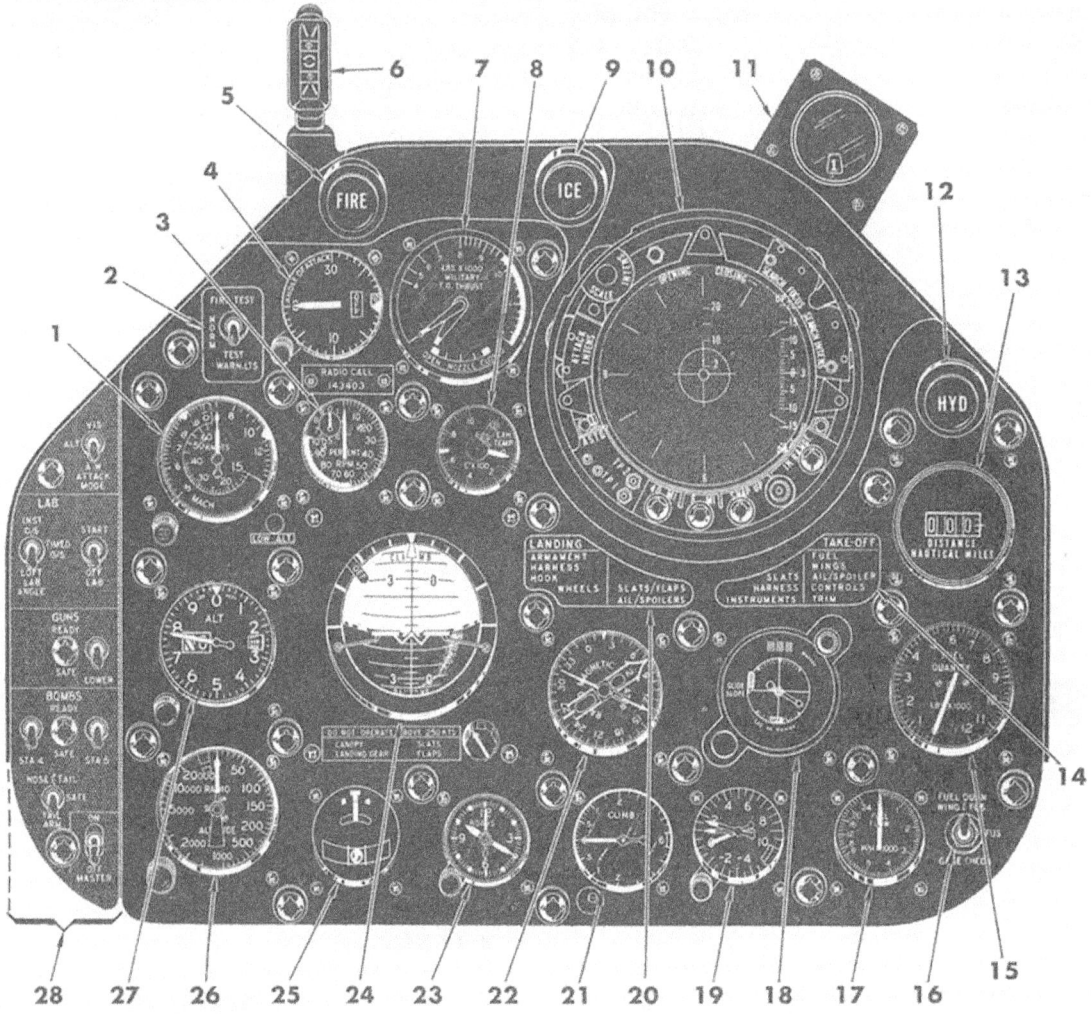

1. AIRSPEED AND MACHMETER
2. WARNING LIGHT AND FIRE (WARNING) TEST SWITCH
3. TACHOMETER
4. ANGLE-OF-ATTACK INDICATOR
5. FIRE WARNING LIGHT
6. ANGLE-OF-ATTACK INDEXER
7. THRUST AND NOZZLE POSITION INDICATOR
8. EXHAUST TEMPERATURE (E.G.T.) INDICATOR
9. ICE WARNING LIGHT (UPON THE INCORPORATION OF ASC168)
10. AN/APG-51C RADAR SCOPE
11. UHF REMOTE CHANNEL INDICATOR
12. HYDRAULIC PRESSURE WARNING LIGHT
13. TACAN RANGE INDICATOR
14. TAKE-OFF CHECK LIST
15. FUEL QUANTITY INDICATOR
16. FUEL QUANTITY GAGE CHECK SWITCH
17. FUEL FLOW INDICATOR
18. TACAN COURSE INDICATOR
19. ACCELEROMETER
20. LANDING CHECK LIST
21. RATE-OF-CLIMB INDICATOR
22. RADIO MAGNETIC INDICATOR
23. CLOCK
24. ATTITUDE GYRO
25. TURN AND SLIP INDICATOR
26. RADIO ALTIMETER
27. BAROMETRIC ALTIMETER
28. ARMAMENT CONTROL PANEL

FH25-114C

Figure 1-17. Main Instrument Panel

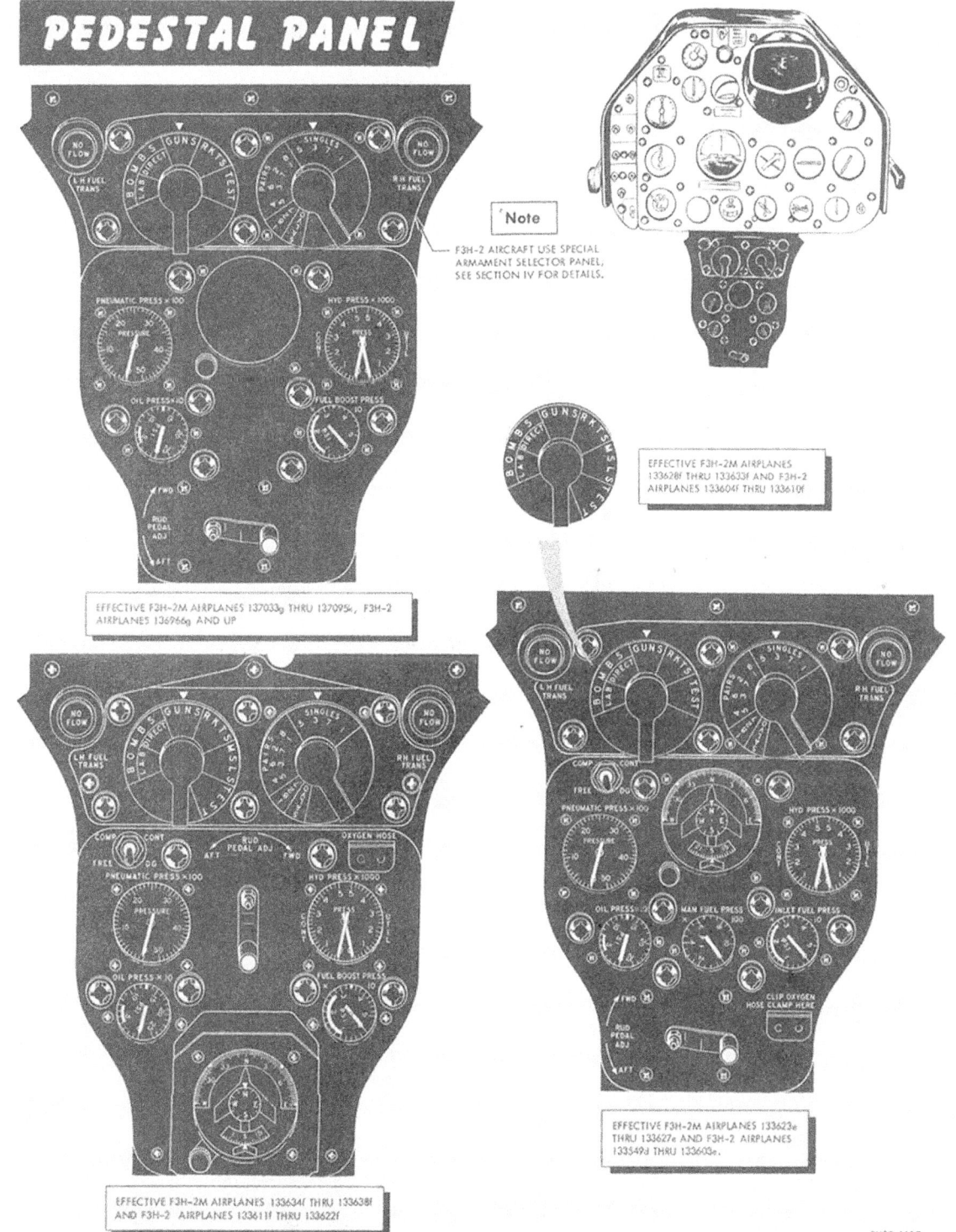

Figure 1-18. Pedestal Panel

INDICATOR LIGHTS

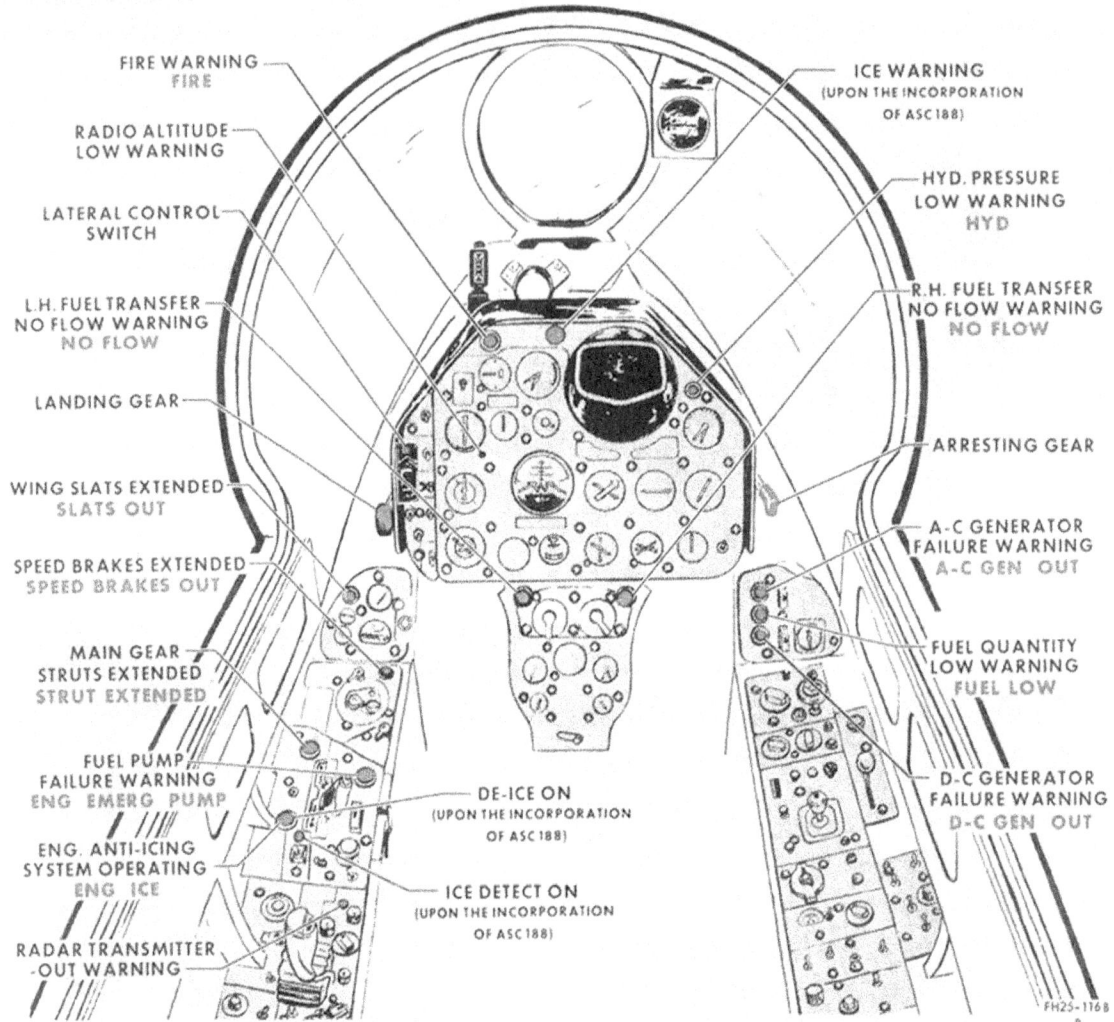

Figure 1-19. Indicator Lights

EMERGENCY EQUIPMENT

FIRE DETECTOR SYSTEM

The fire detector system is an a-c powered, continuous strip type that operates at a predetermined fixed temperature. It consists of a harness of sensing elements in series, a test relay unit, a control unit, a fire detection and warning light and a warning light and fire test switch. The sensing element harness is supported around the engine thermal insulating blanket and is routed longitudinally and circumferentially about the engine, covering the potential fire areas.

Fire Detector Warning Light

The fire detector warning light is located on the main instrument panel (see figure 1-19, this section). If a temperature of 540°F or over occurs, the resistance of the sensing element is reduced to a certain value and measured by the control unit which energizes the warning light. Electrical power to this system is supplied by the primary a-c bus.

WARNING LIGHT AND FIRE TEST SWITCH

The warning light and fire test switch is a three-position toggle switch located on the main instrument panel.

Positions are momentary in FIRE TEST and TEST WARN. LTS. positions; the center position OFF. Holding the switch in FIRE TEST position grounds the sensing element circuit and causes the warning light and control unit to operate in the same manner as a fire signal would, and also effects a continuity check of the wires in the sensing element. If the system is functioning properly, the warning light will glow.

CANOPY

The canopy consists of a transparent plastic closure over the cockpit zone which is moved longitudinally fore and aft by a rack and pinion type mechanism that employs a gear box and a geared track. The geared track is secured to the canopy. An electric motor mounted to gear box normally opens and closes canopy. An air motor is also incorporated on the gear box to aid the electric motor to open or jettison the canopy in an emergency. The air motor cannot close the canopy. Internal and external switches are used to normally open and close the canopy. Because of the irreversible characteristics of the gears within the gear box, no special steps are necessary to lock the canopy after it assumes any position. An internal and external handle is provided to open the canopy in an emergency. An inflatable rubber seal is retained in the cockpit sill and windshield arch. With the canopy closed and the engine in operation, air bled from the engine compressor automatically inflates the seal against the canopy frame. This prevents the loss of cabin pressurization at the canopy edges. Three metal spoilers, attached to the windshield arch, are provided to reduce cockpit noise with the canopy open. The spoilers are automatically extended into the airstream when canopy is opened and retracted when canopy is closed.

INTERNAL CANOPY CONTROLS

Internal Canopy Switch

Normal opening and closing of canopy from within the cockpit is performed by actuating the canopy toggle switch located on the left cockpit sill. This operation uses only the electric motor as the canopy actuator. Limit switches are actuated at the full close and full open positions to stop canopy. Releasing the spring-loaded canopy switch while opening or closing the canopy allows canopy to be stopped at an intermediate position. Electrical power is supplied by the utility d-c bus.

WARNING

Under no condition shall personnel outside the cockpit reach into the cockpit and actuate cockpit canopy switch. Use this switch only when sitting in the pilot's seat.

Internal Canopy Emergency Handle

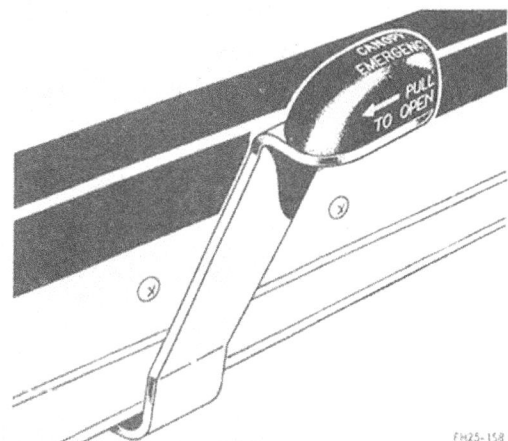

The internal canopy emergency handle is located just below the left cockpit sill. Pulling this handle aft will cause both the air motor and electric motor to open the canopy. (This operation does not jettison canopy.) Structural stops on the gearbox housing stop the canopy in the open position. Returning the handle does not close canopy. There are no emergency controls to close canopy. The canopy can be closed only by the canopy switches after the internal emergency handle has been returned to its forward normal position. The small stop lever located beneath the internal emergency handle must be pushed and held forward to allow handle to be returned to the normal position.

CAUTION

DO NOT RETURN the internal canopy emergency handle to its forward normal position when the canopy is moving or when the air motor or electric motor is running or coasting. Returning this handle to the forward position while either canopy motor is operating will strip gearbox lock. Return the cockpit handle only when both motors are completely stopped.

Canopy Jettison Handle

Effective F3H-2 Airplanes 146709t and Subsequent; also effective all F3H-2 Airplanes 146339s and previous upon incorporation of ASC 132.

An internal canopy jettison handle is installed to accompany the Martin-Baker ejection seat installation (which see). This handle is located on the inside of the left console opposite the radar control panel. When pulled up and aft approximately 35° the canopy air and electric motors are actuated, and the stripper hook is raised, allowing the canopy to ride off its track.

Section I

NAVWEPS 01-245FCB-501

LEFT CONSOLE

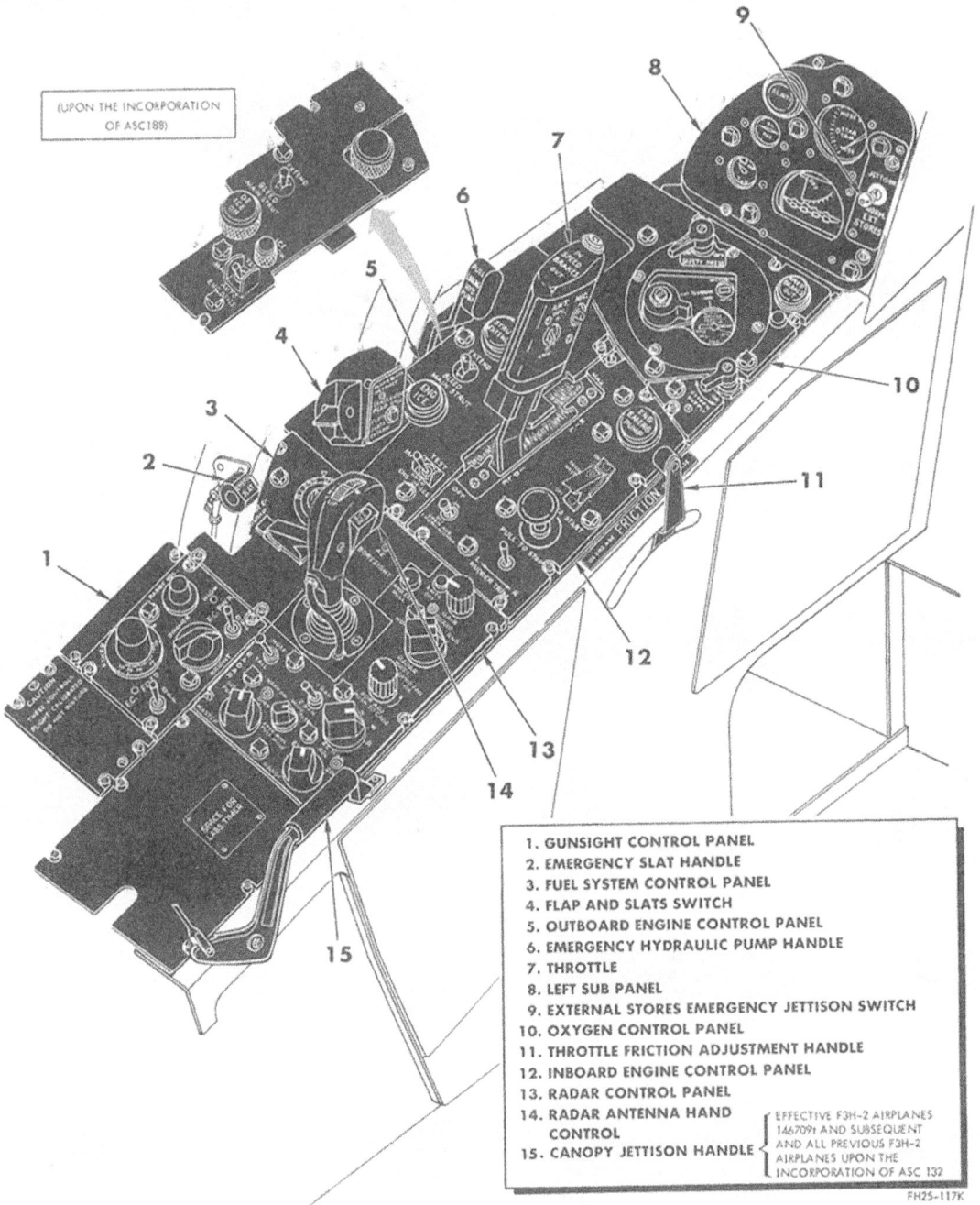

1. GUNSIGHT CONTROL PANEL
2. EMERGENCY SLAT HANDLE
3. FUEL SYSTEM CONTROL PANEL
4. FLAP AND SLATS SWITCH
5. OUTBOARD ENGINE CONTROL PANEL
6. EMERGENCY HYDRAULIC PUMP HANDLE
7. THROTTLE
8. LEFT SUB PANEL
9. EXTERNAL STORES EMERGENCY JETTISON SWITCH
10. OXYGEN CONTROL PANEL
11. THROTTLE FRICTION ADJUSTMENT HANDLE
12. INBOARD ENGINE CONTROL PANEL
13. RADAR CONTROL PANEL
14. RADAR ANTENNA HAND CONTROL
15. CANOPY JETTISON HANDLE

{ EFFECTIVE F3H-2 AIRPLANES 146709t AND SUBSEQUENT AND ALL PREVIOUS F3H-2 AIRPLANES UPON THE INCORPORATION OF ASC 132

FH25-117K

Figure 1-20. Left Console

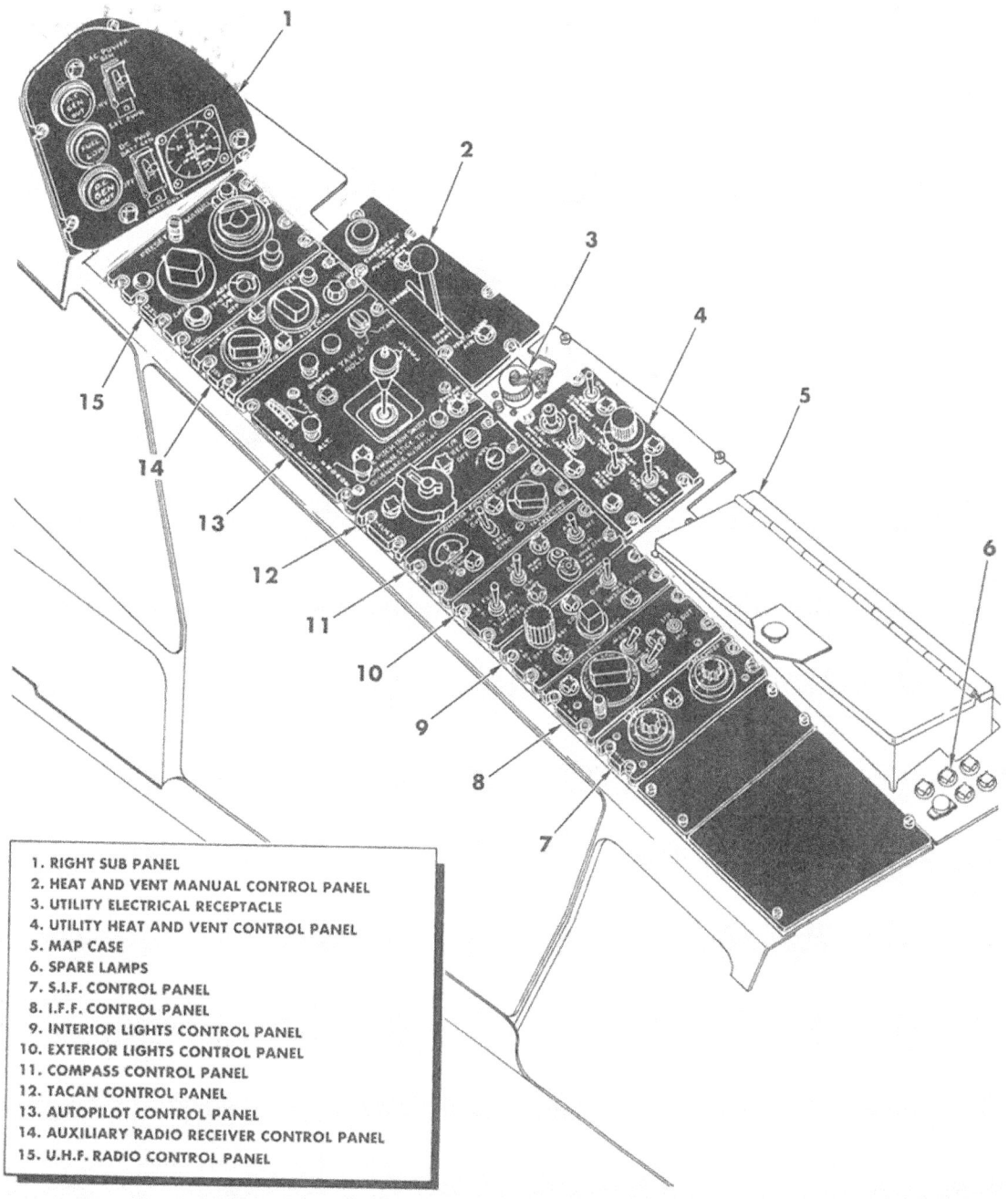

Figure 1-21. Right Console

EXTERNAL CANOPY CONTROLS

External Canopy Buttons

Personnel standing on the ground may operate the canopy by means of two spring-loaded push button switches located on left side of fuselage, forward of wing leading edge. As marked, one is for opening and the other for closing canopy. The cockpit and external canopy switches perform exactly the same operation. All canopy switches are wired in a manner to make it impossible for more than one switch to control canopy movement in case two or more switches are actuated at the same time. Electrical power is supplied by the utility d-c bus.

External Canopy Emergency Handle

The external canopy emergency handle performs exactly the same operation as the internal canopy emergency handle. This handle is located on left side of fuselage near aft end of the canopy and may be reached by personnel while standing on the left wing. In its normal position, the external handle is flush with fuselage skin and pushing the square shaped button just forward of the handle will raise handle. The canopy emergency controls must be returned to their normal position by the internal emergency handle because the external handle does not perform this operation. Also returning either handle does not close canopy.

CAUTION

Use the internal or external canopy emergency handles only during an actual emergency. Pulling either handle aft supplies current to the electric motor switch bypasses the canopy open limit switch. The load imposed on the gearbox by both the air motor and electric motor when the canopy reaches the open position will damage the gearbox and electric motor. DO NOT OPERATE THE CANOPY AT ANY TIME BY THE EMERGENCY HANDLES FOR CHECKING PURPOSES.

Canopy Manual Release Lever

If canopy air pressure and electrical power fails and the canopy cannot be opened by the normal or emergency controls, personnel outside the cockpit may manually pull the canopy open by the pull handle provided on top of canopy tail cone. Either canopy emergency control handle must be pulled first to permit canopy to be manually opened. The canopy cannot be closed manually.

EJECTION SEAT

Effective all F3H-2M Airplanes and all F3H-2 Airplanes 146339s and previous prior to incorporation of ASC 132.

For emergency escape, the pilot's seat is designed so that the seat and pilot may be catapulted together from the cockpit. The seat catapult uses a powder charge which provides sufficient force to insure clearance of the airplane tail structure. The catapult consists of an outer cylinder attached to the seat frame and an inner cylinder secured to the seat track. The catapult firing head is of the cartridge indicating type. When loaded, the knurled red cap of the head mechanism is raised, exposing a white strap approximately 5/16" wide. The word LOADED appears in red letters on this white stripe.

WARNING

The white catapult loaded stripe must appear or the ejection seat will be unsafe for flight.

Holdback hooks located at base of seat catapult normally keep the two cylinders engaged and provide the only means of holding the seat in the airplane. The seat holdback hooks manual release handle, located on the aft side of the headrest, is painted red above the handle's top retaining clip. The seat holdback hooks are properly closed when the bottom edge of the red section on the handle is aligned ± 1/16 of an inch with the top handle retaining clip. Also, white index marks are painted between top left side of seat frame and headrest armor plate. When aligned, the white index marks indicate that the seat assembly is properly installed for engagement of the holdback hooks. Inverted flight will allow seat to fall against or through canopy if the white index marks were not in alignment or the red section on holdback hooks manual release handle was not positioned as described before flight. Upon ejection, the explosive cartridge forces the holdback hooks open and forces the catapult cylinders apart with only the inner cylinder and seat track remaining in the airplane. The seat is built to accommodate a back pack type parachute, PK-2 pararaft kit, and a SP-1 seat pan. The seat is equipped with an automatic-opening safety belt and shoulder harness. Foot stirrups and leg braces are provided on seat to hold pilot's feet in place for clearance and prevent spreading of the legs from wind blast during ejection. A composite plug and receptacle is located beneath seat which connects oxygen, anti-G suit pressure and various electrical components to seat. These items are automatically disconnected during ejection. However, the pilot must manually disconnect his oxygen mask line and radio leads from oxygen trunk line before separation from seat.

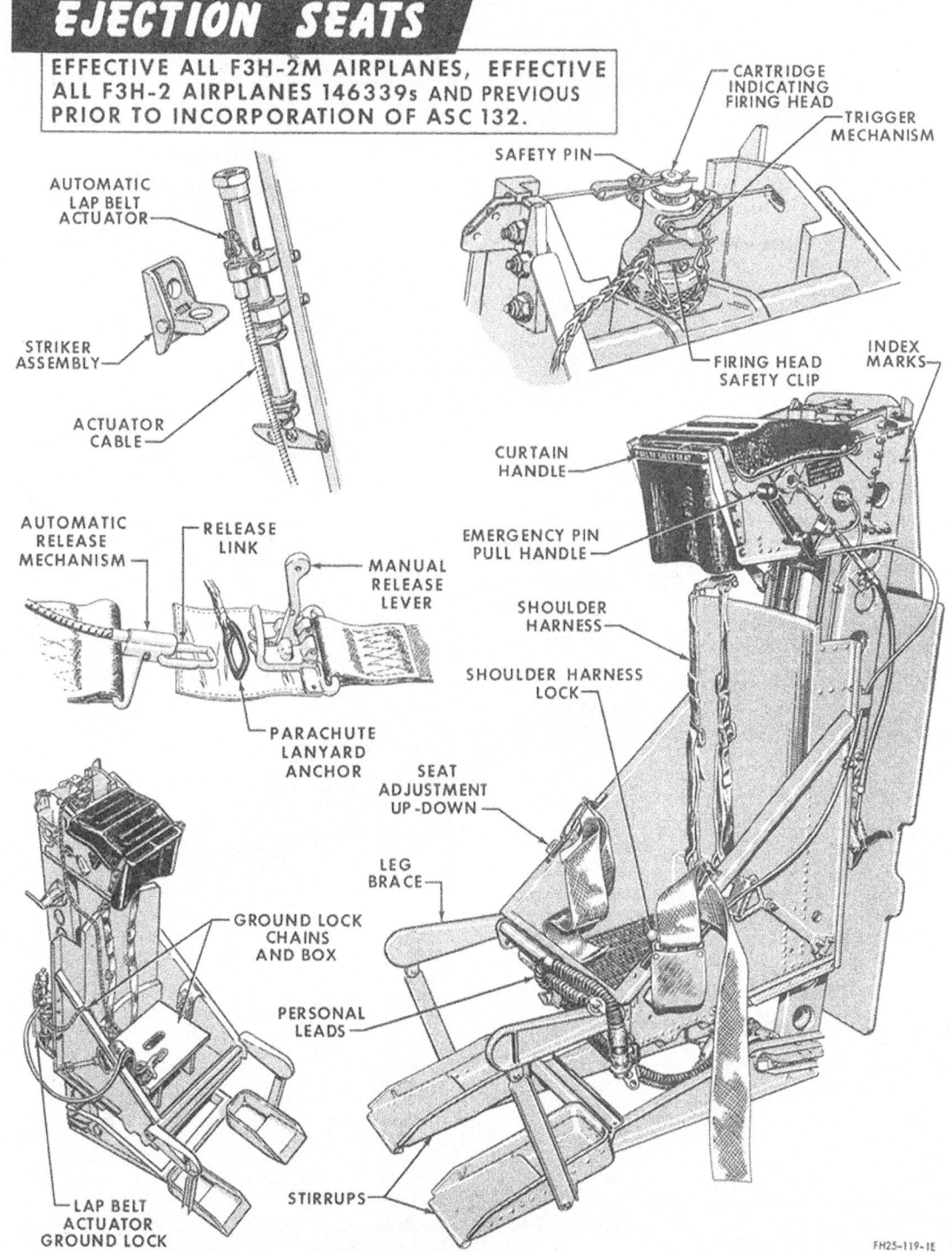

Figure 1-22. Ejection Seats

SEAT ADJUSTMENT SWITCH

The seat bucket may be adjusted vertically by actuating the switch provided on right side of seat. The pilot may raise or lower the seat as desired during flight. It is not necessary to adjust the seat height to any certain position before ejection. Electrical power is supplied by the secondary d-c bus.

WARNING

If the canopy is inadvertently jettisoned or lost in flight, the seat catapult will be armed and ready to fire. Immediately after landing, it is imperative that the safety pin be reinstalled in the catapult firing mechanism.

FACE CURTAIN PULL HANDLE

The pull handle for the ejection seat face curtain is located at the top of seat headrest, projecting forward and providing a grip surface for the pilot. Pulling the face curtain handle down to the first stop, which is approximately half of the curtain travel, actuates the canopy jettisoning linkage. This simultaneously raises a stripper hook and starts the canopy air motor and electric motor into operation. As the canopy approaches the normal open position, this stripper hook strips the canopy stop from the end of the canopy track and allows the canopy track to pass completely through the gearbox, thus jettisoning the canopy. As the canopy leaves the airplane, cable linkage from a reel attached to the canopy pulls the safety pin from the seat catapult firing mechanism which arms the catapult and removes the curtain stops. Pulling the face curtain the remainder of the way down trips the catapult firing mechanism to eject the seat. During ejection, the rubber impregnated nylon face curtain provides support for pilot's body, aids in retaining his head in proper position, protects his face against wind blast and prevents the oxygen mask and helmet from blowing away. The curtain is designed to cup around pilot's face when pulled down and will rewind onto drum when released after ejection.

WARNING

Face curtain handle should be pulled firmly but not hard.

MANUAL SAFETY PIN PULL HANDLE

The seat catapult cannot be fired until the safety pin has been pulled from the firing mechanism. A manual safety pin pull handle is located on left side of seat headrest. Pulling this handle forward AT ANY TIME WILL ARM THE SEAT CATAPULT. This enables pilot to manually pull seat catapult safety pin should the canopy fail to do so when it jettisons. Also, the handle disconnects the canopy air and electric motors, insuring that the canopy will not move when the face curtain is pulled. This gives the option of through-the-canopy ejection. Added hard points on the seat headrest insure complete breakage of the canopy plexiglas. (Refer to bail-out procedure in Section III.)

WARNING

If canopy fails to jettison, do not attempt ejection through canopy unless it remained completely CLOSED. At a partially open or full open position, the canopy frame will cause severe personal injury. Climbing over the side is the only means of escape in this situation.

SHOULDER HARNESS INERTIA REEL

The pilot's shoulder harness is connected by a cable to an electromagnetic inertia reel secured to the seat. The reel is electrically released when the secondary d-c bus is energized which permits the reel cable to unwind and rewind as the pilot leans fore and aft. If the aircraft encounters an impact force in any longitudinal direction, an inertia switch mounted on the seat will instantaneously cut off power to the reel. With power off the reel, it is locked and the cable cannot unwind. This prevents the pilot from being thrown into the instrument panel. Also, upon ejection of the seat, the reel will be locked because the plug supplying power to the reel will be automatically disconnected at the instant the seat starts up the guide rails.

Inertia Reel Manual Control Handle

As an added safety feature a manual control handle for the inertia reel is furnished on the left side of seat bucket. The inertia reel is LOCKED with handle forward and RELEASED with handle aft. Refer to various emergency procedures in Section III which require the pilot to preset this handle to the reel locked position. An electrical power failure to the inertia reel will allow reel to be locked when the manual control handle is forward or aft. Therefore, in this situation, the pilot must hold the handle at the center position when it is necessary to lean forward.

Note

When the secondary bus is first energized, the reel will remain locked until the control handle is moved to the CENTER position and then pulled aft.

AUTOMATIC OPENING SAFETY BELT

An automatic opening safety belt assembly bolted to the ejection seat, permits automatic separation of the pilot from the seat after the seat clears the aircraft during ejection. A two-piece adjustable belt and a belt actuator comprise the automatic belt assembly. A manually operated buckle is incorporated on the free end of the left belt half, and a cable locked automatic buckle is incorporated on the free end of the right belt half. For normal use, the belt is manually fastened and unfastened by a left and right movement of the manual latch on the left belt. The belts are locked by a link, with the right end of the link normally retained at all times in the automatic latch. The left end of the link locks or unlocks into the manual latch. Shoulder harness loops are positioned over the link before the belt is locked. If the automatic parachute is being used, the parachute lanyard anchor (ring shaped) is inserted over the link after the shoulder harness loops.

Note

The automatic opening safety belt assembly was designed as a "one-shot" installation. In the event of inadvertent actuation of the firing mechanism with cartridge installed, the actuating assembly will distort due to powder pressure. Once the firing mechanism has been actuated, the belt assembly cannot be reused and must be replaced with a new assembly.

Automatic Opening Safety Belt Operation

During seat ejection, the upward movement of the seat causes the firing pin to release and strike a powder cartridge primer. Expanding gases from cartridge discharge forces a small piston to move upward. The piston pulls the cable assembly (leading to the automatic release lock) and unlocks the belt. Tension on the belt will easily cause the belt to separate. The shoulder harness will release with belt separation. The parachute lanyard anchor will be retained by the seat belt as the pilot leaves the seat. The resulting pull on the lanyard will actuate parachute deployment.

WARNING

When the automatic lap belt is manually opened, the automatic parachute actuator is no longer automatic. To deploy the parachute in this case, either the arming cable must be pulled manually to arm the actuator or the parachute rip cord must be pulled manually.

MARTIN-BAKER EJECTION SEAT

F3H-2 Airplanes 146709t and subsequent are equipped with the Martin-Baker ejection seat, type MK M-5 (figure 1-23). Upon incorporation of ASC 132, all F3H-2 airplanes will also be equipped with the Martin-Baker seat, in somewhat modified form. The seats previously installed by the airplane contractor are not presently being modified, hence illustrations and text coverage following will reflect both Martin-Baker seats. The Martin-Baker seat is, in fact, a complete escape system, since it offers fully automatic separation and parachute deployment through high altitude ground level ejections. The manner in which these high and low altitude ejections occur is shown in figure 3-6. The lightweight seat unit is stressed for high "g" loads. Ejection power is provided by a 3-section telescoping catapult which is propelled by a triple charge. Initial firing of one charge provides primary thrust, and further impetus is given by the sequential firing of the remaining charges as the catapult extends. Ground level ejection is possible through the use of this high velocity catapult. The occupant is given sufficient altitude for safe ground level ejection providing the airplane speed is sufficient to deploy the parachute (minimum 125, maximum 300 knots). At higher altitudes no minimum airspeed is imposed, but the maximum speed for safe ejection is 525 knots. A double-drogue stabilizing parachute system is deployed automatically upon the seat clearing the airplane, insuring rapid deceleration with minimum tumbling. A body harness and leg restraining system, also deployed automatically upon ejection, insures proper support and protection for the seat occupant. A time delay mechanism is incorporated, as well as a barostatic altitude control and accelerometer. The occupant will not separate from the seat until minimum time (1 1/4 to 1 3/4 seconds), maximum acceleration (4 1/2 "g's"), and maximum altitude (10,000 to 13,000 feet) conditions have been met. All features are discussed in greater detail as this description progresses.

EJECTION CATAPULT

The seat catapult uses a powder charge which provides sufficient force to insure clearance of the vertical stabilizer. The expanding gases from this cartridge exert a force upward on the inner and intermediate tubes releasing the latch mechanism. Upward movement of both inner and intermediate tubes expose two auxiliary charges which are ignited. The two tubes continue accelerating upward together until the intermediate tube is snubbed to a stop. The inner tube and seat continue rising together until the full 72" stroke is reached and the inner tube and seat leave the intermediate tube and cylinder barrel which remain in the airplane.

STABILIZER DROGUE

As the seat moves up the barrel guide rails, two links between the seat and airplane structure are pulled to operate the drogue gun and time delay mechanism sears. The leg restraint cord is anchored to the cockpit floor by a shear rivet. As the seat rises the cord is pulled taut, pulling the legs into the proper position for cockpit clearance. When the limit travel is reached, the anchoring rivet shears, freeing the cord. The legs are restrained by a snubbing unit until separation from the seat. Approximately 1/2 second after ejection from the airplane, the drogue gun cartridge will fire propelling a piston attached to the controller drogue chute away from the seat. This piston deploys the controller drogue chute which in turn extracts the larger stabilizer drogue chute. The stabilizer drogue tilts the seat into a horizontal attitude and reduces forward speed without a great loss of altitude.

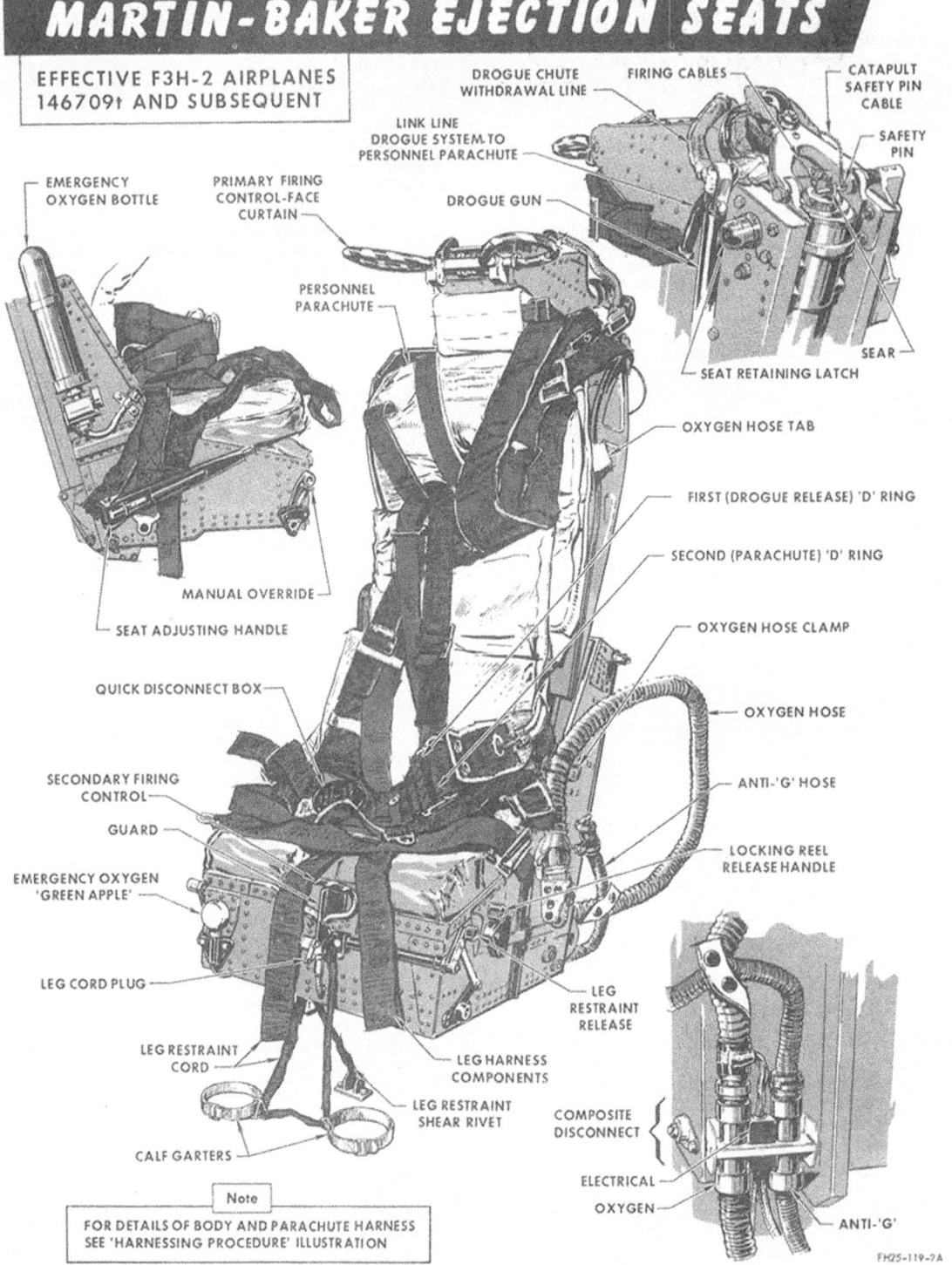

Figure 1-23. Martin-Baker Ejection Seats (Sheet 1)

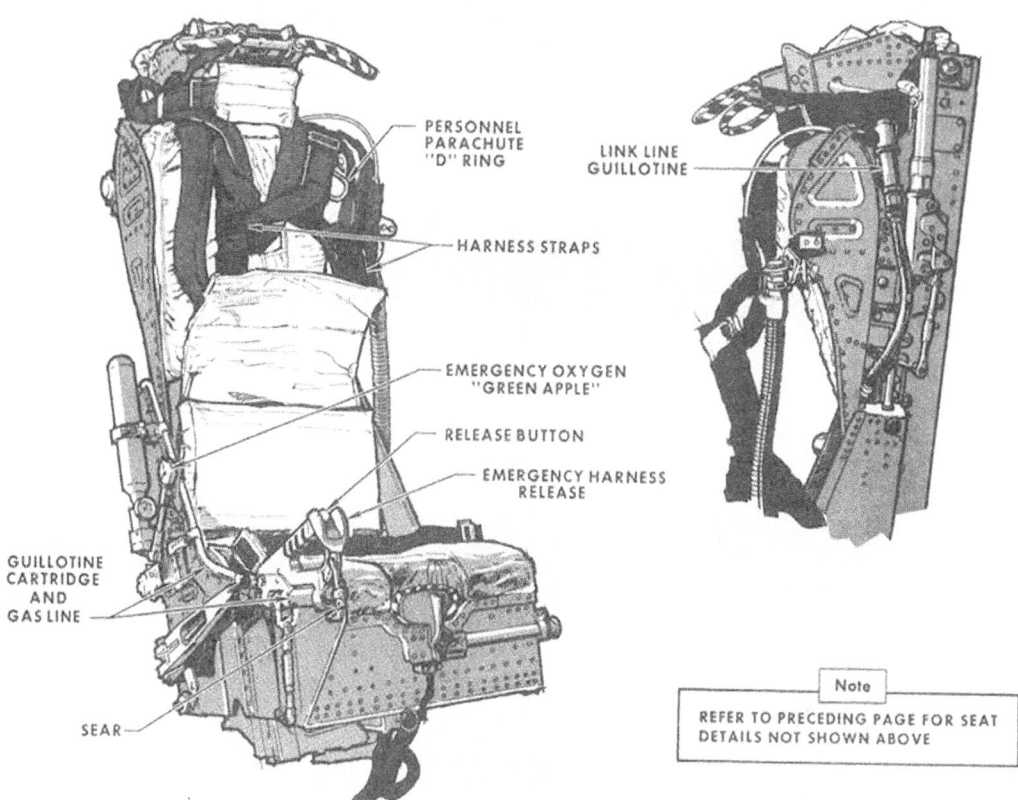

Figure 1-23. Martin-Baker Ejection Seats (Sheet 2)

SEAT SEPARATION MECHANISM

Approximately 1 1/2 seconds after ejection, the time delay mechanism will actuate releasing the harness leg restraints and the drogue chutes. The occupant is now held in the seat only by two sticker clips. As the drogues leave the seat they pull the personnel parachute out of its horseshoe container, and the occupant will be pulled free of the sticker clips and out of the seat upon opening of his personal parachute. He then makes a normal descent to the ground. If ejection is made at a high altitude, a barostatic control attached to the seat delays separation of the occupant from the seat and prevents the pilot's parachute from opening. This permits the occupant and the seat to descend quickly through the cold rarified atmosphere to a more tolerable altitude (10,000 +3000, -0000 ft.) where the automatic mechanism will separate the occupant from the seat and deploy the personnel chute. At very high ejection speeds the opening of the personal parachute is delayed by a switch and the pilot remains strapped in the seat, which is steadied by the pilot drogue chute and main drogue parachute until the seat has decelerated to a safe speed (4.5 "g's" or less).

SEAT CONTROLS

The seat catapult may be fired by either the Primary Firing Control (Face Curtain) or the Secondary Firing Handle located between the pilot's legs. Both the Primary and Secondary Firing Controls perform the same function. Through cable actuation either control will pull the sear from the firing mechanism.

Section I NAVWEPS 01-245FCB-501

Seat Adjustment Handle

Height adjustment of the seat assembly is accomplished by a handle approximately 18 inches long, located on the right side of the seat. Height adjustment is accomplished by depressing a plunger type button at the end of the adjustment handle and moving the handle in the desired direction of seat movement. After adjusting the seat to the desired height the adjusting handle should be positioned to permit the plunger-retracted lock pin to engage one of the seven retaining holes in the seat securing strut, which are spaced one inch apart.

WARNING

A retaining hole is not engaged and the seat is not locked unless the thumb button protrudes approximately 1.5 inches beyond the end of the adjustment handle. This protrusion is approximately .5 inch in the unlocked condition. Failure to observe this warning may result in violent movement of the seat when vertical accelerations are encountered.

WARNING

The seat height adjustment handle must not be operated without an occupant in the seat. Because of the tension of the compensating bungees the seat will spring upward violently when the lock pin is released. Without a balance weight in the seat this could cause injury to anyone in its path.

FACE CURTAIN PULL HANDLE

The face curtain pull handle is located at the top of the seat headrest and will be used for normal seat ejection. When ejection is desired, the face curtain pull handle is pulled forward and downward until full travel is reached. This pulls the face curtain over the face of the pilot and removes the wedge-shaped sear from the ejection gun firing head, firing the main charge and ejecting the seat.

Secondary Firing Handle

The secondary firing handle is located on the front of the seat bucket and consists of a metal ring handle whose lower portion is secured in a receptacle at the seat front. The secondary firing handle is safetied in the seat while on the ground by a dual purpose safety guard. When the guard handle is placed in the vertical position, it covers the handle opening preventing inadvertent grasping of the handle. Also, when the guard is positioned vertically the guard pivot lockbolt is rotated in such a manner that a cam shaped portion of the bolt projects into a detent of the secondary firing control lower stem. This prevents the handle from being pulled out of its receptacle. When the guard is swung down, it clears the handle opening and rotates the pivot bolt cam out of the handle shank detent.

Drogue Release Handle

Installed in F3H-2 Airplanes 146709t and subsequent, two "D" rings are retained in pouches on the quick release box tab of the seat harness. The first of these which comes to hand when the right hand is passed across the body is the drogue release handle. When grasped and pulled free of its yellow and black striped retaining flap, this control separates a link in the drogue chute/personnel chute connecting line. The control must be actuated in manual separation from the seat, and must be deployed BEFORE the manual override lever, discussed below.

Note

The second "D" ring on the body harness is the familiar "rip cord" or personnel parachute "D" ring.

Manual Override Lever

Installed in F3H-2 Airplanes 146709t and subsequent, the manual override lever is located on the right forward corner of the seat bucket. This handle is used by the pilot to manually separate from the seat in the event the automatic time release mechanism accelerometer or barostat fail to operate. The manual override lever performs the same functions as the time release mechanism.

CAUTION

The Manual Override must not be actuated until the Drogue Release Mechanism (First "D" ring on body harness) has been actuated. Failure to accomplish these steps in proper sequence will result in the seat not separating from the occupant after manual parachute deployment.

Emergency Harness Release

In the ejection seats installed upon incorporation of ASC 132, both the drogue release handle and manual override lever are replaced by a single handle, located on the right forward corner of the seat pan. The handle is protected by both a safety pin and a locking button which must be depressed before the handle may be pulled. When the handle is pulled, two actions take place: (1) A cartridge is fired and the gas pressures liberated are piped to a guillotine which severs the drogue chute/personnel parachute connecting line, (2) the manual override functions are performed releasing the occupant from the seat. The guillotine is located on the upper left side of the seat back. With incorporation of this control, the personnel parachute "D" ring is relocated on the upper left harness strap.

Manual Emergency Oxygen Knob

The manual emergency oxygen knob is located on the front of the seat bucket. It is used by the pilot to open the emergency oxygen valve in the event of main oxygen system failure. This handle is located on the aft right side of the seat bucket upon the incorporation of ASC 132 (figure 1-23).

SEAT HARNESS

Since the personnel parachute is not worn by the seat occupant before he enters the airplane, the body harness provided is somewhat different than that which is found in conventional arrangements. The ejection seats installed in F3H-2 airplanes 146709t and subsequent are equipped with a complete body and parachute harness system which will suitably restrain an individual dressed in ordinary flight clothing. The seats installed by ASC 132 utilize the much simplified integrated harness, and it is necessary that the occupant wear a special garment equipped with the required hardware and strap arrangement for use of the seat harness. The Suit, Integrated Torso Harness, MS 22015, is worn with flight clothing or anti-exposure suit. The procedures which must be utilized in taking either seat are shown in figure 1-24.

Shoulder Harness Locking Reel

Used only in F3H-2 airplanes 146709t and subsequent, the shoulder harness locking reel is a device located below the headrest which attaches by a strap to the pilot's harness assembly. One end of the strap is connected to the body harness, the other end passes through a snubbing unit and is then wound and secured to a spring-loaded reel. The snubbing unit prevents any forward movement of the strap unless release is effected by pulling aft on the release handle. The spring-loaded reel keeps the strap under tension and takes up any slack as the occupant sits back.

Locking Reel Release Handle

The locking reel release handle is located on the left side of the seat bucket. It is spring-loaded forward, which is the normal and locked position of the locking assembly. The aft position of the handle unlocks the reel assembly. When the handle is pulled aft, and held, the reel assembly will permit normal forward and aft movement of the pilot's shoulders. When the handle is released, it will spring forward to the locked position and the reel will prevent forward movement. Should the pilot be leaning away from his seat when he releases the handle and locks the reel and then moves or bounces back toward the seat, the reel assembly automatically takes up the slack and locks the reel in successive locked positions.

Shoulder Harness Inertia Reel

In the seats installed by ASC 132, a conventional inertia reel replaces the locking reel. This reel may be locked to preclude any movement, and will also automatically lock when the seat and occupant are subjected to the high "g" forces which would be associated with sudden stoppage or ejection.

Inertia Reel Handle

Although it is mounted in the same place, the inertia reel handle does not function in the same manner as the locking reel handle. This handle is mechanically linked to a two-position cam and must be mechanically moved to the unlocked (aft) position or the locked (forward) position.

LEG RESTRAINTS

A leg restraint assembly is provided on the seat to hold the pilot's legs in place and to prevent them from flailing during ejection. The leg restraint assembly consists of garters worn by the pilot and the leg restraint line contained on the seat. The garters are strapped on to the leg just below the knee. The leg lines running from the bottom of the seat passes through the metal ring on each garter, and then plugs into the leg lock on the front of the seat pans. When the seat is ejected the leg restraint line tightens up automatically securing the pilot's legs to the front face of the seat pan where they are firmly held until the harness is released and the pilot is separated from the seat. A manual release ring on the front left side of the seat allows free leg movement while the pilot is in the airplane.

SURVIVAL KIT

A modified PK-2 survival kit is attached to the parachute seat by a conventional strap-harness. The contents of this kit are the same as for a normal issue PK-2, but the packing arrangement has been changed to suit the requirements of the seat. The following is a list of contents of this kit:

Note

The emergency provisions included in the PK-2 survival kit are subject to local option and may be altered at the discretion of the area commander.

Pararaft with inflation bottle, sleeve type sea anchor and lanyard.
Metallic radar reflector assembly (disassembled)
Solar distillation unit
De-salter kit (tablets)
Water storage bag
Signal mirror
Bailing sponge
50 feet of nylon line
2 packs dye marker
Poncho with reflective surface
Canned rations
Can of sunburn ointment.
Emergency code instruction sheets.

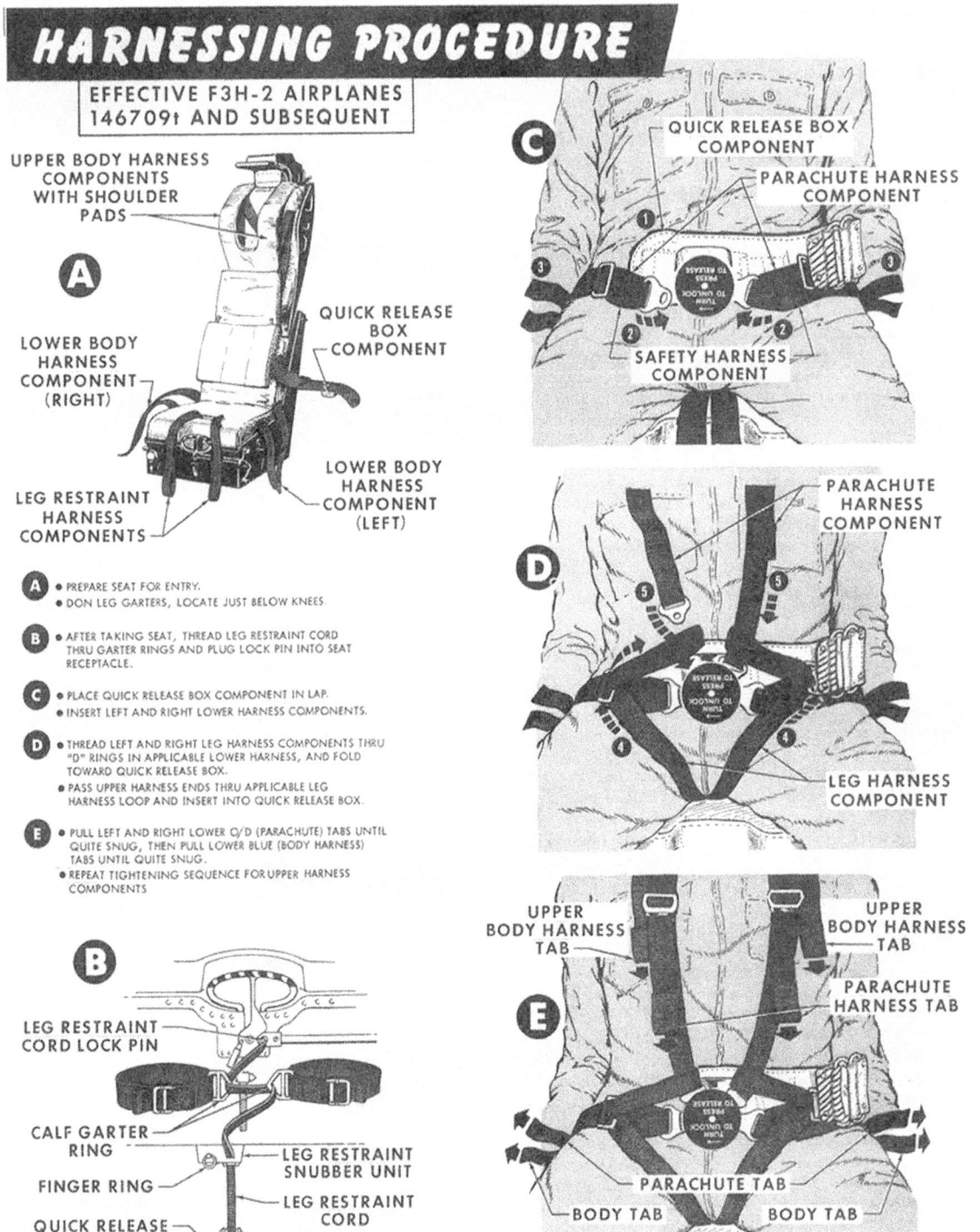

Figure 1-24. Harnessing Procedures (Sheet 1)

EFFECTIVE F3H-2 AIRPLANES 146339s AND PREVIOUS UPON INCORPORATION OF ASC 132.

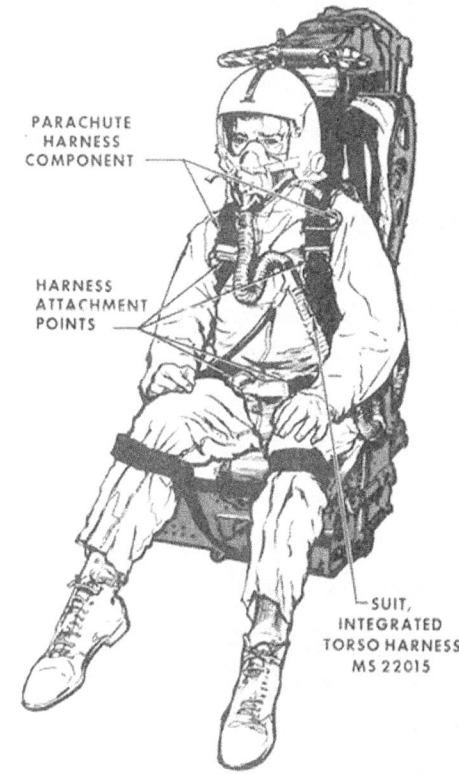

All items except the pararaft and its associated gear are packed in a zipper-enclosed soft case; this packet is then packed into another outer soft case along with the pararaft gear. The survival kit is opened by withdrawing its lacing wire by means of the ring provided when the pararaft and loose equipment packet may be withdrawn for use.

Note

The pararaft will not deploy automatically; its inflation bottle must be manually actuated.

AUXILIARY EQUIPMENT

Information concerning the following operational equipment is supplied in Section IV of this handbook. Cabin Pressurization and Air Conditioning, Communication and Electronic Equipment, Automatic Pilot, Lighting, Oxygen, Anti-G Suit.

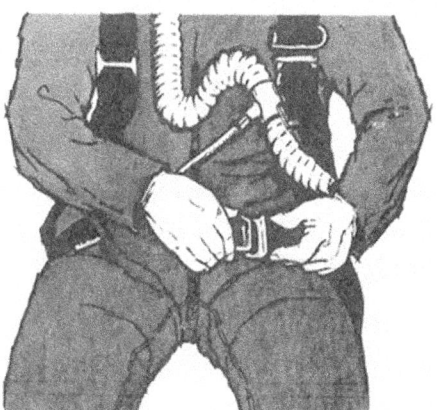

Figure 1-24. Harnessing Procedures (Sheet 2)

SERVICING DIAGRAM

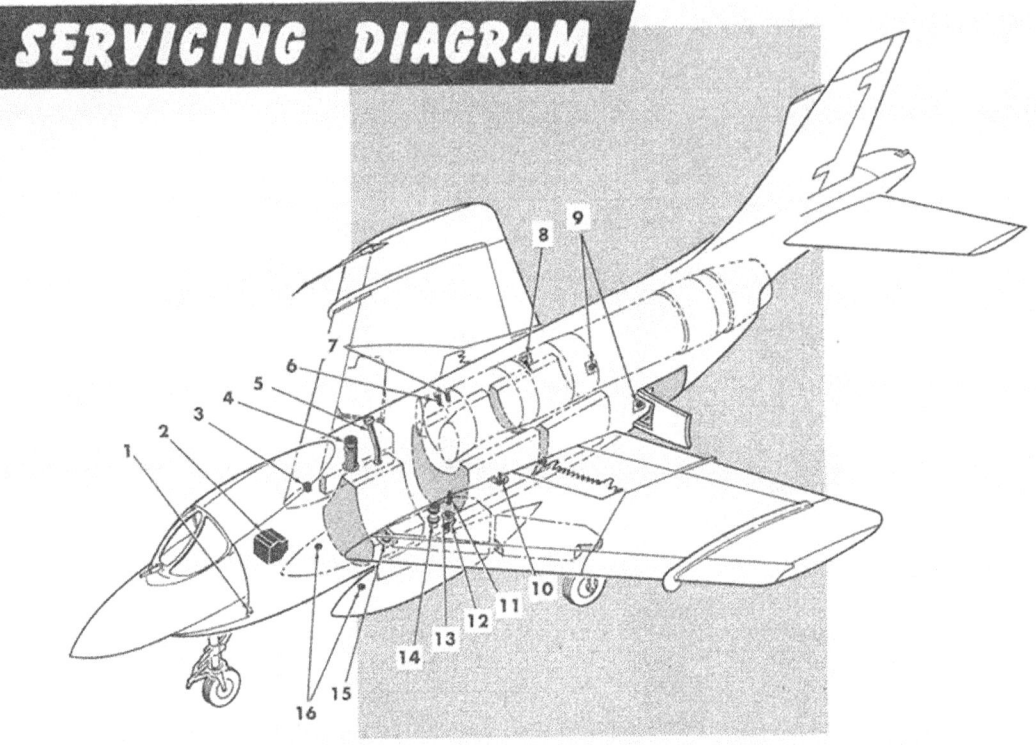

1. **OXYGEN SUPPLY**
   CHARGE TO 1800 PSI (± 50) THROUGH NOSE GEAR DOORS. CHECK AT PREFLIGHT.

2. **BATTERY**
   SERVICE PER MAINTENANCE INSTRUCTION HANDBOOK.

3. **EXTERNAL ELECTRICAL POWER RECEPTACLE**
   DOOR NO. 77 FOR ACCESS TO A-C & D-C POWER RECEPTACLES. CLOSE DOOR AFTER DISCONNECTING POWER.

4. **HYDRAULIC RESERVOIR (UTILITY)**
   SERVICE THROUGH ACCESS DOOR 20 WITH HYDRAULIC FLUID SPECIFICATION MIL-O-5606 (RED). FILLER CAPACITY 2.8 U.S. GALLONS.

5. **FORWARD FUEL TANK**
   SERVICE THROUGH ACCESS DOOR 21 PER AUTHORIZED FUELS TABLE, BELOW. TANK CAPACITIES 858 U.S. GALLONS. (FWD AND CENTER TANKS).

6. **ENGINE HYDRAULIC OIL TANK**
   SERVICE THROUGH ACCESS DOORS 35R WITH HYDRAULIC FLUID MIL-O-5606 (RED). CAPACITY 6 QUARTS.

7. **ENGINE OIL TANK**
   SERVICE THROUGH ACCESS DOOR 35R WITH MIL-L-7808. CAPACITY 8 U.S. GALLONS. CHECK LEVEL WITHIN 5 MIN. AFTER SHUTDOWN.

8. **AFT FUEL TANKS**
   SERVICE THROUGH ACCESS DOOR 47 PER AUTHORIZED FUELS TABLE, BELOW. TANK CAPACITY 342 U.S. GALLONS.

9. **ARRESTING GEAR CYLINDERS**
   CHARGE TO 550 PSI (HOOK-UP) THROUGH ACCESS DOORS 52L AND 52R.

10. **AFT PRESSURE FUELING**
    SERVICE THROUGH ACCESS DOOR 38 PER AUTHORIZED FUELS TABLE, BELOW. TANK CAPACITIES 840 U.S. GALLONS. (CENTER AND AFT TANKS ONLY).

11. **PNEUMATIC SYSTEM**
    CHARGE TO 3000 PSI THROUGH ACCESS DOOR PRIOR TO EACH FLIGHT.

12. **STARTER**
    CONNECT COMPRESSED AIR STARTER AT DOOR 33.

13. **WING FUEL TANKS**
    SERVICE PER AUTHORIZED FUELS TABLE, BELOW. TOTAL WING TANKS CAPACITY 306 U.S. GALLONS.

14. **HYDRAULIC RESERVOIR (POWER CONTROL)**
    SERVICE THROUGH ACCESS DOOR 34 WITH HYDRAULIC FLUID SPECIFICATION MIL-O-5606 (REG) FILLER CAPACITY 1.5 U.S. GALLONS.

15. **FORWARD PRESSURE FUELING**
    SERVICE THROUGH ACCESS DOOR 26 PER AUTHORIZED FUELS TABLE, BELOW. CAPACITY, ALL TANKS, 2054 U.S. GALLONS. EXCLUDING EXTERNAL TANKS, 1490 U.S. GALLONS.

16. **EXTERNAL FUEL TANKS**
    SERVICE PER AUTHORIZED FUELS TABLE, BELOW. TOTAL EXTERNAL TANKS CAPACITY 564 U.S. GALLONS.

AUTHORIZED	FUEL
ASHORE	MIL-F-5624 JP-3, JP-4, JP-5 *
AFLOAT	MIL-F-5624 JP-5
EMERGENCY	MIL-F-5572 AVGAS

* IF STOCKED AT SHORE ACTIVITY

Figure 1-25. Servicing Diagram

SECTION II
NORMAL PROCEDURES

BEFORE ENTERING COCKPIT

FLIGHT RESTRICTIONS

Refer to Section V for detailed airplane and engine limitations.

PREFLIGHT PLANNING

Refer to Appendix I to obtain necessary operating data to complete proposed mission.

WEIGHT AND BALANCE

Refer to Section V for weight limitations. For loading information, refer to Handbook of Weight and Balance Data, AN 01-1B-40. Before each flight, check the following:

1. Check take-off and anticipated landing gross weight and balance.
2. Check "yellow sheet" to determine flight status of aircraft and make sure aircraft has been properly serviced for contemplated mission.
3. Check Form F for weight and balance clearance.

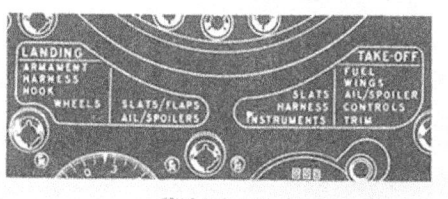

Figure 2-1. Check Lists, F3H-2 Airplanes

CHECK LISTS

The check lists in figure 2-1 are reproductions of the TAKE-OFF and LANDING check lists located on the main instrument panel. Since these lists indicate in general terms only what to check, the pilot must be thoroughly familiar with the procedures outlined in this handbook so as to know how these items should be checked.

EXTERIOR INSPECTION

Perform exterior inspection as outlined in figure 2-1.

Inspect for proper main gear extension, hydraulic leaks and pneumatic leaks when the main landing gear is extended to provide additional deck clearance for external stores during field and carrier take-offs.

ACCESS TO COCKPIT

Normal entry into the cockpit is by means of a metal ladder which hooks over the cockpit sill when canopy is open. An alternate method is by means of the three retractable steps in the fuselage below the canopy. To use the steps, climb upon the wing at the tip, being careful to avoid the NO STEP area, and walk inboard to the fuselage. Place LEFT foot on first step, etc.

WARNING

Prior to each flight, visually check the following seat and canopy items:

Section II NAVWEPS 01-245FCB-501

EXTERIOR INSPECTION

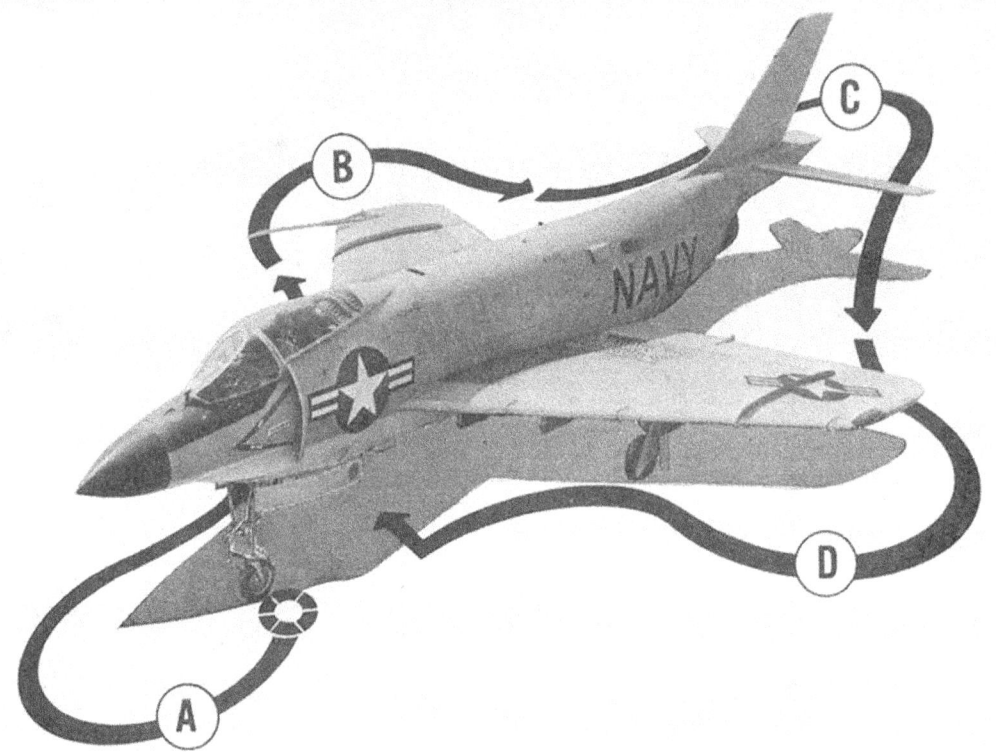

Ⓐ

NOSE GEAR
- ANGLE OF YAW PROBE COVER REMOVED.
- TIRE INFLATION (250 PSI ASHORE, 350 PSI AFLOAT), CONDITION, SLIPPAGE, OIL.
- STRUT EXTENSION (7 INCHES), CONDITION.
- WHEEL WELL.
- HYDRAULIC LEAKS.
- APPROACH LIGHT.
- SHIMMY DAMPER SERVICED.
- GROUND WIRE ADJUSTMENT.
- SAFETY PIN REMOVED.

FUSELAGE - STB'D FWD
- AIR INTAKE COVERS REMOVED, INTAKE DUCTS CLEAR.
- ACCESS DOORS SECURE.
- ANGLE-OF-ATTACK PROBE COVER REMOVED.
- EMERGENCY HYDRAULIC PUMP DOOR SECURE.

MAIN LANDING GEAR - STB'D
- ACCESS DOORS SECURE.
- TIRE INFLATION (250 PSI ASHORE, 300 PSI AFLOAT, CONDITION, SLIPPAGE, OIL.
- STRUT EXTENSION (2 INCHES), CONDITION.
- WHEEL WELL.
- HYDRAULIC LEAKS.
- SAFETY PIN REMOVED.

WING - STB'D LEADING EDGE
- ACCESS DOORS SECURE.
- INSPECT SLATS.
- JURY STRUT REMOVED. (IF WINGS FOLDED)
- WING LOCKED. (IF WINGS SPREAD)
- NAVIGATION LIGHT
- WING SURFACE FREE OF FROST AND ICE.
- WING STATIC BOOM COVER REMOVED

Figure 2-2. Exterior Inspection (Sheet 1)

EXTERIOR INSPECTION

WING - STB'D TRAILING EDGE
- INSPECT AILERONS, FLAPS AND SPOILERS.
- FUEL DUMP LINE.
- FUEL, HYDRAULIC LEAKS.
- ACCESS DOORS SECURE.

FUSELAGE - STB'D AFT
- SPEED BRAKE SAFETY STRUT-REMOVED.
- ARRESTING GEAR AND SPEED BRAKE SWITCHES - "NORMAL".
- HYDRAULIC LEAKS.
- AIR GAGE PRESSURE - 550 PSI - WITH ARRESTING GEAR-UP.
- ACCESS DOORS - SECURE.
- ARRESTING HOOK SAFETY STRUT - REMOVED.
- TAIL SKID-CHECK.

MAIN LANDING GEAR - PORT
- ACCESS DOORS SECURE.
- TIRE INFLATION (250 PSI ASHORE, 300 PSI AFLOAT), CONDITION, SLIPPAGE, OIL.
- STRUT EXTENSION (2 INCHES), CONDITION.
- WHEEL WELL.
- HYDRAULIC LEAKS.
- SAFETY PIN REMOVED.

WING - PORT TRAILING EDGE
- INSPECT AILERONS, FLAPS AND SPOILERS.
- FUEL DUMP LINE.
- FUEL, HYDRAULIC LEAKS.
- ACCESS DOORS SECURE.

TAIL SECTION - STB'D AND PORT
- EXHAUST COVER REMOVED.
- EXHAUST NOZZLE "OPEN".
- TAIL PIPE CLEAR OF GAS, OIL, ALL OBJECTS.
- BLAST CONE AND ACCESS DOORS SECURE.
- INSPECT CONTROL SURFACES.
- HYDRAULIC LEAKS.
- NAVIGATION LIGHT

FUSELAGE - PORT AFT
- AIR GAGE PRESSURE - 550 PSI - ARRESTING GEAR-UP.
- HYDRAULIC LEAKS.
- SPEED BRAKE SWITCH - "NORMAL".
- ACCESS DOORS - SECURE.

WING - PORT LEADING EDGE
- ACCESS DOORS - SECURE.
- NAVIGATION LIGHT
- JURY STRUT - REMOVED (IF WINGS FOLDED).
- WING - LOCKED (IF WINGS SPREAD).
- INSPECT SLATS.
- WING SURFACE FREE OF FROST AND ICE.

FUSELAGE - PORT FWD
- AIR INTAKE COVERS REMOVED, INTAKE DUCTS CLEAR.
- ACCESS DOORS SECURE.
- PITOT TUBE COVER REMOVED.
- ENGINE ACCESSORIES COOLING AIR INLET COVER REMOVED.

Figure 2-2. Exterior Inspection (Sheet 2)

Section II NAVWEPS 01-245FCB-501

ACCESS TO COCKPIT

Figure 2-3. Access to Cockpit

1. Aircraft log book - CHECK
   Log book should indicate that seat catapult is loaded with personnel cartridge, and automatic lap belt cartridge is installed.
2. External canopy emergency handle - LOCKED
   Handle must be flush with fuselage skin.
3. Effective all F3H-2M airplanes; also effective F3H-2 airplanes 133549d thru 146339s, prior to incorporation of ASC 132, ejection seat - CHECK
   a. Alignment - CHECK
      White index marks between top left side of seat frame and headrest armor plate must be aligned. Seat is installed with holdback hooks which may be released by a manual handle; the bottom edge of the red painted portion of this handle must be 1/16 inch from the handle's top retaining clip.
   b. Seat catapult safety pin - INSTALLED
      Check that safety pin is properly installed and attached by attendant cable linkage to reel on canopy and pull handle on headrest
   c. Seat catapult - CHECK
      Insure that seat catapult is loaded and cocked with firing cable properly connected to arm on face curtain bearing. Also, vertical yellow index marker in alignment across catapult cylinder, lock ring and knurled face of firing mechanism.
   d. Face curtain - CHECK
      Check face curtain properly rolled and folded on drum; face curtain pull handle firmly in place under retaining clips.
4. Effective F3H-2 airplanes 146709t and subsequent; also effective F3H-2 airplanes 133549d thru 146339s, upon incorporation of ASC 132, ejection seat - CHECK
   (see figure 2-4).
   a. Seat installation - CHECK
      Insure that the seat retaining latch is in place and safetied.
   b. Personnel parachute link - CHECK
      Check the link between the seat drogue system and the personnel parachute for security. In seats installed by ASC 132, insure that parachute link line passes through guillotine. Insure that the drogue chute withdrawal line passes OVER all other lines.

c. Firing cables - CHECK
   Insure that both primary (face curtain) and secondary (D ring) firing control cables pass through the catapult firing head sear. Insure that time release and drogue gun trip rods are in place and secure.
d. Seat and harness - CHECK
   Check mounting and integrity of body harness, leg restraints and quick release mechanism. Insure proper mating of pilot's composite disconnect. Check canopy jettison handle in stowed position.
e. Safety banner - REMOVED
   Check safety banner and all five locking pins; face curtain, catapult sear, drogue gun, manual override (or emergency harness release, as installed), and oxygen bottle are removed.
5. Interior canopy emergency handle - FORWARD
   Manually check handle in full forward position.
6. Canopy stop assembly - LATCHED
   Check stop assembly firmly latched to forward end of canopy gear track.
7. Canopy stop and stripper hook - CHECK
   Use normal canopy switch to fully open canopy from full closed position; canopy must stop in normal full open position.
8. Automatic seat belt actuator - CHECK
   Check index marks for proper alignment, piston arm safety wired to upper mounting fitting, actuator arm and stripper in proper positions for engagement.
9. Instrument panel mounting - CHECK
   Insure that the pin holding the top of the hinged main instrument panel is properly installed. The panel is free to fall backward upon acceleration if this pin is not installed and secure.

ON ENTERING COCKPIT

INTERIOR CHECK (ALL FLIGHTS)

Before external power source is connected, make a left-to-right check of the cockpit; observe the following:

1. D-C power switch - OFF
2. Seat height - ADJUST
   Depress the thumb button to retract the detent pin; then move handle in direction of seat movement. With seat adjusted, move handle to permit the lock pin to engage one of the seven retaining holes provided, which are one inch apart.

WARNING

A retaining hole is not engaged and the seat is not locked unless the thumb button protrudes from the adjusting handle approximately 1.5 inches. This protrusion is approximately .5 inch in the unlocked condition. Failure to observe this warning may result in violent movement of the seat when vertical accelerations are encountered.

3. Body harness - ADJUST
4. Rudder pedals - ADJUST
5. Personal equipment - CONNECT
   Connect radio gear, anti-g suit, oxygen hose and bailout oxygen bottle, or composite disconnect.

Note

Clip the main oxygen hose sufficiently high to permit freedom of movement.

6. Oxygen mask - CHECK
   Check oxygen supply line and mask for leaks, flow indicator and safety pressure lever for operation, check oxygen control panel as follows:
   a. Oxygen supply lever - ON
   b. Safety pressure lever - ON
   c. Oxygen regulator lever - NORMAL OXYGEN
7. External stores jettison switch - FULL DOWN
8. Circuit breakers - IN
9. Radar Master Switch - OFF

CAUTION

Do not operate the radar on the ground for longer than 1 1/2 minutes unless ground cooling unit is attached, as the system is dependent upon ram air for cooling.

10. Gun sight control switch - OFF
11. Emergency slat handle - FULL UP
12. Starter button - FULL UP
13. Engine master switch - OFF
14. Throttle - OFF
15. Throttle friction adjustment - AS DESIRED
16. Open nozzle emergency A/B switch - OFF
17. Engine de-ice switch - AUTO
18. Emergency hydraulic pump handle - FULL FORWARD
19. Landing gear control handle - DOWN
20. Armament master switch - OFF
21. Lateral control pilot switch - AUTO
    Set manually dimmable lateral control warning light to full bright.
22. Airspeed indicator - SET
    Set airspeed indicator index markers.
23. Altimeter - SET
    Set altimeter for field elevation.
24. Clock - SET
    Wind and set clock; reset accelerometer.
25. Instrument flood lights - OFF
26. Arresting gear - UP
27. A-C power switch - GEN
28. D-C power switch - OFF

CAUTION

Retain d-c power switch in OFF position when external power supply is connected. This prevents overcharging and excessive gas formation in the battery.

Section II
NAVWEPS 01-245FCB-501

MARTIN-BAKER EJECTION SEAT SAFETY PINS — INSPECTION POINTS

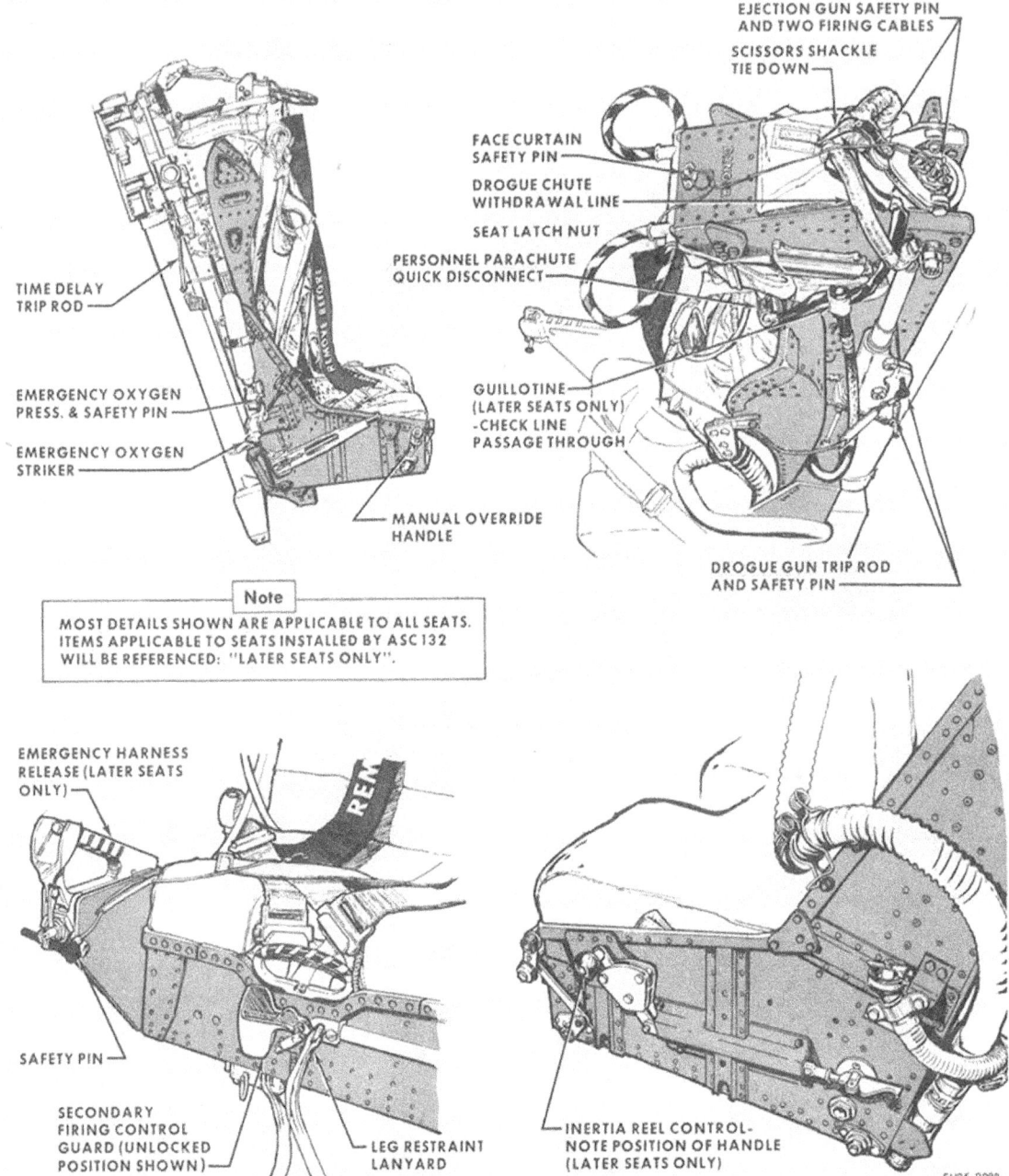

Figure 2-4. Martin-Baker Ejection Seat Inspection Points

29. UHF radio - OFF
30. Autopilot engage switch - OUT
31. Emergency vent control - FULL DOWN
32. Radio compass selector switch - OFF
33. Standby compass switch - OFF
34. Pitot heat switch - OFF
35. Daylight flood light switch - OFF
36. Cabin temperature control switch - AUTO
37. Cabin pressure switch - NORM
38. Exterior lights master switch - OFF
39. Interior lights control switch - OFF
40. IFF master switch - OFF
41. IFF destruct switch - DOWN
    Where installed, this switch must be down and its guard safety wired.
42. S-2 compass switch - SLAVED GYRO

Note

Upon initial application of power to the airplane, the S-2 compass switch must be in the SLAVED GYRO position, and the inverter circuit breaker must be in. If these controls are not in their proper positions upon application of d-c power, the fast slaving feature of the S-2 compass will be lost.

INTERIOR CHECK (NIGHT FLIGHTS)

In addition to the preceding checks, perform the following for night operation:

1. Exterior lights master switch - AS DESIRED
2. Interior lights control switch - ON
   Adjust lights to desired brilliance.

Note

Insure that flashlight is included in personal gear on night flights.

EXTERNAL POWER SUPPLY ON-BEFORE STARTING ENGINE

1. A-C power switch - EXT PWR

CAUTION

Do not place a-c power switch in EXT PWR position until external power supply has been connected and has had time to reach its rated voltage and frequency.

2. D-C power switch - OFF

CAUTION

Retain d-c power switch in OFF position until external power source has been disconnected.

3. Wing tank dump and purge switch - NORMAL
4. Fuel transfer selector switch - FUS

Note

In F3H-2 airplanes 136983h thru 143462n and F3H-2M airplanes 137041i thru 137095k it will be impossible to transfer wing fuel with the landing gear extended. A limit switch in the landing gear mechanism renders the transfer pumps inoperative.

CAUTION

F3H-2M airplanes 133623e thru 137040g and F3H-2 airplanes 133549d thru 136982g are not equipped with the landing gear limit switch, and are capable of wing transfer at any time, however, it is not recommended to transfer wing fuel with the landing gear extended since the maximum speed for flight with the landing gear extended is the minimum speed for wing fuel transfer.

Note

* Effective F3H-2 airplanes 143463o and subsequent, wing fuel transfer will be possible with the landing gear extended, provided the landing gear control is in the UP position.

* The landing gear limit switch in these airplanes has been moved from the gear uplocks to the control handle. This feature permits wing fuel transfer in the event of a landing gear malfunction, and is to be considered an EMERGENCY PROCEDURE ONLY.

* Both fuselage transfer pumps are inoperative with the fuel selector switch in any position other than FUS.

5. Fire warning lights test switch - CHECK
   Check that fire warning light illuminates when switch is held in the FIRE TEST position. All other warning lights (except radio altitude, low altitude and strut extend lights) illuminate when switch is held in TEST WARN LTS position.

Note

Effective F3H-2 airplanes 133549d thru 133564d, the d-c power switch must be placed in BATT-GEN position to accomplish the above check. Return d-c power switch to OFF when the check is completed.

6. Fuel quantity switch - CHECK
   Check for response of fuel quantity indicator.

Section II NAVWEPS 01-245FCB-501

DANGER AREAS

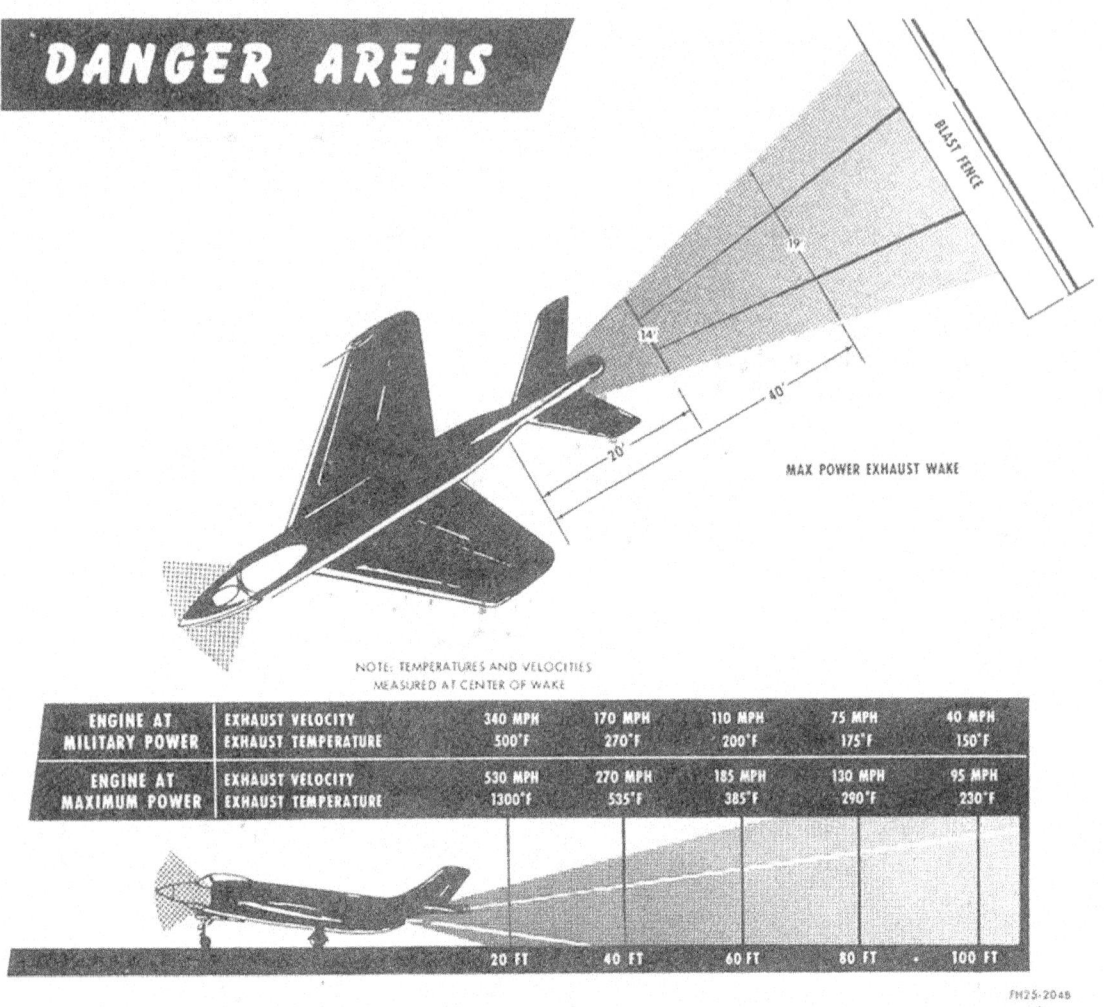

Figure 2-5. Danger Areas

The airplane should be headed into the wind in an area where no loose objects can be drawn into the engine and where the jet blast will cause no damage. See figure 2-5.

WARNING

Before starting engine, be sure that fore and aft engine danger areas are clear of personnel.

External starter air supply must be connected and placed in operation. Refer to Starter Compressor Unit, Section VII.

Note

When necessary, the engine may be started without external electrical power.

STARTING ENGINES

1. D-C power switch - OFF
2. Engine master switch - ON
3. Fuel boost pressure - CHECK
   Pull a-c and d-c boost pump circuit breakers. Negative "g" boost pump pressure 15.0 to 22.5 psi. A-C boost pump circuit breaker in. Boost pressure 20 to 30 psi. Pull a-c circuit breaker; d-c boost pump circuit breaker in. Boost pressure 20 to 30 psi. All circuit breakers in. Boost pressure 20 to 30 psi.

4. Starter button - DEPRESS
   Depress button for approximately 3 seconds, or until holding coil retains button depressed.

> **CAUTION**
>
> Pilot controlled starts are recommended. Electrical connection from the aircraft starter circuit external receptacle located adjacent to the external air connection, to the gas turbine ground power unit is to be made prior to starting to insure automatic shutoff of the air supply at the correct starter cutout speed. Hand signals or ground controlled starts are not recommended for initiation and/or shutoff of the ground air supply. Time delay inherent in this method will result in overspeed of the starter causing failure or damage. Failure of a starter due to overspeed could be hazardous to operating personnel. If automatic shutoff of the air supply cannot be achieved due to malfunction of equipment, pilots and crewmen are cautioned that the starter air supply must be manually shut off at a speed not to exceed 38% rpm. The control valve in the gas turbine ground power unit will not shut off the air supply automatically unless the unit is connected electrically to the aircraft starting circuit.

Note

While engine rpm is building up, make sure there is some indication of oil pressure.

5. Ignition switch - DEPRESS
   When engine rpm reaches approximately 6% depress ignition switch and hold.
6. Throttle - ADVANCE
   At approximately 12 to 14% rpm, advance throttle to IDLE while holding ignition switch down.

> **CAUTION**
>
> If there is no indication of an increase in turbine outlet temperature within 10 seconds after rpm reaches 17% or within 5 seconds after manifold pressure rises above 0, "light-off" has not been affected. Release ignition button, retard throttle to OFF, pull starter button full up, and engine master switch to OFF position. Allow ignition system to cool for three minutes before attempting another start.

Note

In event of three aborted starts, dump tank must be drained prior to next attempted start.

7. Throttle - ADJUST
   Compressor stall during engine starting may be encountered under standard to hot ambient temperature conditions and should be dealt with by throttle modulation below the idle detent. After "light-off", release ignition button and adjust the throttle as required to prevent exceeding the turbine outlet temperature limits. This modulation should be done while monitoring both fuel flow and exhaust temperature. The fuel flowmeter should be used as a guide in modulation to prevent inadvertent shut off of fuel flow. Place throttle in idle detent after engine RPM reaches 60%.

> **CAUTION**
>
> • Failure of the engine starter button to "pop up" automatically or failure of the ground crewman to close the air bleed and shutoff valve at the proper time (36 to 40% engine rpm) may result in overspeeding the starter with a possibility of disintegration or seizure of the starter turbine.
>
> • After "light-off", if there is not an increase in rpm within 10 seconds or if the turbine outlet temperature threatens to exceed limits, release ignition button, retard throttle to OFF, pull starter button full UP, and return engine master switch to OFF. Accomplish the ENGINE CLEARING PROCEDURE, listed below, prior to attempting restart.

8. Starter button - UP
   Starter button should automatically "pop up" at approximately 36% rpm; if it does not pop up when rpm reaches 40% immediately pull it up manually.
9. Engine instruments - CHECK
   After a successful start has been attained, check engine for adherence to idle operating limits.

> **CAUTION**
>
> If turbine outlet temperature exceeds limits, this is considered a "hot" start. The severity of such starts depends on the degree of overtemperature and the length of time the overtemperature existed. The engine must be shut down immediately if any overtemperature condition occurs.

Note

Refer to Section V for normal operating limits.

10. A-C power switch - GEN
11. External electrical and air supplies - DISCONNECTED
12. D-C power switch - BATT-GEN

STARTING PROCEDURE (BATTERY ONLY)

In the event external electrical power is not available the aircraft can be started on battery power alone.

To perform a battery start, proceed as follows for the airplane effectivity applicable.

Note

On F3H-2 airplanes 133549d thru 133580e and F3H-2M airplanes 133623e thru 133630f, the d-c power switch must be in BATT-GEN position in order to open the fuel shutoff valve during battery start. On all later F3H airplanes, the fuel shutoff valve operates from the utility bus and the airplane may be started with the d-c power switch in the OFF position. For F3H-2M airplanes 133623e thru 133630f and F3H-2 airplanes 133549d thru 133580e, use the following proceedure for starting:

1. Check external air supply connected and in operation.
2. Inverter circuit breaker - PULLED
3. D-C power switch - BATT- GEN

Note

After engine is started with the d-c power switch in BATT-GEN position, pull inverter circuit breaker to reduce electrical load on the battery. After "light-off" push inverter circuit breaker IN. All other unnecessary d-c powered equipment - OFF.

4. A-C power switch - INV
   This causes the a-c generator warning light to remind pilot to reset the inverter circuit breaker.
5. Engine master switch - ON

Note

Oil and fuel pressure indicators will show no indications until d-c generator and inverter are in operation.

6. Starter button - DEPRESS
   Depress starter button for approximately 3 seconds.
7. Complete the battery start by following procedures 5 thru 10 listed above in STARTING PROCEDURE.

For F3H-2M airplanes 133631f thru 137095k, F3H-2 airplanes 133581e and subsequent, use the following proceedure for starting:

1. D-C power switch - OFF
2. Engine master switch - ON
3. Starter button - DEPRESS
   Depress button for approximately 3 seconds.
4. Complete the start as in procedures 5 through 10 in STARTING PROCEDURE, above.

ENGINE CLEARING PROCEDURE

If an unsatisfactory start is made (other than hot starts) the engine must be cleared as follows, prior to attempting a restart:

1. External air and electrical connections - CONNECTED
2. Throttle - OFF
3. Engine master switch - ON
4. Engine start switch - DEPRESS

WARNING

Do not depress ignition button during engine clearing procedure.

When engine reaches 12% rpm, pull starter button full up and allow engine to coast to a stop. Allow 30 seconds for excessive fuel to drain before attempting another start.

CAUTION

If the engine clearing procedure is accomplished without the A.P.U. electrical control line connected, insure that the engine master switch is ON before cranking engine. With the engine master switch off, the fuel shutoff valve will be closed, and the suction created by the engine-driven fuel pumps during cranking may collapse the engine fuel feed lines.

BEFORE TAXIING

Note

During prolonged engine ground operation it, is desirable to keep the stabilator in the neutral position.

Signal ground crew to extend wings and lock. Check red warning post on each wing, posts down and flush with wing indicates locked condition.

Note

The wings cannot be operated from the cockpit and must be actuated by ground personnel.

The pilot will make the following checks and recheck of cockpit control systems with engine running at idle:

1. Radar master switch - STB

CAUTION

To prevent tumbling and possible damage to the roll and pitch control gyro, the radar master switch should be in STB or OPER at any time electrical power is being supplied to the aircraft.

2. Flaps and slats - CHECK
   Cycle flaps and slats, checking travel visually. Reset flaps to take-off position. Check flap indicator. Check slats extended. Check slats out warning light off.
3. Speed brakes - CHECK
   Speed brakes out and in; reset to in, checking visually. Check speed brakes out warning light.

Note

The pilot will have visual contact with ground personnel who relay the flap and slat position, rudder, stabilator, speed brake, and hook position.

4. Rudder pedals - ADJUSTED
5. Roll-yaw damper - CHECK
   Engage roll-yaw damper momentarily to eliminate any trapped signals in the autopilot aileron servos that will leave the ailerons out of neutral. This condition occurs when a-c or d-c power is cut off from the autopilot while the control surfaces are deflected. Trim ailerons to neutral, check that stick is centered. Move control stick through complete control range, check controls visually.

CAUTION

Insure that roll damper is disengaged prior to take-off.

Note

If spoilers are selected for pilot familiarization at low speeds it should be remembered that should a trapped signal (ailerons out-of-neutral) exist in the aileron servos near full authority the airplane will roll at rates that are not controllable with spoilers. Engaging the roll damper momentarily will eliminate this condition. Be certain that the roll damper is disengaged at speeds below 300 KIAS because it will cause a large reduction in the available roll rate while using spoilers.

6. Lateral control switch - CHECK
   With stick held in full deflection left wing down, move lateral control switch to EMERG SPOILERS. Note that stick moves back to approximately 5/8 of normal deflection in aileron mode. Observe that time required to complete shift is approximately two seconds. Move lateral control switch back to AUTO, observe that full stick deflection is regained and that shift time is approximately two seconds. Repeat check in same manner for right wing. Cycle and check controls visually.

WARNING

Insure that the lateral control switch is immediately returned to the AUTO position after ground check, to prevent possibility of take-off under spoiler system control.

7. Controls - CHECK
   Cycle stick laterally and fore and aft, and observe pressure drop on both hydraulic systems. This insures that both hydraulic systems are supplying power to aileron and stabilator.
8. Stabilator trim - SET FOR TAKE-OFF
   Check stick trim button operation; check feel trim indicator set for take-off - "0" indication.
9. Instruments - WITHIN LIMITS
   Check main panel instruments flight instruments operating properly.
   a. Hydraulic pressures.
      (1) Utility - 2850 to 3150 psi
      (2) Power control - 2850 to 3150 psi
   b. Pneumatic pressure - 2650 to 3200 psi
   c. Check all warning lights.
   d. Compass system - CHECK
      Check that the sync signal indicator needle is within the width of the index mark.
   e. Compass control switch - CHECK
      Place switch to COMP. CONT. on G-2 compass systems or to SLAVE on the S-2 compass system.
   f. Engine instruments - WITHIN LIMITS
      Engine instruments normal limits (refer to Section V).
10. A-C power switch - GEN
    Cycle switch from INV to A-C GEN and check for momentary warning light.
11. D-C power switch - BATT-GEN
    Cycle switch to BATT and back to OFF, check for warning light on. This checks the operation of the transformer-rectifier. No light in the off position indicates a possible malfunction.
12. UHF radio - ON
13. Emergency ventilating handle - CLOSED
    a. Emergency vent - CLOSED
    b. Check defrost for operation. Set as required.
    c. Temperature control switch - AUTO
    d. Cycle temperature control clockwise to check response.
14. Radio compass - CHECK
    Check all phases of operation.
15. IFF master switch - STDB
    (Prior to the incorporation of ASC 188)
16. While at idle rpm place the ENG. DE-ICE switch in MANUAL. A slight indication of T.O.T. increase (5 to 10°C.) should be noted. Return the switch to AUTO and observe a slight T.O.T. decrease. If doubt exists con-

cerning the T.O.T. indication, request the plane captain to feel the anti-icing hose through door 35R for the pressure and temperature surge when MANUAL is selected at idle rpm. Return the ENG DE-ICE switch to AUTO and check for deactivation of de-icing system.

(SUBSEQUENT TO THE INCORPORATION OF ASC188)

Actuate the engine de-ice switch to the TEST position and return to AUTO. All de-ice system lights should illuminate. Approximately 20 seconds later the ICE DETECT light may flicker. Approximately 50 seconds after actuation the ICE warning and the DE-ICE ON light should be extinguished.

17. Emergency A/B mod switch - ON. Note RPM increase of 1 to 1 1/2% return switch to OFF.

TAXIING

Observe the following instructions for taxiing:

1. Signal plane captain to remove chocks.
2. Observe plane captain's taxiing signals.
3. Once airplane is moving, taxi at the lowest practical rpm to maintain forward motion and steering control.
4. Taxi on hard surface or areas indicated as adequate for airplane support.
5. Steer airplane by differential braking.

CAUTION

Do not ride brakes. Use positive brake application in direction of desired turn, then release pressure.

6. Check operation of turn-and-slip indicator.
7. Ground operation reduces at a high ratio, time and fuel available for flight.

Note

Plan your flight for a minimum of ground operation.

BEFORE TAKE-OFF

PRE-TAKE-OFF AIRCRAFT CHECK

1. Harness - TIGHT AND LOCKED
2. Personal equipment - CHECK
   Recheck radio gear, anti-G suit, oxygen hose and bail-out oxygen bottle for proper connections.
3. Canopy - OPEN (with Martin-Baker seat, canopy - CLOSED)
4. Fuel transfer selector switch - FUS.
5. Fuel quantity - CHECK
   Check fuel quantity in all tanks.
6. Wings - SPREAD and LOCKED
7. Trim - SET FOR TAKE-OFF
   Rud Pos - T.O.
   Ail Pos - Neutral
   Stab Trim - Neutral
8. Flaps and slats - Slats and 1/4 Flaps

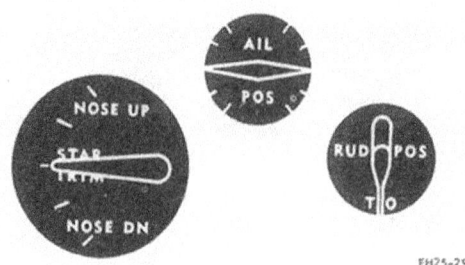

Figure 2-6. Control Trim Indicators

Taxi to run-up area - recheck the following:

9. Speed brakes - IN
10. Arresting gear - UP
11. Controls - CHECK
    Cycle stick full fore and aft and laterally.

PRE-TAKE-OFF ENGINE CHECK

Note

The pilot should select an area for run-up with thought to jet blast area.

1. Hold firm equal brake pressure.
2. Advance throttle to MIL position.
3. Check engine instruments for normal operation.
4. Check turbine outlet temperature to be within limits specified in figure 5-1.
5. Rapidly retard throttle to IDLE.
6. Check time to stabilized idle rpm.
   Observe rpm for undershoot of stabilized idle RPM. Normal deceleration time should be approximately 6 to 8 seconds, with no tendency to undershoot RPM.

CAUTION

This rapid retardation of the throttle is a check of the rigging, throttle quadrant security, fuel control malfunction resulting in engine stagnation or surge, to avoid possible inflight malfunctions. Any of the above observed malfunctions is a cause for corrective action prior to flight. This is a ground check and should not be used in the air. Inflight throttle application should always be smooth and steady.

LAND BASED OPERATION

TAKE-OFF

Note

Refer to Section III for procedure to employ in the event of an emergency during take-off.

1. Request tower clearance to active runway.
2. Line up on active runway, hold position with brakes.

3. Advance throttle to full MIL, allow to stabilize.
4. Stick in trimmed position.
5. Release brakes evenly.
6. Move throttle outboard to MAX (afterburner) position.
7. Maintain directional control with a minimum of brake action. Rudder is effective at approximately 50 knots.
8. Pull aircraft off at approximately 125-135 knots.

TAKE-OFF TECHNIQUE

Take the runway and when in position, roll forward slightly to align nose wheel. Pump brakes to insure positive pressures. Perform all checks as outlined. With satisfactory engine performance in MIL power, release brakes evenly to start take-off run while moving the throttle outboard to MAX position. Correct heading by slight brake pressure until rudder becomes effective. The stick will move aft slightly as ram air enters the bellows on the stabilator. At approximately 125 knots, a slight aft stick force will initiate take-off. Pilots unfamiliar with the control effectiveness will tend to overcontrol in both planes of rotation, lateral and longitudinal. Porpoising or wobble can be stopped by a steady stick pressure. A high rate of climb is available from take-off so a systematic and rapid procedure of establishing climb, retracting gear, retracting flaps and slats must be practiced. The ensuing mission will dictate what climb technique should be used.

Note

The afterburner may be used in much the same manner as JATO bottles are used on other aircraft if the afterburner is cut in for a short period during a take-off that could normally be made with military power. The afterburner should be cut in at 110 knots IAS and cut out at 160 knots IAS. This technique will permit rapid acceleration through the high drag region on take-off with little penalty in fuel consumed. The afterburner should be cut in and allowed to stabilize momentarily during the first portion of the take-off roll on all take-offs as a check in afterburner operation.

CAUTION

This technique should not be used in lieu of continuous afterburner operation from brake release where runway length will not permit a military power take-off.

CROSSWIND TAKE-OFF

1. Release brakes evenly. Maintain directional control by use of brake during initial part of roll.

CAUTION

Do not ride or keep pressure on brakes during crosswind take-off. Brakes should be used sparingly to prevent overheating. Excessive braking will increase take-off run.

2. Rudder control becomes effective at approximately 50 knots.
3. Hold nose gear on runway until flying speed is reached.
4. Pull aircraft off at approximately 135 knots. Aircraft tends to "weather-cock" into the wind at lift-off with controls neutral.

WARNING

In order to counteract airplane drift at lift-off, do not attempt an immediate wing low attitude. The pilot cannot properly judge the wing tip ground clearance on a swept wing type aircraft.

NIGHT TAKE-OFF

For night take-off, it is recommended that the following checks be made in addition to normal daylight take-off procedure.

1. Check exterior lights, adjust cockpit and instrument lights to desired brilliancy.
2. When aligning the aircraft with the runway, pick a reference by which to guide the take-off run in order to hold directional control.

AFTER TAKE-OFF

When airplane is definitely airborne:

1. Retract landing gear.
   a. Handle - UP
   b. Check indicators and warning light in gear handle.

WARNING

Due to the close proximity of the landing gear control and the lateral control switch, extra care must be exercised in avoiding inadvertent actuation of the lateral control switch when extending or retracting the landing gear.

2. Close canopy.
3. Retract flaps and slats.

CAUTION

Do not retract flaps and slats until reaching 170 knots. This insures positive take-off and climb technique and will provide best control characteristics.

4. Establish best climbing speed; see climb data in Appendix I.
   If climb does not require afterburner, retard throttle to MIL after reaching climb speed.
5. Fuel transfer selector to WING or PYLON.

> **CAUTION**
>
> • The minimum airspeed for wing fuel transfer is 250 knots IAS. This limitation is imposed due to the possibility of wing tank collapse if transfer occurs at a lower airspeed.
>
> • No provisions are made for automatic transfer pump shutoff. Immediately upon completion of wing tank transfer the FUS TRANSFER position should be selected to eliminate the possibility of burning out the wing transfer pumps.

Note

• Care should be exercised during normal afterburner modulation not to retard throttle too rapidly. Very rapid reduction of afterburner fuel can cause an afterburner flame-out.

• During a locked throttle climb, engine speed may vary as much as 1 percent.

CLIMB

Climb at full military power unless maximum power (afterburner) is required. Do not exceed turbine out temperature red line. Refer to climb charts for recommended airspeeds and estimated rate of climb to be maintained.

Note

Engine overtemperature may be encountered during warmer weather while in afterburning from sea level to approximately 20,000 feet. This condition is brought about by the mechanical limits of nozzle opening, hence must be controlled by reducing fuel flow. Accordingly engine temperature during afterburning should be controlled by throttle modulation.

FLIGHT CHARACTERISTICS

Refer to Section VI for information regarding flight characteristics.

DESCENT

1. In all descents, the pilot should not exceed any airframe limitations. See Limitations, Section V.
2. Prior to rapid descents from altitude, advance manual heat control lever to the full DEFROST position to prevent possible fogging or icing on the windscreen and canopy.
3. Since rapid descents cannot always be anticipated the maximum comfortable interior temperature should be maintained. This will aid in defrosting the cockpit.

Note

• Refer to Section II for emergency descent from altitude.

• EGT temperatures as low as 135°C may be encountered during a descent with IDLE power.

TRAFFIC ENTRY

Perform the following checks prior to entering traffic pattern:

1. Engine De-Ice Switch - auto
2. Armament switches - OFF
3. Autopilot - DISENGAGED
4. Fuel quantity - CHECK
5. Fuel transfer switch - FUS
6. Radar - STANDBY

> **CAUTION**
>
> Do not select wing fuel transfer below 250 knots IAS. A possibility of tank collapse exists due to insufficient ram air for tank pressurization at low airspeeds.

7. Hydraulic pressure - WITHIN LIMITS
8. Harness - TIGHT AND LOCKED
9. Arresting gear - UP
10. Lateral control switch - AUTO
11. Dump and purge switch - NORMAL

LANDING PATTERN

(See figure 2-7).

1. Landing gear - DOWN AND LOCKED
2. Slats - EXTENDED
3. Flaps - FULL DOWN
4. Canopy - OPEN (with Martin-Baker seat canopy - CLOSED)

> **WARNING**
>
> Under heavy gross weight configurations, the landing pattern must be extended and speeds increased. See figure 2-7, Landing Pattern, and figure 6-1, Stall Speeds.

LANDING TECHNIQUE

Every pilot should develop a landing technique good enough to not only allow him to walk away from every landing, or just to do his share in reducing A.A.R.s to a minimum, but have the satisfaction of knowing

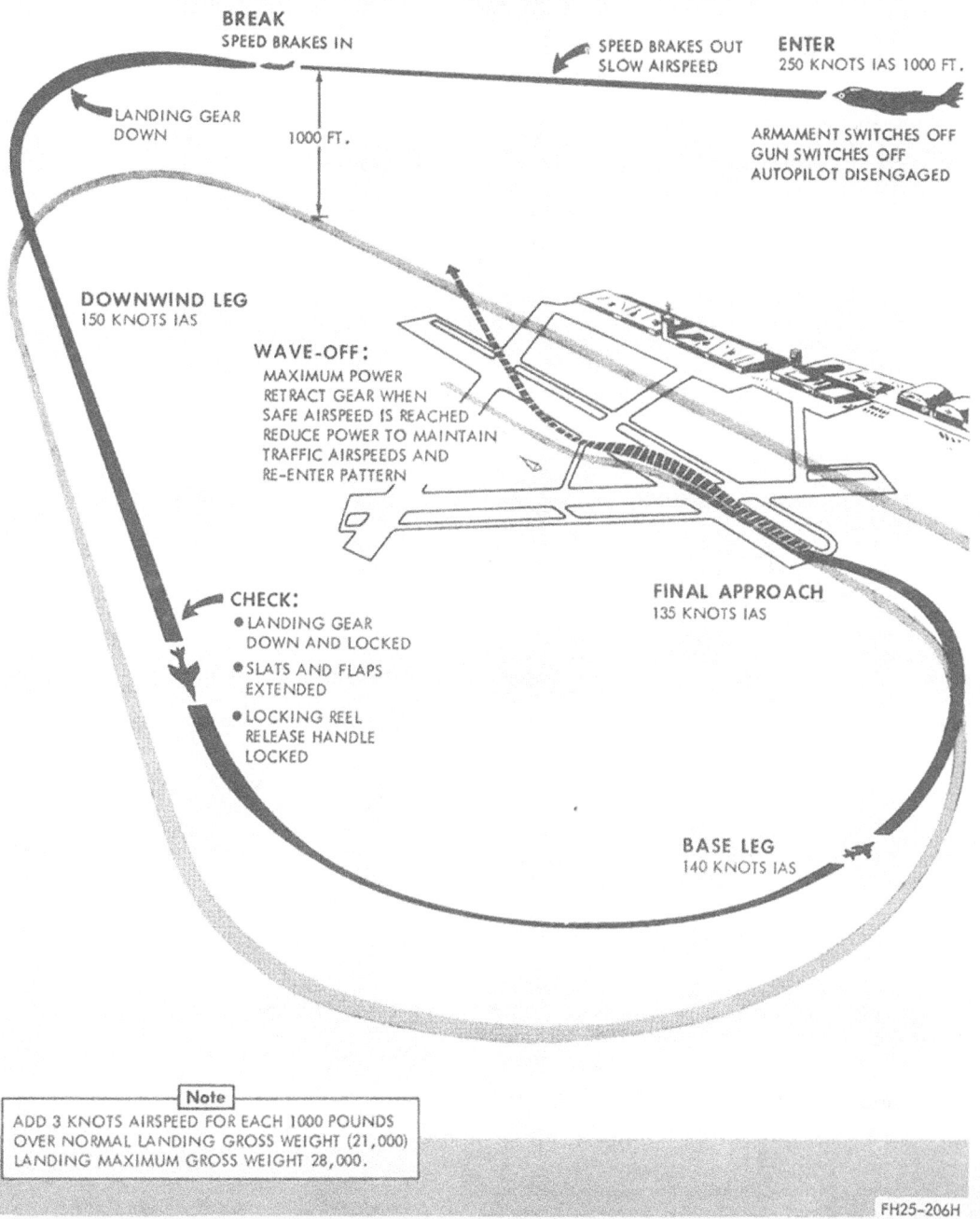

Figure 2-7. Typical Landing Pattern

that he flew the airplane instead of the airplane flying him. Needless to say, a good landing technique is a prerequisite of longevity. Knowledge of the airplane's capabilities, planning and anticipation are the key notes to this, the most dreaded maneuver of all first flights. Assuming that the break will be to the left on the upwind leg and conceding the pilot the prerogative of flying a comfortable pattern, let's fly our version of the illustrated landing pattern (see figure 2-7). Enter the pattern upwind decelerating to 250 knots IAS using the speed brakes and throttle as necessary. Continue on your upwind leg far enough to allow sufficient time on the downwind leg to perform all the prelanding checks. Roll into the downwind leg and drop the gear, power should be increased enough to maintain altitude and prevent a drastic decrease in airspeed. By the time the gear is down and locked you should be indicating about 200 knots, which is a good time to extend your slats and flaps and start a mild rate of descent. After rechecking gear down and locked, slats and flaps extended, canopy open and shoulder harness and safety belt locked, roll into your base leg with a moderate rate of descent and maintain about 140 knots IAS. Plan the base leg to allow yourself about 1/2 mile straight-away with sufficient altitude to establish a mild rate of descent and an attitude that will allow a flare-out. The minimum airspeed "across the fence" is 130 knots IAS. You will have to carry a power setting sufficient to maintain this attitude and provide enough thrust to allow acceleration in event of wave-off. Cut the power when the landing is assured. It is imperative to establish the correct power setting, airspeed and rate of descent; this will create your attitude. It should be readily seen that if the power is too much - you'll be landing long; too little - short. The airspeed too high, you'll float, too low - you'll sink. The rate of descent too great, you'll drive the gear up into the wing, too little, and - you'll overshoot the field. Excessive airspeed should be lost by a combination power reduction and nose-up, followed by a power increase to maintain this attitude. It is the latter power increase that pilots tend to forget.

CAUTION

Do not attempt a full stall landing. The angle of attack attitude will result in dragging the tail skid.

Landing Roll

On landing roll, hold nose wheel off as long as possible to take advantage of aerodynamic braking (excellent above 90 knots IAS). Maintain directional control with the rudder. The nose wheel will rock to the three-point attitude at approximately 80 knots IAS; directional control is then maintained by slight brake pressures.

Note

Braking will be required to decelerate the airplane rapidly below 90 knots IAS.

AFTER LANDING

After clearing active runway, perform the following checks while taxiing to parking area:

1. Flaps and slats - RETRACT
2. Speed brakes - IN
3. All trim controls to neutral, check feel trim indicators.

ENGINE SHUTDOWN

1. Radar master switch - OFF
2. Throttle - OFF

Note

- Any time full MIL or MAX power is ground checked, a delay of 2 minutes at idle rpm is required for cooling before shutdown.

- Pilot should not rely on throttle friction control to accomplish full off position. Pilot should hold throttle in the off position until certain no shutdown fire exists.

3. Engine master switch - OFF
   Engine master switch off when rpm is below 10 percent.
   All switches - OFF

BEFORE LEAVING AIRPLANE

Before leaving airplane, make following checks:

1. Wheels - CHOCKED
2. Ejection seat safety pins - INSTALLED
3. Canopy - CLOSED - Using external switches
4. Landing gear safety pins - INSTALLED
5. Flight forms - COMPLETED

CARRIER OPERATION

Refer to caution under Exterior Inspection prior to entering aircraft.

CATAPULT SPOTTING

Spotting can be accomplished satisfactorily by taxiing from directly astern the catapult or by taxiing from the deck centerline at an angle of approximately 40 degrees. A nose wheel steering bar is recommended to facilitate spotting.

Note

The nose wheel has a tendency to swivel during high wind conditions or when taxiing slowly.

CATAPULT CHECK

1. Harness - TIGHT AND LOCKED
2. Personal equipment - CONNECTED
3. Canopy - OPEN
4. Fuel transfer selector switch - FUS.
5. Fuel Quantity - CHECK
   Check fuel quantity in all tanks.
6. Wings - SPREAD AND LOCKED
7. Flaps - FULL DOWN
8. Slats - EXTENDED
9. Trim Settings - The following trim setting recommendations (figure 2-8) are the results of tests, and are based on the expected catapult, end airspeed. These settings can be checked at altitude by trimming the aircraft for level flight at reduced airspeed at the weight involved, with wheels and flaps down, slats extended, and power settings as near to take-off conditions as practicable.
10. Speed brakes - IN
11. Hook - UP
12. Catapult hold-back handle - DOWN
13. Cycle stick through full throw fore and aft and laterally.

CATAPULT LAUNCH

OPTIMUM PILOT TECHNIQUE DURING LAUNCH

Select the optimum trim settings for the anticipated end airspeed (see figure 2-8). Position the stick five (5) inches forward of the full aft position and hold this stick position until aircraft rotates to the required angle of attack for level flight.

If partial or full back stick is held, there is danger of over-rotating after leaving the bow. Airplane nose-down response is appreciably slower than airplane nose-up response because of differences in stabilator rate of movement. If the pilot is not careful with stick movement during the power stroke and after leaving the bow, it is possible to over-rotate the airplane to the point where full forward stick would not produce a rapid enough recovery, resulting in a large loss of altitude.

POSTLAUNCH PILOT TECHNIQUE

On afterburner launches in order to conserve fuel, reduce power from combat to military thrust as soon as possible.

POWER

MIL power shall be used on all launches when the gross weight is 36,000 lbs. or below, except as follows: When carrying the Mark 7 store; when wind over the deck or operational conditions require the use of MAX (afterburner) power. (Refer to applicable Aircraft Launching Bulletins for further details.)

	EXPECTED END AIRSPEED (KNOTS)		
	122-140	141-145	146-160
AILERON TRIM (MARKS)	0	0	0
RUDDER TRIM (MARKS)	0	0	0
STABILATOR TRIM (4 GRADUATIONS)	1 N.U.	¼ N.U.	½ N.U.
STABILATOR TRIM (10 GRADUATIONS)	2½ N.U.	2 N.U.	1¼ N.U.

Figure 2-8. Catapult Launch Trim Setting

LANDING GEAR STRUT EXTENSION

1. Normal except with Mark 7 store.
2. With Mark 7 store main gear fully extended (9").

SIGNALS

Know the routine exchange of signals. The catapult officer shall confer with the pilots to insure that he will stand at the correct station on the deck to enable the pilots to clearly see the catapult signals.

HEADREST

The headrest should be used when catapulting. An uncomfortable neck jerk, possibly producing temporary loss of control, will result if the head is not held firmly against the headrest during the launching run.

AIRCRAFT EQUIPMENT

Looseness of the throttle and similar controls shall be avoided by a check of adjustments to ascertain that they are sufficiently stiff to prevent easing back during launching.

CARRIER LANDINGS

LSO APPROACH

When making an LSO approach, the carrier landing pattern and glide path are identical to the pattern and glide path flown when using the mirror system. After the "RELEASE" signal (cut) is given by the LSO, the pilot flies the airplane to the deck exactly the same as when using the mirror.

MIRROR APPROACH

When flying a mirror pattern the altitude during the downwind leg is approximately 400 ft. and the airspeed is approximately 10 kt above the final approach speed. A level turn at 20 to 24° angle of bank is begun 4 to 5 seconds after passing abeam of the ramp. The 400 ft. altitude is maintained until the "meat ball" is picked up and the final approach down the glide path is begun.

As the on-glide-path position is approached the power is reduced 1 to 1 1/2% rpm and the airplane is held on the glide path to touchdown. Recommended final approach speeds are the same as for LSO landings. Airspeed varies between 124 and 133 kts IAS in the airplane gross weight range of 24,000 to 27,000 lb.

Note

Care must be taken to begin the rate of descent with the proper final approach airspeed because airplane response to small power changes is slow.

CAUTION

- Carrier landings on angled deck ships should be made with particular attention to achieving a good line up and avoiding landings with right to left drift which, when associated with the increased runout of angled deck arresting gears can result in the aircraft coming to rest in the port catwalk even though a pendant is engaged.

- A burble effect, present under all wind conditions, produces a definite tendency for the right wing to drop as the airplane approaches and passes the ramp at the aft end of the landing area on angled deck ships.

WAVE-OFF

The use of MAX (afterburner) power is recommended for standard wave-off procedure, although MIL power is satisfactory for wave-offs at light gross weights (24,000 lbs.). With MAX power, sink rate can be stopped almost immediately and the airplane accelerates very rapidly. The minimum distance for a mirror wave-off should be approximately twice that for an LSO wave-off.

SECTION III
EMERGENCY PROCEDURES

ENGINE FAILURE

Engine failure of jet aircraft, in all probability, will be caused by improper fuel scheduling due to malfunction of the fuel control system or incorrect techniques used during critical flight conditions. Engine instruments and the fuel low warning light often provide indications of fuel control system failures before the engine actually stops. In the event engine failure is caused by improper fuel management or incorrect operating techniques, an air start can usually be accomplished, provided time and altitude permit. If engine failure can be attributed to some obvious mechanical failure within the engine proper, do not attempt to restart engine.

CAUTION

If engine icing conditions are encountered or expected, place the engine de-ice switch in the MANUAL position and pitot heat switch to ON.

Note

To maintain control effectiveness, the emergency hydraulic pump must be extended in the event of partial power loss as well as complete power loss.

AIR START

If engine flame-out occurs when the engine is at Military rpm, which may possibly occur during gunfire operation, immediately initiate the following starting procedure while the engine is above 72% rpm and at altitudes above 28,000 feet:

1. Retard throttle to OFF immediately.
2. Press ignition switch on.
3. Advance throttle to idle before engine drops below 72% rpm.
4. Release ignition switch when engine reaches idle rpm.
5. Advance throttle to attain desired rpm.

WARNING

If throttle is advanced beyond idle detent during ignition, a mild explosive relight may take place producing one or more audible "bangs". This does not necessarily preclude a successful start, therefore, the pilot should check for rpm response to throttle movement. These explosive light-offs can result in guide-vane damage.

When flame-out occurs at engine rpm's other than Military, air starts during flight are more readily obtained below 28,000 feet. An air start attempt should be made as soon as possible in accordance with the following procedure:

1. Retard throttle to OFF position.
2. Extend EMERGENCY HYDRAULIC PUMP.
3. Establish glide to attain 200 to 250 knots IAS.
4. At approximately 10% to 15% windmill rpm (28,000 feet or below) press the ignition switch on.
5. Advance throttle to IDLE position.
6. Release ignition switch when temperature rise indicates ignition.

Note

For altitudes above 28,000 feet, modulate the throttle as required to maintain turbine outlet temperature between 400° and 450°C. This modulation may be required at approximately 40% rpm.

7. Advance the throttle to the desired speed.

Note

During an attempted restart, if ignition is not evident within 30 seconds after throttle is advanced, promptly release ignition button and retard throttle to OFF to allow ignition system cooling and fuel drainage. Maintain glide slope for recommended rpm and repeat air start procedure. Air start is evident by rise in turbine outlet temperature and accompanying increase in rpm. On high altitude restarts, the engine may be on the verge of compressor stall with throttle at idle position. In this case, advance throttle carefully during restart, keeping turbine outlet temperature within limits. If restart cannot be accomplished pilot must select forced landing or ejection. See Forced Landing and Ejection Instructions in this section.

Air starts under water/ice ingestion conditions can be successfully accomplished below approximately 28,000 feet using NORMAL airstart procedure. If flame-out occurs above 28,000 feet, an air start attempt should be made immediately. However, if relight is unsuccessful, descent to 28,000 feet should be expedited since engine and guide-vane icing becomes more critical at windmill rpm possibly as low as 10 to 15%. The only characteristics peculiar to an airstart in precipitation is a slower rpm acceleration after light-off.

CAUTION

There may be a delay of 5 to 10 seconds after actual ignition before rpm starts to rise and the pilot should not assume by this that the start has been unsuccessful.

ENGINE FAILURE DURING TAKE-OFF

Before Airborne

If engine failure occurs during take-off run and sufficient runway remains for an emergency stop, perform the following as rapidly as possible:

1. Throttle - OFF
2. Apply brakes as required to stop.
3. Engine master switch - OFF
4. External load - JETTISON (if necessary)
   a. Landing gear handle must be in the UP position.
5. D-C power switch - OFF

CAUTION

- With engine failure, or failure of either hydraulic systems, approximately three full brake applications will exhaust the system. With the system exhausted, braking will still be available, but without boost from the utility system, brakes will require very high pedal pressure.
- With engine failure, or failure of either hydraulic systems, do not attempt to check brakes prior to touchdown.

After Airborne

If engine failure occurs after aircraft becomes airborne, accomplish as much of the following as time permits:

1. Throttle - OFF
2. Emergency hydraulic pump - EXTENDED
3. Engine master switch - OFF
4. Landing gear - UP
5. External stores - JETTISON
6. Flaps - FULL DOWN, slats - EXTENDED
   If flaps and slats have been retracted, extend slats pneumatically.
7. D-C power switch - OFF
8. Land straight ahead if possible.

WARNING

All forced landings will be made with gear up unless adequate space and surface is available.

ENGINE FAILURE DURING FLIGHT

1. Throttle - OFF
2. Emergency hydraulic pump - EXTENDED
3. Establish glide.
4. Determine cause of failure.
5. Attempt air start.
   Refer to Emergency Air Start Procedure.
6. If air start fails, set up forced landing pattern.
   Refer to Forced Landing.
7. If bail-out is necessary, use procedure outlined in Emergency Bail-Out Procedure.

WARNING

When operating in precipitation areas, either with or without the afterburner operating, do not automatically retard the throttle to OFF on a mistaken assumption that the engine has flamed out. See RPM DROOP AND RECOVERY IN HEAVY PRECIPITATION.

SIMULATED FORCED LANDING

Landings with engine inoperative may be simulated without actually securing the engine by observing the following procedure:

1. Reduce airspeed to best glide speed - 230 knots, IAS
2. Speed brakes - OUT
3. Emergency hydraulic pump - EXTEND

4. Use following power vs. altitude settings:

if above 20,000 feet   use 90% engine rpm.
from 10,000 to 20,000 feet   use 86% engine rpm.
from sea level to 10,000 feet, use 82% engine rpm.

All airplane feel and reaction normal to actual forced landings will be reproduced through the use of this procedure. Simulated forced landings may be made from approximately 40,000 feet to 5,000 feet altitude, in both clean glide and landing configurations. The altitudes, airspeeds and identification points shown on figure 3-2, Forced Landing - Dead Engine, should be used for forced landing practice.

CAUTION

Do not perform forced landing practice at too low an altitude. Landing practice may be accomplished at 5,000 feet as easily as "on the deck".

AFTERBURNER FAILURE

AFTERBURNER FAILURE DURING TAKE-OFF

Failure of afterburner during take-off is not critical, though the aircraft requires more runway to accomplish take-off. Afterburner failure is evidenced by loss of thrust together with a loss in turbine outlet temperature and then a rapid rise. If afterburner fails during ground roll, and runway length permits, continue take-off using MIL power. If runway length does not permit, use procedure outlined in Engine Failure During Take-Off. If afterburner failure occurs after lift-off, immediately move throttle to MIL position. This will recycle the afterburner system, allowing a relight to be attempted. Landing gear should be retracted immediately after take-off upon loss of afterburner, and after minimum safe airspeed is attained, retract slats and flaps.

AFTERBURNER FAILURE IN FLIGHT

Should the afterburner flame out in flight in a relatively calm atmosphere, the loss of thrust will be noticed instantly. Immediately retard the throttle to the MIL position. A relight may be attempted unless the flame out can be attributed to some mechanical failure or atmospheric condition (see below) which would prevent a successful relight.

RPM DROOP IN HEAVY PRECIPITATION

When entering precipitation areas where freezing conditions will be encountered, place pitot heat switch ON and de-ice switch to MANUAL. A slight turbine outlet temperature rise (5° to 10°C) may be noted as the de-ice switch is placed in MANUAL (similar to the TOT rise noted in ground de-ice check), indicating that the de-icing air valve is functioning properly. The turbine outlet temperature may rise above the engine red-line temperature but normally will not remain above this limit for more than 2 to 3 seconds as the amplifier responds and opens the exhaust nozzle to reduce the temperature.

Note

The possibility of rpm droop will be considerably reduced if flight through precipitation is made in the MIL range. 95% is recommended; see IN THE STORM, SECTION IX.

Flight tests have shown that heavy precipitation while in afterburner can result in considerable rpm reduction and possibly cause the afterburner to blow out, even with an operative de-ice system. This drop in rpm is basically caused by (a) fuel-control pressure-sensing aneroid blockage by ice which decreases the fuel available to the engine, and (b) increased mass flow and engine cooling due to ice and/or water which increases the fuel required to run. Greater precipitation and higher indicated airspeeds tend to promote droop. A full rpm droop is characterized by a rapid (5 to 20 seconds) decrease in rpm to about 83 to 85% where the inlet guide vanes close, exhaust nozzle opens and the turbine outlet temperature will drop to 520° to 600°C. The result is a cycling condition in which the inlet guide vanes and nozzle both oscillate, accompanied by a very small rpm change (approximately ±1%). A less critical rpm droop is characterized by a rapid reduction of 1 to 3% as the fuel control pressure-sensing probes become blocked. At this point the rpm may either stabilize or continue to decrease very slowly. In either case, once the rpm decreases below the fuel control-governor break point (95 to 96%), droop will continue rapidly to approximately 85%. Under still less critical conditions, droop may never extend below 96 to 98% rpm. However, the pilot should be aware that full droop is possible.

CAUTION

A nose down trim condition may result during flight through icing conditions. This is caused by icing of the ram air pick up line of the stabilator feel trim system.

RPM DROOP RECOVERY PROCEDURE

Recovery from an rpm droop to 85% should be effected by moving the throttle from afterburner to a position slightly below full Military. This will result in quicker recovery and a higher stabilized rpm than that obtainable at full MIL. The rpm will increase during droop recovery and stabilize between 96 and 98% within 30 seconds until the fuel control pressure-sensing probes become unblocked, at which time the rpm will fully recover. Although the F3H has all-weather capability as demonstrated in actual severe weather flight tests, prudence dictates that areas of very heavy precipitation be avoided. If droop is encountered, the proper recovery procedures will produce almost full Military engine power within 30 seconds. Departure from the area of precipitation will then permit normal engine operation, at which time maximum power (afterburner) may be resumed.

WARNING

Do not retard throttle to OFF on a mistaken assumption that the engine has flamed out. If engine flame-out has occurred, engine rpm will fail to respond to throttle movement and the turbine outlet temperature will quickly drop to approximately 300°C and continue to decrease.

VARIABLE NOZZLE CONTROL FAILURE

A nozzle control system failure may be electrical, hydraulic, mechanical or combinations thereof. The failure may be noticed by any one or combinations of the following indications:

1. Excessively high or low turbine outlet temperature.
2. Loss of thrust.
3. "Dead-band" of throttle movement about last throttle position.
4. Compressor surge or stall.
5. High or low engine rpm.
6. Nozzle position indicator.

Should the exhaust nozzle fail in the fully OPEN position, afterburning may be initiated in the normal manner providing engine rpm is 98 percent or above. This feature provides afterburner thrust in a situation where sustained flight would be difficult without afterburning. The clean airplane is only capable of maintaining an altitude of from 6,000 to 10,000 feet (dependent upon gross weight), if the nozzle fails open and the guide vanes fail closed (compressor "unloaded" position).

CAUTION

The emergency afterburner modulation system should be used only when a malfunction has caused the exhaust nozzle to fail in the open position during non-afterburning operation.

OPERATION OF EMERGENCY AFTERBURNER MODULATION SYSTEM

Assuming a hydraulic failure allows the exhaust nozzle to go open, afterburning has been initiated, and the throttle is at full MAX, use the following procedure for thrust modulation in the landing power range.

CAUTION

- Emergency afterburner modulation is provided to permit reduction of thrust while in afterburning under failed jet nozzle conditions; not to ffect emergency lighting of afterburner. Therefore, select emergency afterburner modulation only after normal afterburning has been established.

- If emergency afterburner modulation switch is selected before normal afterburning is established, compressor bleeds will open and entrance guide vanes will close, causing reduction of thrust to approximately 30% of military if afterburner fails to light.

Note

Sufficient power will be available at Military rpm with failed open nozzle to maintain level flight in clean configuration up to 10,000 feet.

1. Place emergency modulation switch ON when entering landing pattern.
2. Retard throttle to obtain the required power. The throttle may be retarded below the MAX range without stopping the afterburner down to approximately 6,000 pounds thrust. Retard throttle to obtain the required power. The throttle may be retarded to idle without the loss of afterburner, and acceleration without stagnation can be accomplished due to the automatic energizing of a fuel enrichment solenoid valve. Expect an unusual rumbling sound from the engine when near idle position because of the afterburner operation. Refer to Afterburner Emergency Modulation System and Afterburner Emergency Modulation Switch, Section I.
3. If rpm is inadvertently reduced too low and stagnation develops, place emergency modulation switch OFF, accelerate to full speed, and repeat the above procedure to regain modulated thrust.

Note

The engine may overspeed momentarily up to 109 percent rpm but will stabilize at approximately 103 percent. Though this is an emergency procedure, speed limits still apply.

4. To check the emergency modulation system at any time without danger of overspeeding, or during an emergency condition if time allows, reduce rpm to 82 to 84 percent and place the emergency modulation switch ON.
5. Cautiously advance throttle until afterburner fires. After afterburner fires immediately reduce rpm to minimize possible high compressor blade vibratory stress with open bleeds at high rpm.
6. Use 1/4 flaps for approach and landing to reduce drag.

TERMINATION OF EMERGENCY AFTERBURNER MODULATION

If the throttle is above full MIL position, afterburning should be terminated by placing the afterburner emergency modulation switch in the OFF position and immediately retarding the throttle. If the throttle is below MIL position, afterburning may be discontinued simply by placing the switch in the OFF position.

CAUTION

When returning to the field in emergency afterburner, anticipate the need to terminate emergency afterburner system immediately after normal landing.

ENGINE TEMPERATURE CONTROL AMPLIFIER FAILURE

Failure of the temperature control amplifier has no effect on engine operation up to and including full MIL power, as long as overtemperature conditions are not present. Should overtemperature conditions occur in this range, retardation of throttle will be necessary to prevent overtemperature. Although it is possible to initiate afterburning with a "dead" amplifier, this action should in no case be attempted since overtemperature is inevitable, and sustained afterburning impossible. A complete amplifier failure during afterburning will result in the loss of MAX (afterburner) power and the nozzle area being returned to the MIL area. Other types of failure within the amplifier will be indicated by nozzle oscillation, resulting in overtemperature and/or undertemperature. An a-c power failure to the amplifier during afterburning will not result in a complete loss of afterburner power due to simultaneous de-energizing of an emergency nozzle position relay which causes the nozzle override valve to be energized through the demand switch, allowing the nozzle to be automatically positioned and held in the wide open position. Approximately 1300 pounds thrust is lost while in normal afterburner with nozzle failure.

Note

A normal corrective nozzle "hunt" is usually present on this engine while temperature is being limited by the amplifier. This "hunt" will usually stay within 1/2% total rpm fluctuation, however, excessive "hunt" may occasionally be noticed. This excessive hunting condition is usually due to improper lubrication of the nozzle segments, and will be evidenced by rpm fluctuations of 1% or more. Any excessive nozzle "hunt" should be brought to the attention of maintenance personnel.

CAUTION

Normal afterburner modulation from full MAX down to low portion of MAX range (93 degrees) should not be attempted during a-c power failure since the nozzle is held full open and retarding the throttle reduces fuel flow. An afterburner flame-out would result.

The emergency afterburner modulation system may be placed into effect to modulate thrust for landing purposes. (Refer to Operation of Emergency Afterburner Modulation System, this section.) Since the nozzle override valve is energized through the demand switch during a-c power failure, afterburning may be initiated normally.

OIL SYSTEM FAILURE

An oil system failure is recognized by a decrease or a complete loss of oil pressure. If an oil system malfunction has caused prolonged oil starvation of engine bearings, the result will be a progressive bearing failure and subsequent engine seizure. This progression of bearing failure starts slowly and will normally continue at a slow rate up to a certain point at which the progression of failure accelerates rapidly to complete bearing failure. The time interval from the moment of oil starvation to complete failure depends on such factors as: Condition of bearings prior to oil starvation, operating temperatures of bearings, and bearing loads. A good possibility exists for an additional 10 to 30 minutes of engine operation after experiencing a complete loss of lubricating oil. Bearing failure due to oil starvation is generally characterized by a rapidly increasing vibration, and when the vibration becomes moderate to heavy, complete failure is only seconds away.

CAUTION

Since the generator oil supply is taken from the engine supply tank, a generator warning light illumination could be an early indication of engine oil starvation even before an appreciable decrease in oil pressure is indicated on the oil pressure gage. Consequently, if a generator warning light illuminates, the oil pressure gage should be monitored until the possibility of oil starvation is determined.

Upon first recognition of sustained oil system failure, (above or below oil pressure limits), complete the following:

1. Maintain power as necessary to reach nearest field.
2. Avoid further throttle movement.
3. Make precautionary flame out approach.
4. Land as soon as possible.
5. As soon as stopped, shut down engine.

MAXIMUM GLIDE

See figure 3-1 for maximum glide distance.

FIRE

Note

There is no fire extinguishing equipment on this airplane.

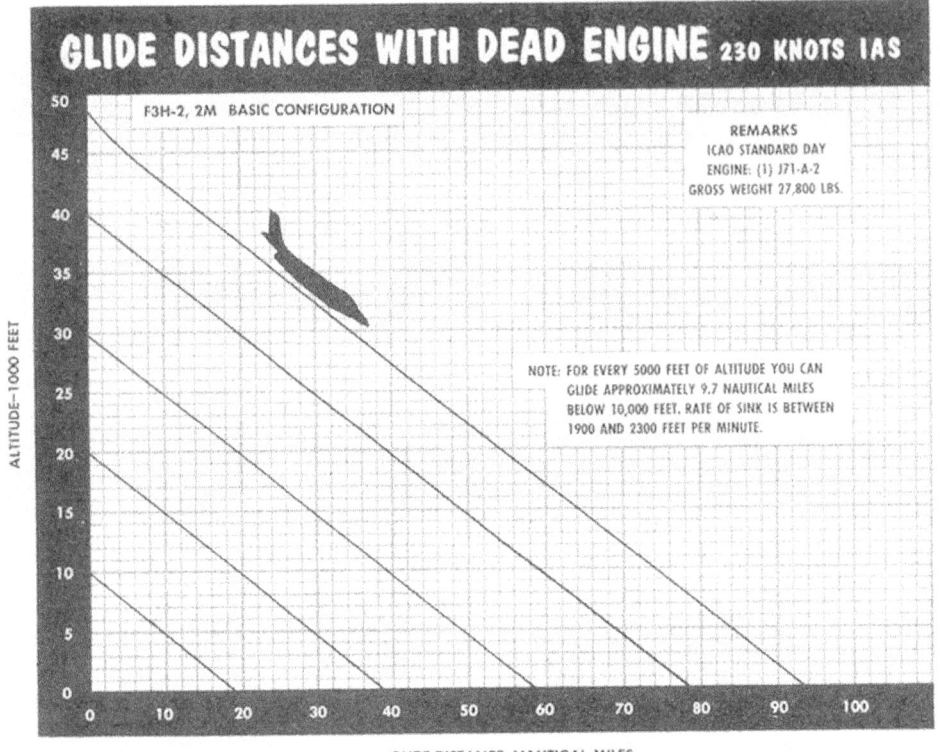

Figure 3-1. Glide Distance

ENGINE FIRE WARNING SYSTEM

The airplane is designed with a fire warning system which indicates to the pilot a fire condition.

CAUTION

Do not assume defective wiring is responsible for warning light until all other possibilities have been explored.

ENGINE FIRE DURING STARTING

If fire warning light illuminates or any evidence of fire while starting, perform the following:

1. Ignition switch button - RELEASE
2. Throttle - OFF
3. Engine master switch - OFF
4. All electrical power - OFF
5. Prepare to abandon aircraft if ground personnel cannot extinguish fire.

Note

Do not attempt restart until cause of fire is corrected and excessive engine fuel drained.

ENGINE FIRE DURING FLIGHT

If fire warning light illuminates in flight:

1. Reduce throttle setting to lower EGT.
2. Reduce speed.
3. If warning light does not go out, check for trailing smoke.
4. If conditions warrant, prepare to abandon aircraft. See Ejection Procedures.
5. If light goes out, return to field with minimum required power.

ELECTRICAL FIRE

Circuit breakers and fuses protect all electrical circuits to minimize electrical fires. Should an electrical fire occur, place d-c power switch to OFF and a-c power switch to INV. position. This de-energizes all electrical buses except the utility bus. If source of fire can be determined, eliminate faulty circuit from bus system by pulling circuit breaker or placing applicable control switch to OFF, then return power to remaining bus system.

ELIMINATION OF SMOKE AND FUMES

If smoke or undesirable fumes enter cockpit, proceed as follows:

1. Pull emergency ventilation control knob.
2. Oxygen regulator lever to 100% OXYGEN.

Note

If below 250 knots and emergency ventilation does not give satisfactory clearing, the canopy may be opened to clear cockpit.

When cockpit clears, return oxygen regulator lever to NORMAL OXYGEN. At the 100% OXYGEN position, the system's supply is rapidly exhausted. (See figure 4-15.)

LANDING EMERGENCIES

The high stress cockpit design in jet aircraft makes forced landings more feasible than in older aircraft. The pilot is protected by structure and seated firmly to resist the deceleration loads. If forced landing is necessary, proceed as follows:

FORCED LANDING

Note

See figure 3-1 for recommended airspeeds for maximum obtainable distance or minimum sink angle in dead engine glide.

1. Throttle - OFF
2. Emergency hydraulic pump - EXTENDED
3. Establish glide for intended landing area.
4. Engine master switch - OFF
5. Dump remaining wing fuel.
6. External stores - JETTISON

Note

Speed brakes and flaps will not be available with the complete loss of the engine. Pilot should govern approach speed accordingly. Slats should be selected using the emergency system. Refer to Emergency Slat Extension.

CAUTION

If it is possible to complete landing on surfaced runway, landing may be made with gear extended. Should the runway be of insufficient length or no surfaced area is available, land with gear UP (retracted).

7. Shoulder harness - TIGHT AND LOCKED
8. Landing gear - DOWN for runways, UP for an unprepared surface.
9. When below safe ejection altitude - OPEN CANOPY

CAUTION

DO NOT LOWER GEAR UNLESS CERTAIN THAT A SUITABLE LANDING AREA IS AVAILABLE.

Note

The lowering of the gear will increase the glide angle of the aircraft.

CAUTION

With engine inoperative, do not attempt to check brakes prior to touchdown.

10. Prior to contact with the ground, place d-c power switch to OFF, and a-c power switch to INV.

Note

- With complete engine loss or failure of utility hydraulic system, approximately three full brake applications will exhaust brake accumulator system. There will be a brake action with exhausted system but pressure will not be boosted and will require considerable pilot effort.

- The field may have arresting gear installed on the runway in which case it is advisable to make an arrested landing. Approximately 2 seconds is required to extend the tail hook.

BRAKE FAILURE

If one brake has failed, land on side of runway corresponding to failed brake, i.e., right brake failure - land on right side of runway. Use the remaining brake for directional control only. Any attempt to STOP the airplane with only one brake is sure to result in loss of directional control. After touchdown, engine shutdown.

Both Brakes

Land in center and as close to the end of the runway as possible, hold nose gear off until it falls through. Prior to contact with runway, retard throttle to OFF, engine master switch to OFF, d-c power switch to OFF.

Note

- If landing is made under crosswind conditions and the crosswind is from the side opposite the failed brake, it may be inadvisable to land close to the side of the runway.

- The field may have arresting gear installed on the runway in which case it is advisable to make arrested landing.

- Upon loss of the utility or power hydraulic systems, do not pump the brakes prior to touchdown or during roll-out. The limited capacity of the brake system accumulator requires that the brakes be used in one steady, positive application whenever possible.

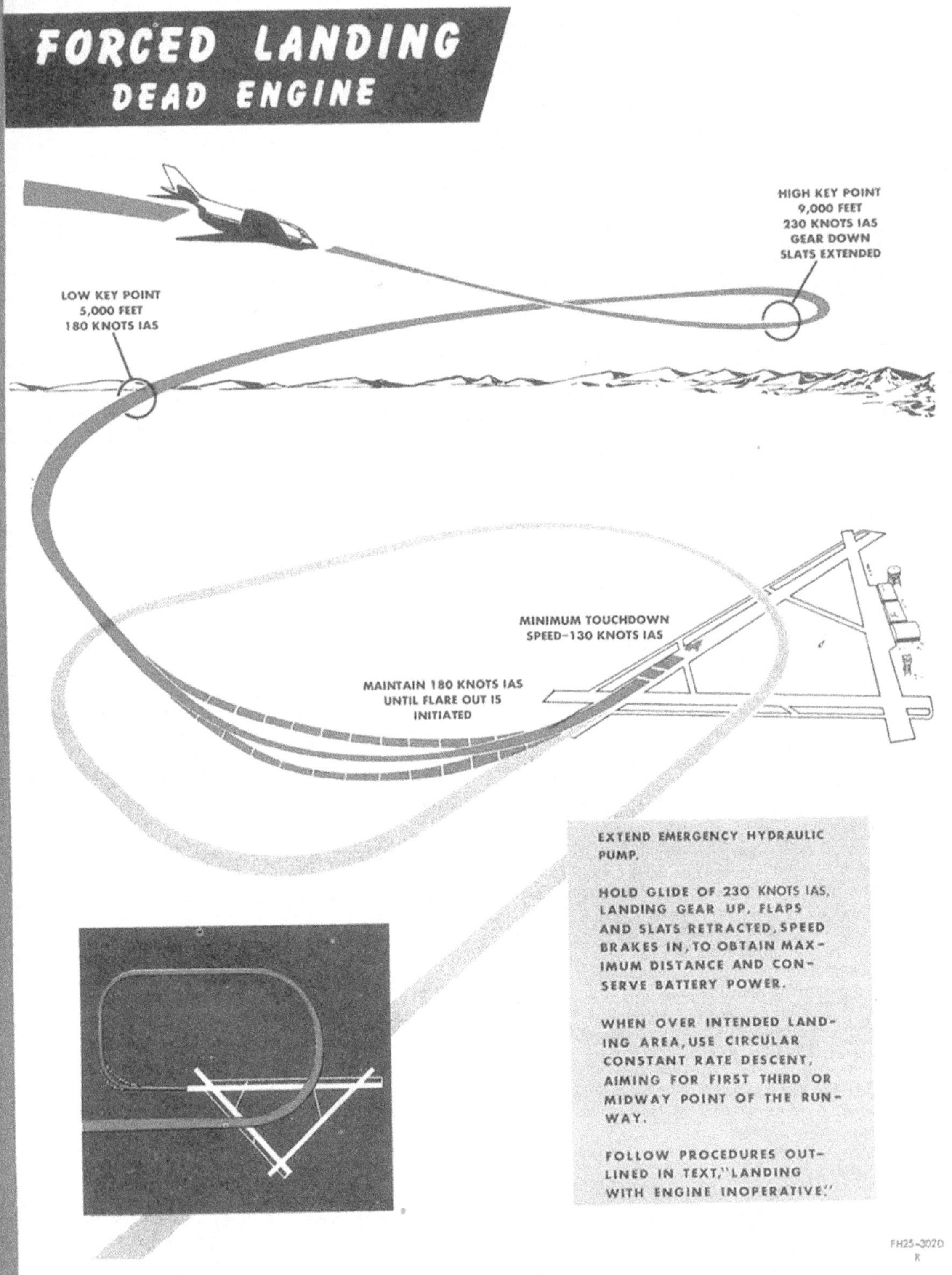

Section III
NAVWEPS 01-245FCB-501

FORCED LANDING
DEAD ENGINE

HIGH KEY POINT
9,000 FEET
230 KNOTS IAS
GEAR DOWN
SLATS EXTENDED

LOW KEY POINT
5,000 FEET
180 KNOTS IAS

MINIMUM TOUCHDOWN
SPEED—130 KNOTS IAS

MAINTAIN 180 KNOTS IAS
UNTIL FLARE OUT IS
INITIATED

EXTEND EMERGENCY HYDRAULIC PUMP.

HOLD GLIDE OF 230 KNOTS IAS, LANDING GEAR UP, FLAPS AND SLATS RETRACTED, SPEED BRAKES IN, TO OBTAIN MAXIMUM DISTANCE AND CONSERVE BATTERY POWER.

WHEN OVER INTENDED LANDING AREA, USE CIRCULAR CONSTANT RATE DESCENT, AIMING FOR FIRST THIRD OR MIDWAY POINT OF THE RUNWAY.

FOLLOW PROCEDURES OUTLINED IN TEXT, "LANDING WITH ENGINE INOPERATIVE."

FH25-3020
R

Figure 3-2. Forced Landing

TIRE FAILURE

Flat Nose Wheel Tire

Hold nose gear off as long as possible on landing roll.

One Main Gear Tire Flat

Make normal landing on side of runway opposite to flat tire, i.e., right tire flat - land on left side of runway.

Both Main Gear Tires Flat

Make normal landing in center of runway, using brakes with caution.

LANDING UNDER SPOILER CONTROL

The possibility of multiple failures of the various components of the lateral control system is very slight, however, should such failures occur, leaving the aircraft in the spoiler mode, the pilot may select from three control conditions for landing. The conditions are listed below in the order of best effectiveness, and should be utilized in this order whenever possible. It must be emphasized that landing under the best (first) of these conditions is hazardous due to decreased effectiveness of lateral control at low airspeeds, and that the effectiveness of control diminishes rapidly in the succeeding conditions. Use the last condition only when absolutely necessary.

1. Land under spoiler system control with landing flaps EXTENDED.
2. Land with autopilot ENGAGED, utilizing the stick controller for aileron control. This will allow approximately 15° aileron deflection.
3. Land under spoiler system control with landing flaps RETRACTED.

It is recommended that a landing pattern slightly wider than normal be flown, flying the base leg at 170 knots IAS, and the final approach at 150 knots IAS. The use of the leading edge slats is left to the pilot's discretion.

LANDING WITH ASYMMETRICAL SLAT EXTENSION

The possibility of improper extension of the leading edge slats, i.e., one or more slat segments failing to extend, is very slight. However, should this occur the only limitation which need be observed is the minimum speed requirements for a clean wing, with no slats and no flaps. Clean wing landings and approaches should be flown approximately 20 knots faster than the speeds quoted in figure 2-8, Section II, with a flare speed of 150 knots IAS (at landing gross weight).

LANDING WITH FORWARD CENTER-OF-GRAVITY

It may become necessary under certain conditions to make field landings with external store configurations (full pylon tanks, for example) that will create a very forward C.G. condition. Pilots should be cognizant of the fact that this condition is not too noticeable until power is removed prior to touchdown. At this point full aft stick may not rotate the airplane or hold the power-on attitude constant. The recommended procedure to be followed during field landings with a known forward C.G. location is: (1) Flare the airplane before removing power, or (2) Increased the approach speed approximately 15 knots IAS at the point power is to be removed. In any event the pilot should familiarize himself with the landing characteristics by simulating a landing approach at altitude when an extreme C.G. location is suspected.

BELLY LANDING

If a belly landing is imminent, accomplish the following:

1. External stores - JETTISON
2. Dump wing fuel.
3. Canopy - OPEN
4. Speed brakes - AS REQUIRED
5. Flaps and slats - EXTENDED
6. Landing gear - UP
7. Shoulder harness - TIGHT AND LOCKED
8. Emergency hydraulic pump - EXTENDED
9. Arresting gear - DOWN
10. Before contact with the ground, retard throttle to OFF, engine master switch to OFF; if time permits, turn all electrical systems OFF.
11. Touchdown in normal attitude - maintain directional control.
12. Abandon the aircraft as soon as possible.

LANDING GEAR UP OR UNLOCKED

If any one gear will not extend or lock down, and landing is to be made on other than smooth ground or runway, retract gear and make belly landing. If landing is to be made on smooth ground or runway and arresting gear is not available, leave gear down and proceed as follows:

1. Jettison external stores.
2. Dump wing fuel.
3. Set up normal approach with
    a. FLAPS & SLATS EXTENDED
    b. SHOULDER HARNESS LOCKED
4. Open canopy
5. Plan approach to touchdown as near end of runway as possible.
6. After touchdown, retard throttle to OFF, hold unlocked gear off as long as possible, easing it down before controls become ineffective.
7. Do not use brakes if you can stop without them.

GEAR WILL NOT RETRACT

No provisions are made for emergency retraction of the landing gear. In the event that the gear cannot be retracted, an immediate return to base is recommended. Do not exceed 250 knots IAS with the gear extended. If it is not possible to effect an immediate return, some problem exists concerning fuel scheduling. The maximum airspeed limitation of 250 knots for flight with the landing gear extended was imposed due to the possibil-

EMERGENCY OPENING OF CANOPY

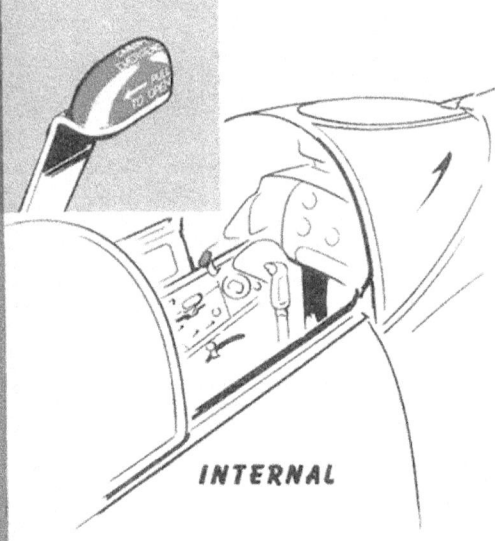

INTERNAL

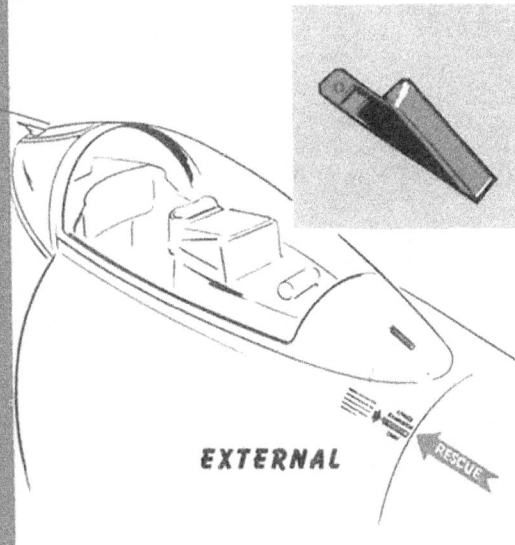

EXTERNAL

Figure 3-3. Emergency Opening of Canopy

ity of structural failure at higher airspeeds. The MINIMUM airspeed at which wing fuel may be transferred is again 250 knots IAS. This limitation was imposed to preclude the possibility of wing fuel tank collapse due to insufficient ram air pressure in the tanks at lower airspeeds. In F3H-2M airplanes 133623c thru 137040g and F3H-2 airplanes 133549d thru 136982g wing fuel may be transferred at any time, regardless of the position of the landing gear. The pilot is urged only to keep his airspeed as close as possible to 250 knots during wing fuel transfer. F3H-2 airplanes 143403m thru 143462n, F3H-2M airplanes 137041i thru 137095k, and F3H-2 airplanes 136983h thru 137032k are equipped with limit switches designed to eliminate the possibility of tank collapse by limiting wing fuel transfer to flight with the gear retracted. In these airplanes wing fuel transfer will not be possible with the landing gear extended. F3H-2 airplanes 143463o and subsequent have had this limit switch moved from the gear uplocks to the gear control handle. In these airplanes wing fuel transfer will be possible with the landing gear extended, but only if the gear control handle is placed in the UP position.

EMERGENCY ENTRANCE

To open the canopy from the cockpit in an emergency:

Pull red canopy emergency handle full aft to actuate pneumatic system.

To open canopy from exterior in an emergency:

1. On left side of fuselage, extend red emergency handle and pull aft to actuate pneumatic system.
2. If canopy does not actuate extend red manual pull handle on rear of canopy assembly, pull handle aft.

Note

Emergency handle on left side of fuselage must be actuated prior to use of manual system. See illustration, figure 3-3.

DITCHING PROCEDURE

Effective all F3H-2M Airplanes; also effective F3H-2 airplanes 146339s and previous prior to incorporation of ASC 132.

Ditching the airplane should be the pilot's last choice. If ditching is unavoidable, proceed as follows:

1. Canopy - OPEN (use canopy emergency handle)
2. External stores - JETTISON
3. Dump wing fuel.
4. Personal equipment - DISCONNECT
   Disconnect all personal equipment except oxygen hose.
5. Oxygen regulator - 100% OXYGEN
6. Gear - UP
7. Speed brakes - IN
8. Flaps and slats - EXTENDED

9. Arresting hook - DOWN
10. Body harness - LOCKED
11. Land parallel to any uniform swell.
12. Make power approach maintaining nose-high attitude. When hook contacts water - throttle OFF, engine master switch OFF, and d-c power switch - OFF.
13. Abandon the aircraft as soon as possible.

DITCHING PROCEDURE, MARTIN-BAKER SEAT

Effective F3H-2 Airplanes 146709t and subsequent; also effective all F3H-2 Airplanes and F3H-2 Airplanes 146339s and previous upon incorporation of ASC 132.

Ditching should be the pilot's last choice; however, if ditching is unavoidable, proceed as follows: Prepare for the ditching by performing steps 1 through 11 of the earlier procedure. At this point, the pilot must elect from two methods of abandoning the aircraft. These are:

1. Leaving the aircraft with life vest only.
2. Leaving the parachute, pararaft and survival kit still attached to his person.

In the first instance, egress from the cockpit is made easily and quickly and the option to go back after survival equipment is available if time permits. The latter method, if somewhat slower, does guarantee the pilot the use of his survival equipment. With the combining of manual override and drogue system release functions into one control (emergency harness release) on the ejection seats installed by ASC 132, the drogue chute disconnection cannot be performed in the air (first "D" ring procedure). Hence, a different procedure for each method of egress is necessary in both seats. For the seats installed on F3H-2 airplanes 146709t and subsequent, the following procedures apply:

To perform the first method:

1. Before touchdown, pull manual leg restraint release, anti-g connector, emergency oxygen lanyard and first "D" ring on body harness.
2. Immediately upon coming to rest in the water, slap harness quick release button and undo harness.
3. If time permits, actuate manual override.
4. Leave cockpit immediately.
5. If time permits, a sharp jerk will dislodge parachute and survival kit from sticker clips.

To abandon aircraft by the second method:

1. Before touchdown, pull manual leg restraint release, anti-g connector, emergency oxygen lanyard, and first "D" ring on body harness.
2. Immediately on coming to rest in the water, pull manual override.
3. Stand up sharply to dislodge sticker clips.
4. Abandon cockpit, being careful that gear does not foul cockpit protuberances.

The ditching procedures for airplanes with ASC 132 incorporated are as follows:

To perform the first method:

1. Before touchdown, pull manual leg restraint release, anti-g connector and emergency oxygen lanyard.
2. Immediately upon coming to rest in the water, actuate integrated harness quick disconnects.
3. If time permits, pull emergency harness release.
4. Leave cockpit immediately.
5. If time permits, a sharp jerk will dislodge parachute and survival kit from sticker clips.

To leave airplane by the second method:

1. Before touchdown, pull manual leg restraint release, anti-g connector and emergency oxygen lanyard.
2. Immediately on coming to rest in the water, pull emergency harness release.
3. If survival kit alone is desired, actuate upper harness quick disconnects.
4. Stand up sharply to dislodge sticker clips.
5. Abandon cockpit, being careful that gear does not foul cockpit protuberances.

EJECTION PROCEDURE

Effective All F3H-2M Airplanes; also Effective F3H-2 Airplanes 146339s and previous prior to incorporation of ASC 132.

See Ejection Procedures, figure 3-4.

WARNING

• Do not pull the manual pin pull handle when attempting a normal ejection. In addition to arming the catapult, the handle deactivates the canopy jettisoning mechanism, making through-the-canopy ejection mandatory.

• Before ejecting at low altitude use all excess speed to zoom to higher altitude whenever possible.

Note

If the manual pin pull handle should inadvertently be pulled, it will not be possible to return the handle and its related mechanism to the normal condition.

WARNING

Do not attempt ejection through canopy unless it remains fully closed. At any other position, the canopy frame will cause severe personal injury.

Section III NAVWEPS 01-245FCB-501

EJECTION PROCEDURE

F3H SEAT

1. SIT ERECT AND WELL BACK IN SEAT WITH HEAD PRESSED AGAINST HEADREST, SPINE STRAIGHT AND FEET PLACED HARD AFT IN FOOT STIRRUPS . . .

2. REACH OVERHEAD, WITH PALMS AFT, AND KEEPING ELBOWS TOGETHER GRASP FACE CURTAIN HANDLES . . .

SHOULD SEAT FAIL TO FIRE, ALLOW CURTAIN TO PARTIALLY REWIND AND WHILE HOLDING CURTAIN WITH ONE HAND, PULL EMERG. PIN PULL WITH OTHER HAND. AGAIN GRASP FACE CURTAIN HANDLES WITH BOTH HANDS AND PULL DOWN HARD.

3. PULL FACE CURTAIN . . .

DO NOT EJECT THROUGH A PARTIALLY OR FULLY OPENED CANOPY AS THE CANOPY FRAME WILL CAUSE SEVERE PERSONAL INJURY.

4. . . . FIRE SEAT.

SHOULD CANOPY REMAIN FULLY CLOSED, RATHER THAN JETTISONING, AND EJECTION THROUGH THE CANOPY IS DESIRED, PULL THE EMERGENCY PIN PULL PRIOR TO PULLING FACE CURTAIN TO FULL DOWN POSITION.

Figure 3-4. Ejection Procedure F3H Seat

EJECTION PROCEDURE
MARTIN-BAKER SEAT

1. SIT ERECT IN SEAT-BUTTOCKS AGAINST BACKREST. HEAD AGAINST HEADREST, SPINE STRAIGHT, THIGHS FIRMLY AGAINST SEAT PAN, FEET EXTENDED FOREWARD.

2. A. JETTISON CANOPY (PILOT'S OPTION)
   B. REACH OVERHEAD PALMS DOWN, ELBOWS TOGETHER-GRASP FACE CURTAIN HANDLES

3. PULL FACE CURTAIN

4. FIRE SEAT.

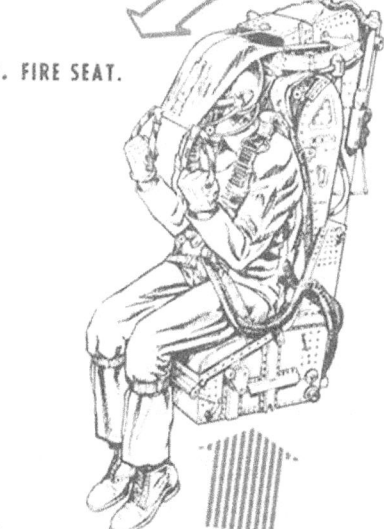

CAUTION

THE SECONDARY FIRING HANDLE "D" RING ON SEAT SHOULD BE USED ONLY WHEN IT IS IMPOSSIBLE TO REACH THE FACE CURTAIN PULL HANDLE.

Figure 3-5. Ejection Procedure Martin Baker Seat

EJECTION SEQUENCE

MARTIN BAKER EJECTION SEAT

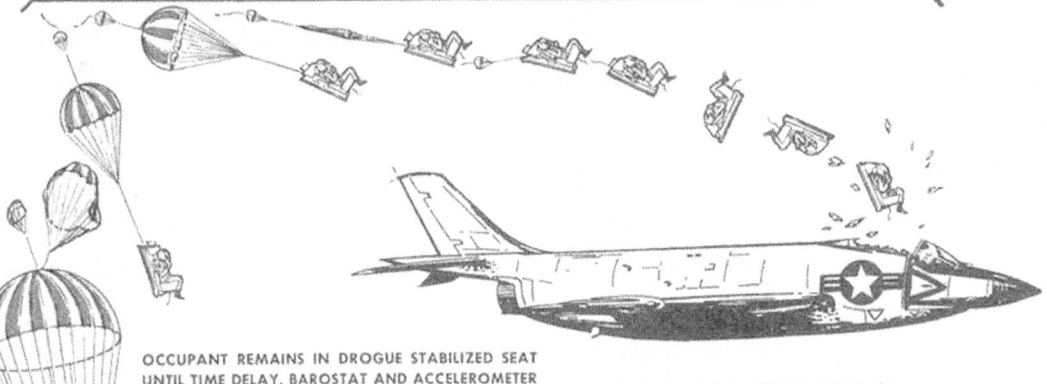

DROGUE GUN FIRES, WITHDRAWING DROGUE PILOT CHUTE AND DROGUE CHUTE.

OCCUPANT REMAINS IN DROGUE STABILIZED SEAT UNTIL TIME DELAY, BAROSTAT AND ACCELEROMETER FUNCTIONS DEPLOY, AFTER WHICH OCCUPANT IS RELEASED FROM SEAT AND HIS PERSONNEL PARACHUTE IS WITHDRAWN.

HIGH ALTITUDE SEQUENCE

BLOSSOMING OF PERSONNEL PARACHUTE WILL DISLODGE STICKER CUPS AND SEPARATE SEAT.

Note
CANOPY MAY BE JETTISONED AT PILOT'S OPTION

10,000 FT........ IF NECESSARY PROCEED WITH......

LOW ALTITUDE SEQUENCE

DROGUE GUN FIRES; SEAT AND OCCUPANT REMAINS DROGUE STABILIZED ONLY UNTIL TIME DELAY MECHANISM DEPLOYS AND SEAT DECELERATES TO LESS THAN 4 "g"s.

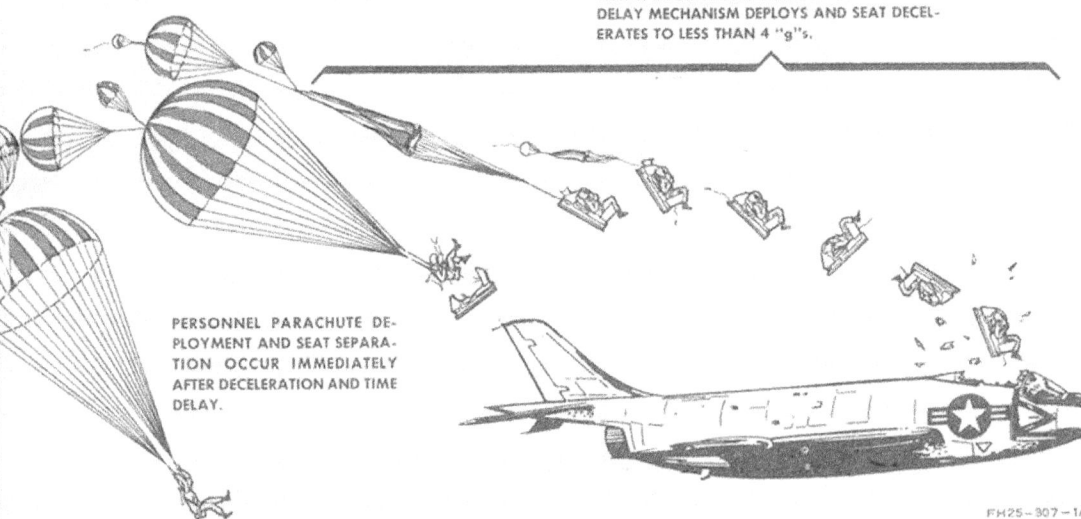

PERSONNEL PARACHUTE DEPLOYMENT AND SEAT SEPARATION OCCUR IMMEDIATELY AFTER DECELERATION AND TIME DELAY.

Figure 3-6. Ejection Sequence (Sheet 1)

NAVWEPS 01-245FCB-501 Section III

PREPARATION FOR EJECTION

1. Reduce airspeed if situation and time permit.
2. At altitude, pull "green ball" on parachute seat pack for emergency oxygen supply. Dump cabin pressurization to preclude a rapid decompression at canopy jettison.
3. Disconnect oxygen and radio leads.

AFTER EJECTION

As the ejection seat slides upwards on the track, a small metal arm mounted on the track contacts the trigger mechanism on the automatic-opening lap belt actuator. At a point approximately halfway up the seat track, the actuator delay cartridge is thus fired. Gas pressure generated by the cartridge acts upon a piston and cable assembly, which unlocks the belt lock link at the lap. The belt should be fully unlocked after a 3/4 second delay, and the following procedure should be followed:

1. After automatic lap belt has opened, kick away from seat.
2. When escape is accomplished at high altitude, it is recommended that pilot free fall to an altitude of 18,000 feet or less before opening his parachute in order to avoid effects of hypoxia and cold.

CAUTION

Do not pull rip cord while in seat.

Note

If an automatic opening device is used, its arming mechanism will be actuated upon seat separation, and rip cord will be pulled at the altitude and/or time the device is set for.

ALTERNATE EJECTION (THROUGH-THE-CANOPY)

If the canopy fails to jettison in the normal manner, or if lack of time dictates, a through-the-canopy ejection may be performed. Pulling the manual pin pull handle forward to its lower detent will:

1. Arm the seat catapult.
2. Disconnect the canopy jettisoning mechanism.
3. Remove the face curtain stop, allowing a continuous pull to fire the seat catapult.

WARNING

Though a through-the-canopy ejection may be considered a safe method of escape, it is still retained as an EMERGENCY method only. A canopy jettisoned ejection is the primary means of escape from this aircraft.

..... MANUAL SEPARATION

IN F3H-2 AIRPLANES 146709 AND SUBSEQUENT:

A — PULL FIRST "D" RING ON BODY HARNESS
B — PULL MANUAL OVERRIDE
2 — KICK FREE OF SEAT AND PULL PERSONNEL PARACHUTE "D" RING.

MARTIN BAKER EJECTION SEAT

IN ALL F3H AIRPLANES WITH ACS 132 INCORPORATED:

1 — PULL EMERGENCY HARNESS RELEASE
3 — MAKE NORMAL PARACHUTE DESCENT.

Figure 3-6. Ejection Sequence (Sheet 2)

Section III NAVWEPS 01-245FCB-501

Note

The manual pin pull handle cannot be returned to the normal condition once pulled. Through-the-canopy ejection is then mandatory.

All procedures for preparation, ejection and separation after ejection are the same with the manual pin pull handle actuated, except that no face curtain stop is provided and the seat will fire in one uninterrupted pull.

EJECTION PROCEDURE, MARTIN-BAKER SEAT

Effective F3H-2 Airplanes 146709t and Subsequent; Also effective F3H-2 Airplanes 146339s and previous upon incorporation of ASC 132.

The ejection seat installed in these later aircraft provides for ground level and high altitude ejection. In each of these types of ejections two methods of performing the ejection are provided. The primary method utilizes the face curtain mounted in the seat headrest. The secondary method utilizes a "D" ring located between the pilot's knees. Due to the poorer ejection posture and lack of head and face protection, the secondary method should be used only when, for example, under high "g" loads, it is impossible to use the face curtain.

LOW LEVEL EJECTION

1. Reduce airspeed to 300 knots or less, or increase to at least 125 knots as case requires.

WARNING

- Before ejecting at low altitude use all excess speed to climb whenever possible.

- Canopy must be full closed before attempting ejection unless time and conditions permit jettisoning. NEVER attempt ejection through a partially or fully opened canopy.

2. Assume proper ejection posture.
3. Pull face curtain.

Note

If it is impossible to use face curtain, pull "D" ring located between knees.

Time delay mechanism should release approximately 1 1/4 to 1 3/4 seconds after ejection provided acceleration is less than 4 1/2 "g's"; if it does not actuate, in F3H-2 Airplanes 146709t and subsequent:

1. Drogue system release - PULL
   Pull the first "D" ring on the body harness approximately 2 inches. This is the first "D" ring which comes to hands and is protected by a yellow and black striped canvas closure.
2. Manual override - PULL
   Squeeze finger lift and pull this handle approximately 2-1/2 inches aft; release finger lift to detent.
3. Kick free of seat.
4. Pull manual parachute release (second "D" ring).

In all airplanes in which ASC 132 has been incorporated;

1. Emergency harness release - PULL
   Depress the thumb button and fully pull up handle.
2. Kick free of seat.
3. Pull manual parachute "D" ring.

WARNING

Drogue system release must be pulled before the manual override. The seat will not be separated from the drogue linkage if the proper sequence is not followed.

HIGH ALTITUDE EJECTION

Ejection at higher altitudes is accomplished in exactly the same manner as the ground level ejection except that the canopy is jettisoned prior to ejection. This is accomplished by means of the canopy jettison handle located on the inside of the left console opposite the radar panel.

WARNING

Do not confuse the canopy jettison handle with the emergency canopy handle located below the canopy sill. This control opens, but does not jettison the canopy.

A brief outline of the high altitude ejection procedures follows. See ground level ejection for detail procedures.

1. Reduce airspeed to 525 knots or below.
2. Canopy jettison handle - PULL (optional)
   Pull handle up and aft as far as it will go.
3. Assume proper ejection posture.
4. Face curtain - PULL (primary ejection is through the canopy)
   If face curtain cannot be reached, use "D" ring between knees.

Emergency oxygen should deploy automatically at time of ejection; if not, pull the "green apple" at front of seat bucket. Barostat, accelerometer and time delay mechanism will not release occupant until safe speed and altitude are reached. If these components fail, or if peculiar circumstances dictate earlier parachute deployment, in F3H-2 Airplanes 146709t and subsequent:

1. Drogue system release (first "D" ring) - PULL
2. Manual override or emergency harness release (as installed) - PULL
3. Kick free of seat.
4. Pull manual parachute release (second "D" ring).

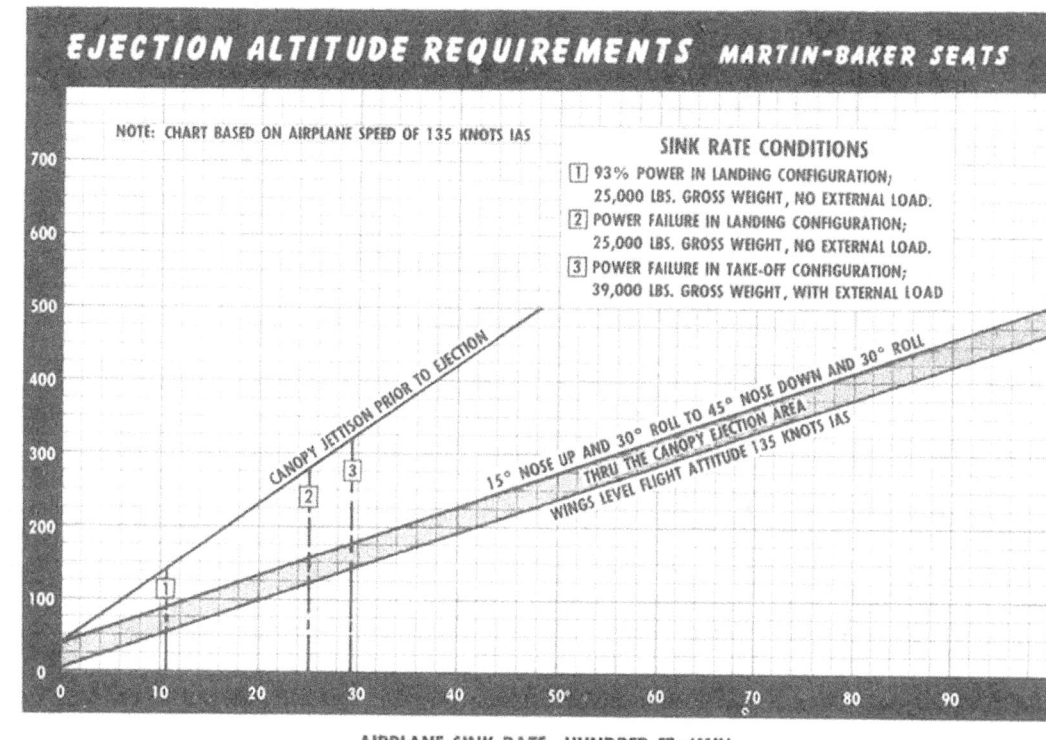

Figure 3-7. Ejection Altitude Requirements

In all airplanes in which ASC 132 has been incorporated:

1. Emergency harness release - PULL
2. Kick free of seat.
3. Pull manual parachute "D" ring.

WARNING

In the event of separation from the seat, emergency oxygen is no longer available.

EJECTION LIMITATIONS (MARTIN-BAKER SEATS)

The Martin-Baker ejection seat is considered to give excellent escape capabilities in a range extending from maximum airplane altitude to ground level. It should be realized, however, that the term "ground level" can be easily misinterpreted. The minimum airspeed of 135 knots quoted for ground level ejection of necessity assumes a near-level aircraft attitude and NO SINK RATES. Extremes of aircraft attitude (roll or pitch) will vary the maximum attainable ejection height, due to the ejection line of the seat being vectored away from the vertical. Taken about the pitch axis, these changes in attitude will also effect the velocity of the ejected seat and occupant. Assuming a maximum ejection catapult velocity of, say, 80 feet/sec., it will be seen that very low rates of descent will have an immediate and extreme effect on the maximum attainable trajectory height. If, for instance, the above mentioned seat were ejected from an airplane which was descending at the same rate of 80 feet/sec. (this represents a glide slope of only 18° at 150 knots), the additional height attained during ejection would be zero; clearly insufficient for safe escape unless considerable altitude were available for parachute deployment. The factors which contribute to sink rate and aircraft attitude are manifold; other factors which will effect safe ejection probability include pilot reaction time and the weight of the ejected mass. In the following chart, no attempt has been made to determine sink rates for all conditions, however, three typical situations are presented, from which interpolation may show probable sink rates for other airplane conditions. To use the chart, enter at the sink rate expected, and read up to one of the three slopes presented. The first line met represents a level flight attitude; the second represents extremes of pitch and roll. The third line shows the added time factor called for in jettisoning the canopy prior to ejection. All three slopes include normal pilot reaction time. At the intersection of the chosen slope, read left to the REQUIRED ALTITUDE scale. This will then be the minimum ejection altitude for the condition selected.

Section III   NAVWEPS 01-245FCB-501

Ditching Versus Ejection

The difficulties presented in ditching an airplane are not as simple as effecting a successful water landing; evacuation of the cockpit is of prime importance, and here time is the critical factor. The airplane ingests water and, of consequence, sinks very quickly. If, as in the case of a ditching in the immediate vicinity of ship or shore, the pilot wishes to leave the cockpit without his survival gear, egress can be made quite quickly. If the ditching were to be made in remote waters, the requirement for survival gear is mandatory, and the time required to evacuate the cockpit with this gear still attached to the pilot's harness, or the elective to return to the cockpit for it rends successful ditching more critical. In the final analysis, it will be seen that the Martin-Baker ejection seat will not accomplish miracles, but that it will provide better low-level ejection capabilities than have ever been realized in this airplane, PROVIDED ITS LIMITATIONS ARE RECOGNIZED AND ADHERED TO. With this in mind, it will be seen that the elective to ditch is not always an elective, but often a necessity.

ELECTRICAL SYSTEM EMERGENCY OPERATION

A-C GENERATOR FAILURE

If the a-c generator fails (warning light), equipment on a-c monitored buses will be dropped and essential instruments will be transferred automatically to the inverter. When a-c power switch is moved to INV. position, warning light goes out. If the inverter should fail, the warning light will illuminate.

Note

- Pilot should return and land as soon as practicable.

- In the event of a-c power failure, engines incorporating the high lift exhaust nozzle cams will realize high (750°) turbine outlet temperature while operating in or near the military power setting.

D-C GENERATOR FAILURE

If the d-c generator fails (warning light), equipment on d-c monitored buses will be dropped. Primary, secondary and utility d-c buses will be supplied automatically with d-c power through the transformer-rectifier by the a-c generator.

D-C ENGINE CONTROL POWER FAILURE

Loss of utility d-c electrical power for engine control, i.e., a popped circuit breaker, will cause the engine's guide vanes to close, and bleed valves to open, resulting in an immediate thrust loss.

WARNING

Engine control d-c power failure will result in immediate loss of from 30 to 40 percent of engine thrust. If electrical power cannot be restored, use of the afterburner may be necessary to maintain level flight under high gross weight conditions, or if operating with external loads.

A possibility exists that loss of the d-c engine control circuit breaker is the result of a shorted solenoid on the 16th stage air shutoff valve which supplies air to the engine air inlet duct water removal system. On recognizing the popped circuit breaker, actuation of the pitot heat switch may eliminate the short, and allow the breaker to be reset.

Note

- Power to the d-c boost pump is supplied by the primary d-c bus, however, the boost pump control is supplied by the d-c monitored d-c bus. Since the boost pump control energizes the boost pump power circuit, loss of the d-c generator will render the d-c boost pump inoperative.

- In the event that the d-c power switch has been placed in the OFF position it may be necessary to momentarily switch to the INV. or EXT. position on the a-c power switch to reconnect the d-c generator to the bus system.

DOUBLE GENERATOR FAILURE

If both generators fail (warning lights), immediately turn off all non-essential equipment (pull circuit breaker if necessary) to conserve battery power. The primary buses are supplied by the battery automatically under these conditions. The secondary d-c bus will be dropped upon selection of the inverter for operation of essential instruments. If equipment on secondary d-c bus must be used, pull secondary bus circuit breakers of equipment not desired, then place d-c power switch to BATT - ONLY position.

Note

In the event of failure of both generators, all fuel boost pumps will be inoperative.

CAUTION

- Since the generator oil supply is taken from the engine supply tank, a generator warning light illumination could be an early indication of engine oil starvation even before an appreciable decrease in oil pressure is indicated on the oil pressure gage. Consequently, if a generator warning light illuminates, the oil pressure gage should be monitored until the possibility of oil starvation is determined.

- With both generators inoperative, the battery will last only a short period.

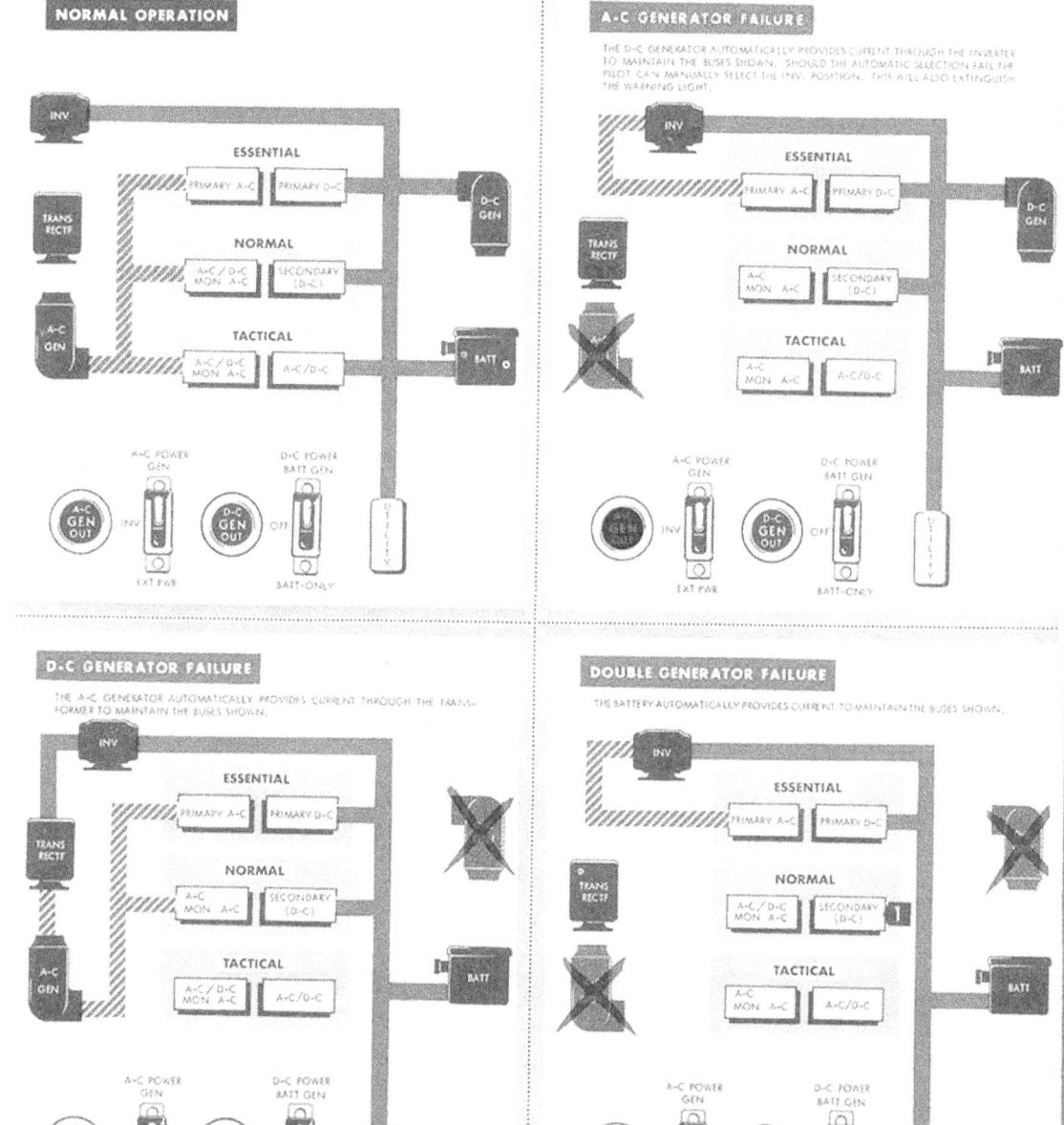

Figure 3-8. Electrical System Emergency Operation

COMPLETE ELECTRICAL FAILURE

Should complete electrical failure occur or it becomes necessary to turn off all electrical equipment, all fuel boost pumps will be inoperative. The pilot will probably have to decrease altitude and airspeed to retain engine performance. Landing should be made as soon as possible.

CAUTION

Do not fly for extended periods at high angles of attack with inoperative boost pumps. The gravity flow necessary for engine feed will be impeded. On FCLP or other flights where the airplane must operate at high angles of attack for protacted lengths of time it is recommended that the aft fuel transfer pump be given a preflight check. Failure of the aft transfer pump can trap as much as 768 pounds of fuel in the aft fuel cell.

LANDING GEAR SYSTEM EMERGENCY OPERATION

LANDING GEAR RETRACTION

There are no provisions for emergency retraction of the gear on this airplane.

LANDING GEAR EMERGENCY LOWERING

1. Reduce airspeed to less than 250 knots.
2. Gear handle down.
3. Gear handle pulled aft - actuating pneumatic system which allows main gear to fall free and actuates nose gear to locked position.
4. Check gear position indicator; if necessary, yaw airplane to lock main gear.

CAUTION

Do not attempt to retract gear after extending by emergency method unless procedure outlined in Section VII is followed.

Note

The tail skid will not extend by the emergency method. The pilot should attempt to keep the tail from touching down during landing after emergency extension.

EMERGENCY SLAT OPERATION

Emergency extension of the slats is accomplished by use of the high pressure pneumatic system. In event of a hydraulic failure (utility or power control) and use of slats is advisable (refer to Flight Characteristics, Section VI), the slats can be extended by pushing emergency slat handle FULL DOWN.

CAUTION

Do not attempt to retract the slats hydraulically after extending pneumatically unless the procedure outlined in Section VII has been followed before extension, and is followed during retraction. Failure to follow this procedure may result in loss of hydraulic system.

HYDRAULIC SYSTEM EMERGENCY OPERATION

Complete failure of both hydraulic systems will prevent pilot from maintaining full control of the airplane. If in level flight at the time of failure, the airplane will probably nose down. This is due to the aerodynamic loads imposed on the stabilator. Should both systems fail as indicated by the hydraulic pressure indicator or airplane attitude, proceed as follows:

1. Pull EMERG HYD PUMP handle AFT.

Note

The emergency hydraulic pump handle requires slightly less force during the first part of its movement than during the latter. The handle must be pulled to its absolute limit in order to effect emergency pump extension.

2. If control is ineffective or inadequate, resulting from insufficient hydraulic power, pilot should eject before airplane enters a maneuver which makes exit difficult. See Ejection Procedure.

PARTIAL FAILURE (ONE SYSTEM)

Partial failure of hydraulic power, in which only one system has failed, can be noted on hydraulic pressure indicator and warning light. Care should be taken to refrain from maneuvers which require excessive power demands on the system.

WARNING

Do not exceed Mach 1.0 with one hydraulic system inoperative.

PARTIAL FAILURE (ENGINE DRIVEN PUMP)

Partial failure of hydraulic power, in which engine has failed but is windmilling, can be noted by sluggish control and by abnormal drop in indicated pressure in both systems. In this event, the emergency hydraulic lever on the left console should be pulled aft, actuating the emergency pump supplementing the normal system. The pump is driven by ram air (see Section I, Emergency Hydraulic Power).

HYDRAULIC SYSTEM EMERGENCY OPERATION

POWER CONTROL SYSTEM
UTILITY SYSTEM

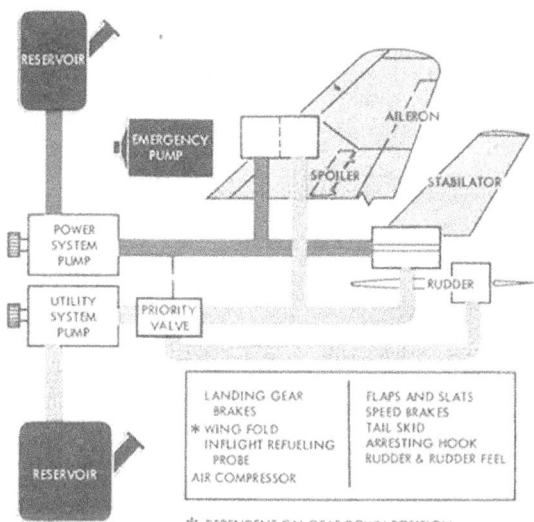
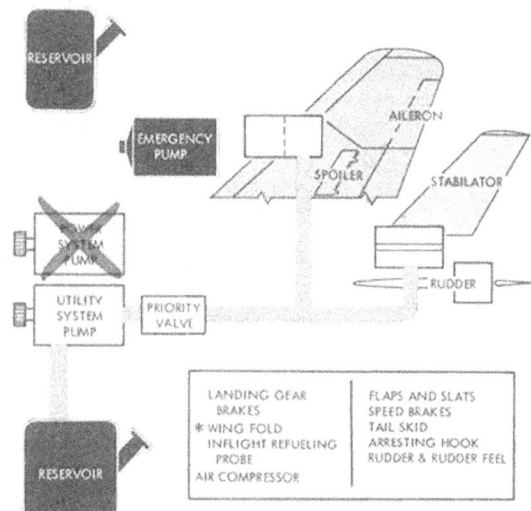
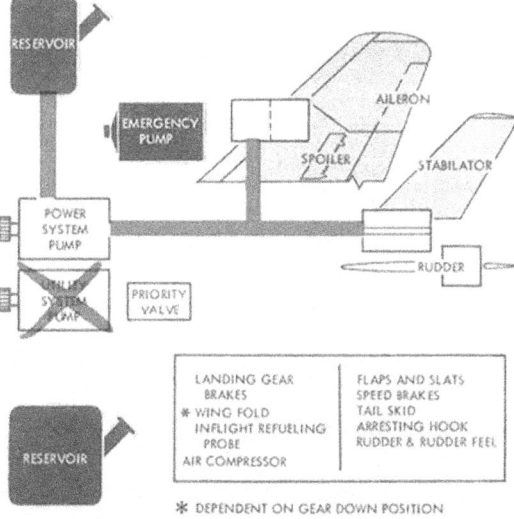
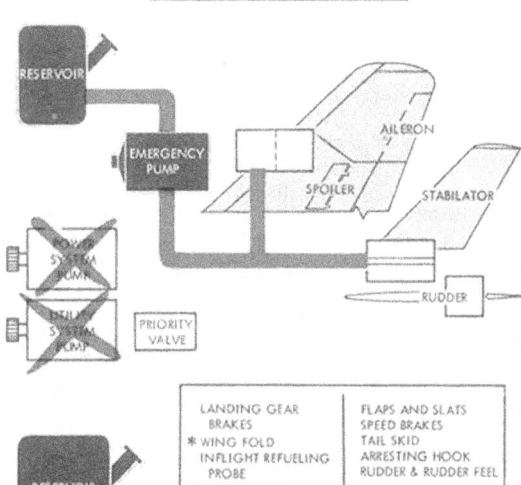

Figure 3-9. Hydraulic System Emergency Operation

POWER HYDRAULIC SYSTEM FAILURE

Upon loss of hydraulic pressure in the power system, the shutoff valve closes and shuts off utility pressure to all units except ailerons and stabilator. The power system will no longer share the load in moving the dual pistons in the ailerons and stabilator and the maximum control deflection will be reduced at high speed flight. The emergency hydraulic pump should be lowered immediately, and if the loss of pressure is not due to a leak in the power system, lowering of the emergency hydraulic pump will restore hydraulic pressure to the power system. Normal operation of the ailerons and stabilator will be regained, and as the pressure in the power system reaches 600 psi, the shutoff valve will be fully open and all other hydraulic units will again receive hydraulic pressure.

UTILITY HYDRAULIC SYSTEM FAILURE

Loss of utility system pressure will also result in a reduction of maximum control deflection obtainable at high speeds, as the utility system no longer shares the load in moving the ailerons and stabilator. Under this condition, pilots should avoid excessive maneuvers and high speed flight. In the absence of hydraulic pressure to the rudder cylinder, an internal by-pass valve opens to allow fluid to pass from one side of the piston to the other, and the cylinder then acts as another link in the rudder system. The rudder can then be moved by pilot effort. Besides sharing the load for actuating the primary flight controls, the utility system operates all other hydraulic units in the aircraft; therefore, when this system fails, operation of essential units will have to be by emergency means.

FLIGHT CONTROL SYSTEM EMERGENCY OPERATION

LATERAL CONTROL SYSTEM FAILURE

Serious loss of aileron control may possibly result from failure of certain components of the autopilot damper control amplifier. Such a failure may result in the unlocking of the aileron servos, allowing up to 7° of "free float" in the ailerons, and the ensuing sloppiness of lateral control. The situation will be recognized on disengagement of damper. Engaging damper may not alleviate this condition, as the return of the autopilot servos to the indexed position may cause excessive roll. It is recommended that if this situation should occur that the damper remain disengaged, and that the d-c power switch be placed in the BATT ONLY position. This will drop the a-c/d-c monitored d-c bus, locking the aileron servos and ensuing positive lateral control. An immediate return to base is recommended.

AILERON FEEL TRIM FAILURE

The ailerons may be controlled by overpowering the spring and manually positioning the aileron. The force required for full aileron travel is 12 1/2 pounds.

STABILATOR FEEL TRIM FAILURE

Bellows Skirt

The bellows skirt is a flexible seal connecting the diaphragm and bellows housing, dividing the bellows into two chambers. As a safety precaution, a primary and secondary skirt are provided.

Partial Bellows Failure

Failure of the primary skirt is not serious in itself but warrants immediate correction. This failure is recognized by a mild nose-down stick force proportional to airspeed, unless the failure occurs during maneuvering flight, at which time it may not be noticeable. Reduced stick centering and reduced pitch stability will occur. If this failure occurs, you should retrim the airplane and then avoid abrupt fore and aft maneuvers as well as high speed flight.

Complete Bellows Failure

A complete bellows failure will produce an abrupt nose-down stick force proportional to airspeed. The airplane will remain under control without danger if the pilot retains a firm grip on the stick at the time of failure. The pilot should trim nose-up until minimum stick force is obtained and then avoid high speed flight and abrupt fore and aft stick movements to prevent overstressing the plane inadvertently.

RUNAWAY FEEL TRIM

The maximum stick force encountered with runaway lateral trim is approximately 6 pounds at all airspeeds. Longitudinal trim system runaway to the maximum nose-down direction produces approximately 35 pounds full force at the stick. The push force with runaway trim to the nose-up direction is approximately 50 pounds. The difficulty in control and the increased stick forces encountered during runaway feel trim may often be corrected by utilizing the trimming capabilities of the autopilot. Minimum airspeeds should be maintained and a return to base expedited. The following procedure should be used to correct runaway trim or trim failure of the longitudinal feel trim system.

1. Engage autopilot.
2. Check the position indicator of the longitudinal feel trim system for indications that autopilot is regaining trim control of the airplane.
3. If the autopilot is regaining or maintaining control of the airplane, the autopilot may be used until the landing configuration is reached.

Note

The automatic trim circuits operate the feel trim actuators at a slow rate, and the autopilot stabilator servo has a limited force capability (approximately 17 pounds at the center of the stick grip). Pilot force should be applied to the stick until the out-of-trim force drops well below 17 pounds. Disengage autopilot if the automatic trim circuits are not effective in relieving the situation.

4. When the airplane is in the landing configuration (gear and flaps extended), pull the stabilator and aileron feel-trim circuit breaker prior to disengaging the autopilot. This will leave the corrected trim in the control system linkage, allowing the landing to be performed with near-normal pilot effort.

EMERGENCY JETTISONING

A lever-lock toggle switch, marked JETTISON and NORM, is provided for jettisoning external stores. This switch, mounted on the left sub-instrument panel supplies power from the battery bus to the external stores jettison circuits when the JETTISON position is chosen. Actuation of this switch supplies the electrical jettison circuit with power from the battery bus. This switch will jettison all stores except those carried on sliding rocket launcher racks.

Note

A microswitch installed in the handle linkage makes it impossible to jettison external stores with the landing gear control in the down position. This interlock feature is valid regardless of the position of the landing gear itself.

This page intentionally left blank.

SECTION IV
AUXILIARY EQUIPMENT

COCKPIT PRESSURIZATION AND AIR CONDITIONING SYSTEM

The cabin is pressurized and air conditioned by air bled from the engine compressor. The same air pressurizes and heats the cabin and also keeps the windshield free of fog and frost. The air is taken from the 11th stage of the engine compressor and routed to the cabin through a duct system containing flow control and temperature control devices. The air enters the cabin through the windshield defrosting tubes and a foot heater valve located forward of the pilot's feet. All controls for the cabin pressurization and air conditioning equipment are located together on the right hand console panel. A rubber seal, which is air inflated from the engine compressor when canopy is closed, prevents the loss of cabin pressurization at the canopy edges.

COCKPIT PRESSURIZATION

With the canopy closed and the engine in operation, the cabin is automatically pressurized above an altitude of 5,000 feet. The pressure in the cabin is maintained by the cabin pressure regulator which controls the outflow of air from the cabin. Below 5,000 feet, the regulator relieves cabin air at a rate to keep the cabin unpressurized. Operation of the pressure regulator is entirely automatic except that the pilot may select a normal or combat pressurization schedule. (See figure 4-2.) An altimeter for indicating pressure altitude of the cabin is located on the right hand subpanel. In event that the cabin pressure regulator fails to open or becomes clogged, a safety valve (dump valve) will automatically relieve the cabin air when the differential pressure reaches 5.25 psi. The same safety valve will also permit atmospheric air to enter the cabin when cabin pressure becomes lower than the outside pressure. A rapid descent from altitude may cause this condition.

Cabin Pressure Switch

This switch with two positions, NORMAL and COMBAT, controls setting of the cabin pressure regulator. With the switch in the NORMAL position the cabin pressure is maintained at a 5 psi differential to atmospheric pressure. At the COMBAT position, a lower cabin pressure differential results, and is 3.3 psi maximum over the outside pressure. The COMBAT setting reduces the chance of personal injury to pilot from explosive decompression if the cabin is ruptured during combat. Below 13,160 feet pressure altitude, the COMBAT position of the switch is not effective and the normal and combat pressurization schedules are the same regardless of switch position. A power failure in the cabin pressure circuit will cause the pressure regulator to stay on COMBAT schedule at all altitudes.

Ventilating Control Handle

This handle manually opens and closes the foot heater valve forward of the pilot's feet. With the handle at DEFROST position, the cabin foot heater valve is full closed and all pressurizing air enters the cabin through the windshield defrosting tubes. The pilot may place the handle at any intermediate position.

Note

When flying in warm humid air with the temperature control set near full cold, the pilot may hear sounds like muffled explosions. These sounds are created when ice accumulates in the lines of the air conditioning system and breaks loose at intervals releasing air pressure. The "explosion" is usually followed by a spray of ice particles from the defrost tubes. Turning the temperature control knob up a small amount will usually eliminate these sounds.

Section IV
NAVWEPS 01-245FCB-501

COCKPIT AIR CONDITIONING, PRESSURIZATION AND VENT SYSTEM

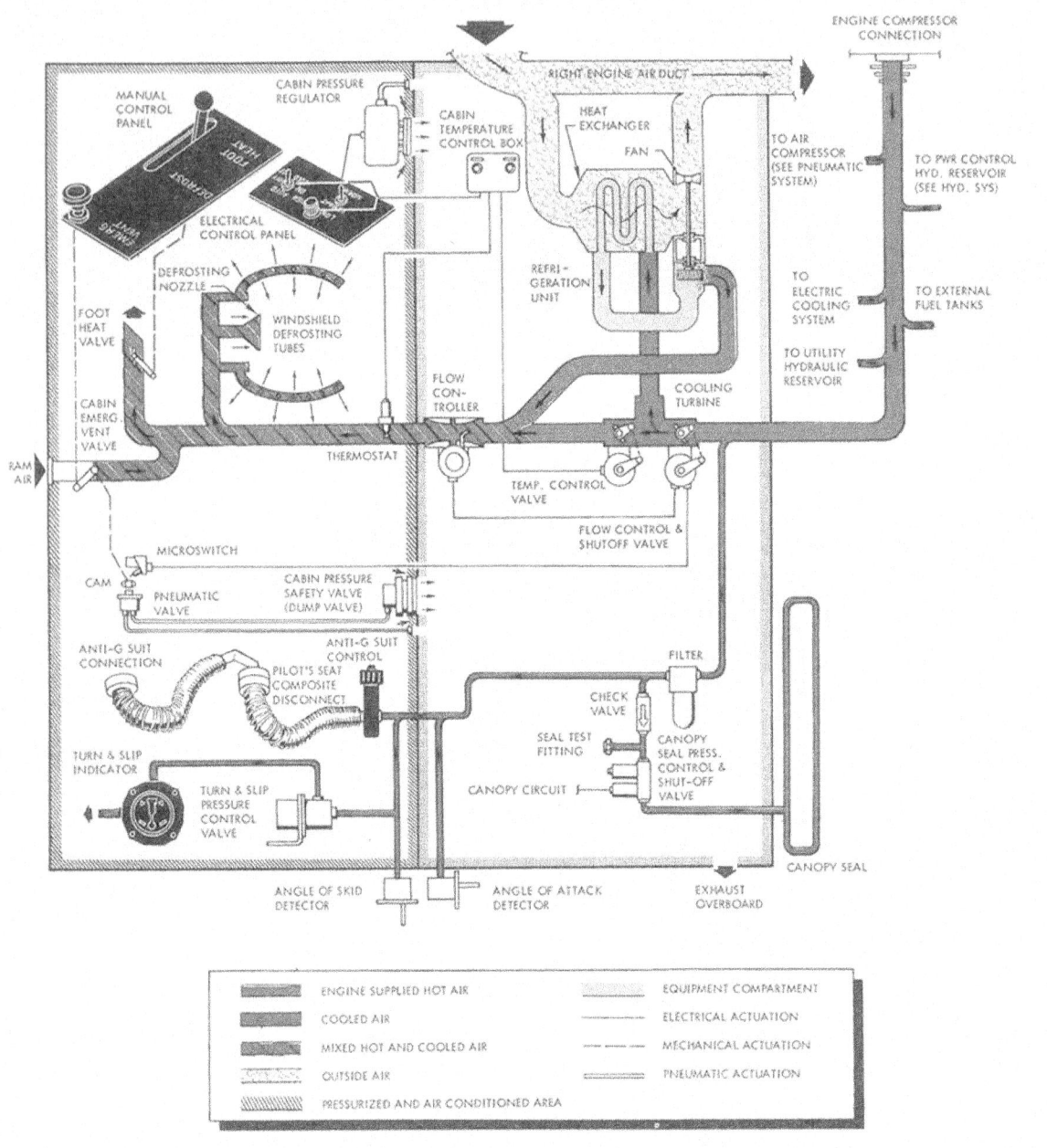

Figure 4-1. Heat, Vent and Pressurization System

Emergency Ventilating Control Handle

The cabin may be cleared of undesired smoke or fumes by pulling the emergency ventilating handle. Push button on top of handle to pull. The handle may be placed in an intermediate position to obtain desired amount of emergency ventilation. When pulled up, three actions occur simultaneously:

1. All heating and pressurizing air from the engine compressor is completely shut off.
2. The cabin safety valve is opened and the cabin becomes completely depressurized.
3. An emergency ventilating valve is opened and atmospheric air is allowed to enter the cabin through the windshield defrosting tubes and the foot heater valve.

Note

Operation of the emergency ventilating control handle is the only method of shutting off bleed air entering cabin from engine, when engine is in operation.

CABIN TEMPERATURE

The cabin air is at a relatively high temperature when it leaves the engine compressor. A certain percentage of this air is diverted by the temperature control valve through the refrigeration unit to be cooled before entering the cockpit. The position of the temperature control valve is controlled by a thermostat located in the cabin air duct and an electronic control circuit. The refrigeration unit is composed of a conventional heat exchanger plus an expansion cooling turbine.

Temperature Control Switch and Rheostat

The temperature control switch has four positions: AUTO, HOT, COLD and OFF. With the switch at AUTO position, the temperature as it enters the cabin will be held within $8 \pm 4°F$ of the temperature selected by pilot at the temperature control rheostat. The rheostat is effective only when the control switch is at AUTO position. The two momentary positions, HOT and COLD, are provided for manual adjustment of cabin temperature should the automatic system fail. Re-

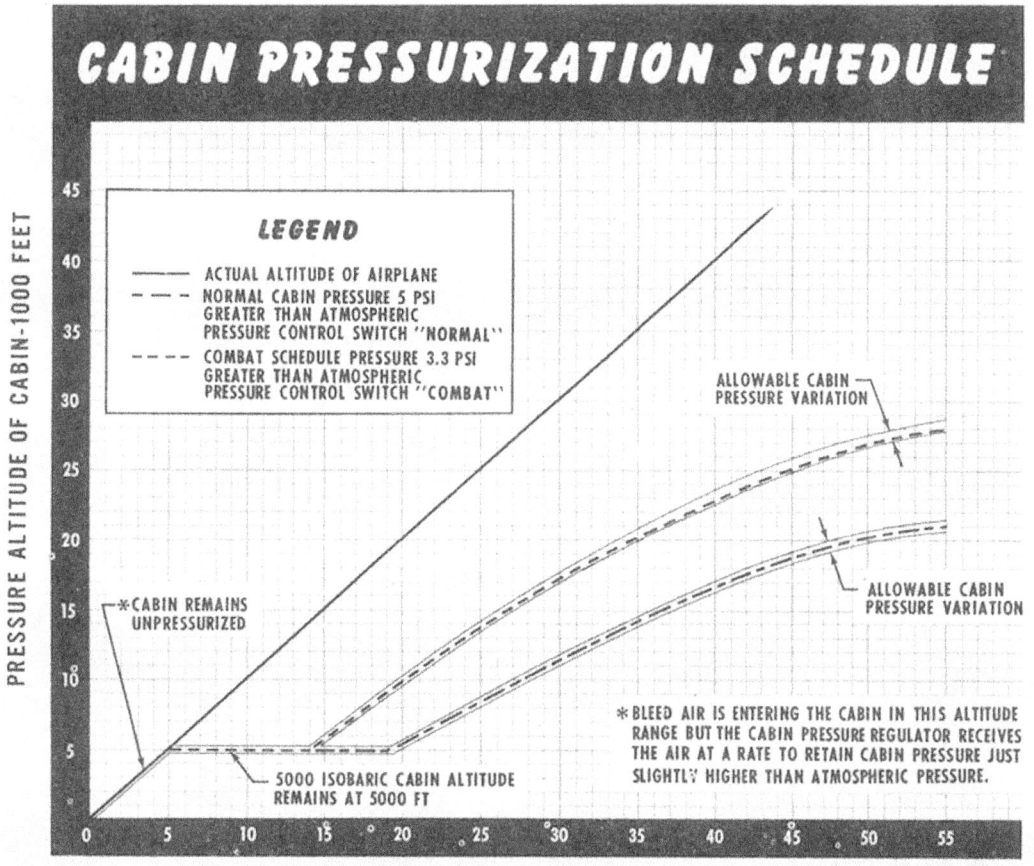

Figure 4-2. Cabin Pressurization Schedule

Section IV NAVWEPS 01-245FCB-501

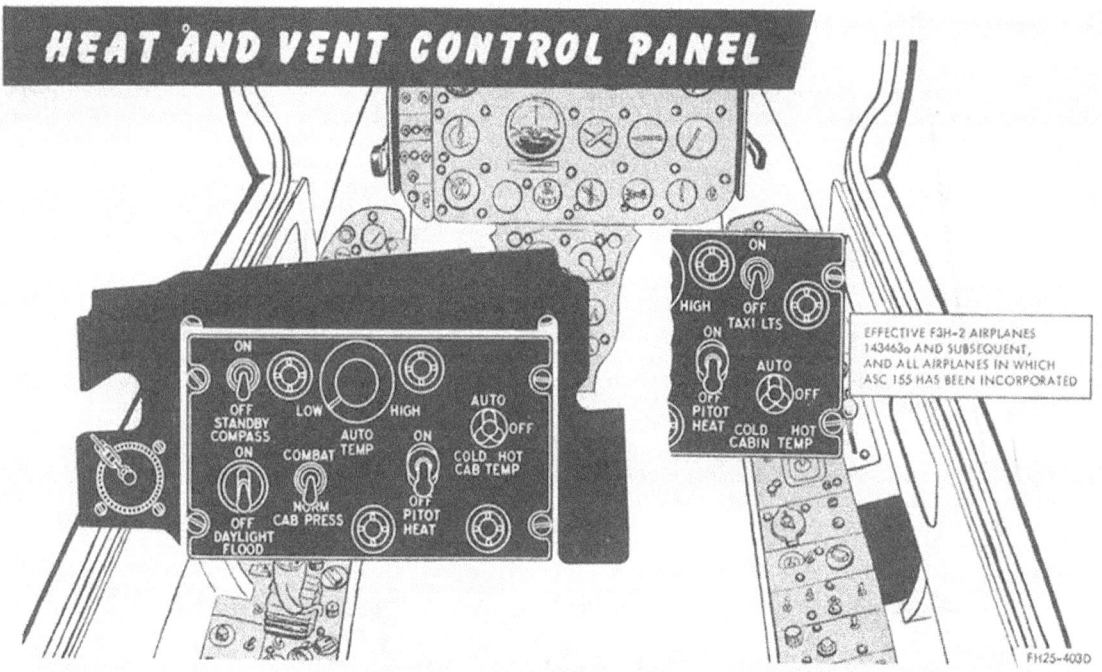

Figure 4-3. Heat and Vent Control Panel

turning the control switch to OFF retains the temperature control valve at a fixed position, but does not shut off the air entering the cabin.

CABIN PRESSURIZING PROCEDURE

1. Keep cabin pressure control switch at NORMAL position when flying in a non-combat area.
2. Preset cabin pressure control switch at COMBAT position before entering probable combat area.
3. For rapid depressurization, pull emergency ventilation control handle. (This also shuts off cabin air from engine compressor and ventilates cabin to atmosphere.)

CABIN HEATING PROCEDURE

1. Place temperature control switch at AUTO position.
2. Adjust temperature control rheostat for desired cabin temperature.
3. Position normal ventilating control handle for personal comfort and effective windshield defrosting.
4. If the automatic temperature control system fails, a temporary temperature adjustment may be obtained by "bumping" the temperature control switch to HOT or COLD position. (Holding this switch at HOT or COLD position for eight seconds obtains the maximum temperature condition.)

WINDSHIELD DEFROSTING PROCEDURE

Level Flight

Fog or frost may form on the windshield and canopy when flying in rain, clouds, or on a day when the relative humidity is high. It usually begins at the aft end of the canopy and moves forward. To obtain maximum windshield and canopy defrosting, perform the following:

1. Place normal ventilating handle at full DEFROST position.
2. Adjust cabin temperature to a hotter condition.

Rapid Descents

Rapid descents from altitude will cause the windshield to fog or frost over. When making rapid descents perform the following:

Note

Keeping the cabin temperature adjusted to maximum comfortable warmth will aid in defrosting when a descent is made.

1. Place the ventilating handle at full DEFROST position.

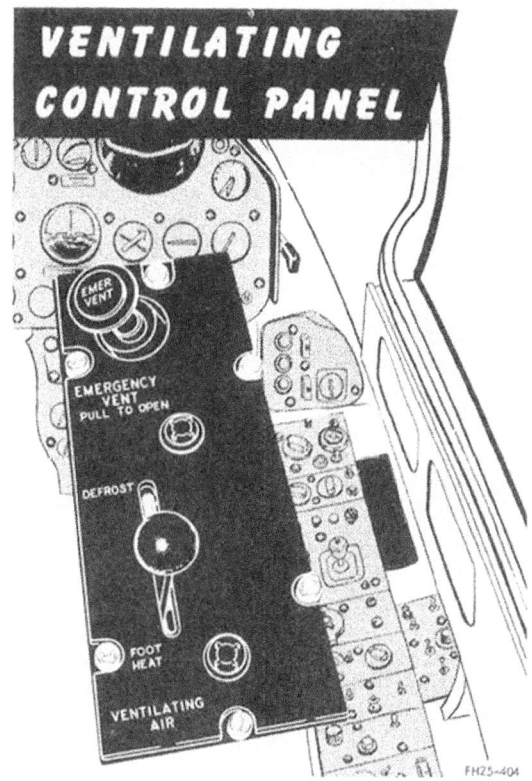

Figure 4-4. Ventilating Control Panel

2. Should excessive frosting or fogging occur, decrease rate of descent if possible, increase engine thrust and adjust cabin temperature to a hotter condition.

CAUTION

If fog or snow is discharged from the windshield defrosting tubes, place the normal ventilating handle at full FOOT HEAT position. Do not place the handle at DEFROST position as this would obscure vision. A higher cabin temperature will dissipate the condensed moisture. If this condition persists, it may be necessary to pull the emergency ventilating handle to maintain vision through windshield.

ENGINE ANTI-ICING SYSTEM (PRIOR TO THE INCORPORATION OF ASC 188)

Engine anti-icing is provided to de-ice and prevent further ice formation on the engine inlet guide vanes. The system is electrically controlled by the engine de-ice switch. This switch has two positions, AUTO and MANUAL. Automatic operation of the system occurs with the switch in the AUTO position. The automatic sequence is dependent on a signal received electrically through a pressure loss in the sensing probe located in the starboard engine air inlet. When this probe is iced over, the pressure switch transmits a signal to the hot air pilot valve. This valve is a solenoid operated valve normally energized closed. The pressure switch signal interrupts the circuit and de-energizes the hot air pilot valve allowing hot air from the engine compressor to flow through the hollow inlet guide vanes and exit into the compressor inlet. Engine de-ice ability varies as a function of engine rpm and therefore the engine rpm should be kept as high as possible within the limits of the paragraph IN THE STORM in Section IX. Pilot indication of automatic anti-icing operation is illumination of a red indicator light marked Eng Ice.

Note

- When the anti-ice system is operating either in automatic or manual, the engine stall range will be increased and the possibility of excessive turbine outlet temperature exists. Extreme caution on the use of throttle settings should be exercised when the anti-ice system is operating.

- If flying in known icing conditions, place pitot heat switch to the ON position. This applies heat to the pitot tubes and the inlet duct water removal system.

CAUTION

If flying in known icing conditions, place the engine de-ice switch at the MANUAL position.

When the engine de-ice switch is placed in the MANUAL position, the sensing switch is by-passed and the hot air pilot valve opens. Simultaneously, the Eng Ice indicator light is illuminated and a heater coil within the sensing probe is energized to de-ice the probe. Anti-ice airflow will be continuous until engine de-ice switch is returned to AUTO position. Returning the switch to AUTO readies the system for a new automatic de-icing cycle. Electrical power for the system is supplied from the utility bus.

ENGINE ANTI-ICING SYSTEM (UPON THE INCORPORATION OF ASC 188)

This system consists of a Cook ice detector, an interpreter, a timer, the engine Anti-ice valve, and three cockpit indicating lights. The Cook ice detector probe is located in the left inlet duct. Ram air pressure on the forward side of the probe and a lower pressure on the aft side create a pressure differential which extends a bellows. In this position the bellows maintain the ice detector in the ARM position. If ice begins to form on the probe, the pressure differential decreases, contracting the bellows moving the contact to the ACTUATE position. This illuminates the ICE WARNING LIGHT on the instrument panel and energizes the probe heater. After 14 to 19 seconds a thermal switch in the ice interpreter de-energizes the probe heater and the ice detector is then recycled to the ARM position. When the engine de-ice switch is in AUTO position and the ice detector moves to ACTUATE (indicated by illumination of the ICE WARNING LIGHT) this de-energizes the engine anti-ice valve open and illuminates the DE-ICE ON light. A time delay maintains the Anti-ice valve open for 30 seconds after the ice detector has recycled. The MAN position of the engine de-ice switch de-energizes the engine anti-ice valve open and illuminates the DE-ICE ON light regardless of conditions sensed by the Cook ice detector. If the ICE DETECTOR ON light fails to come on at approximately idle rpm, the anti-ice system is not armed and will not sense nor activate the engine de-ice system, if icing conditions are encountered. Activate the engine De-Ice switch to the TEST position in order to de-ice the probe and recycle the system.

DE-ICE SYSTEM CHECK

With the engine running at idle rpm or higher, momentarily actuate the de-ice switch to the TEST position and then return to AUTO. All three indicator lights should be illuminated. Approximately 20 seconds later the ICE DETECTOR ON light may flicker as it returns the ice-detector to the ARM position. Approximately 50 seconds after the switch was actuated to the TEST position, the ICE warning light and DE-ICE ON lights should be extinguished.

COMMUNICATION AND ASSOCIATED ELECTRONIC EQUIPMENT

The microphone plug and the headset plug must be inserted into the disconnect assembly, located on the front edge of the pilot's seat, and the secondary d-c bus must be energized before operation of the UHF radio is possible. The secondary d-c and primary 26 volt a-c busses must be energized for operation of the radio compass and the direction finder group. The secondary d-c and monitored a-c busses must be energized for operation of the IFF radar and radar altimeter.

UHF RADIO COMMUNICATION SYSTEM AN/ARC-27A

The UHF radio communication system provides AM telephone communication, in the frequency range of 225.0 to 399.9 megacycles, between aircraft and ship, aircraft and shore, or between aircrafts. The transmitter may be tone-modulated at 1020 cycles per second for emergency or direction finder purposes. The UHF radio communication system provides 1750 frequency channels in the aforementioned range. Provisions have been made for the pilot's remote selection of any one of 20 preset frequencies or operation on a guard channel frequency. Transmission and reception are on the same frequency and by the same antenna. Power is obtained from the airplane's 28 volt d-c electrical system, and is controlled through two radio control panels and a circuit breaker which is mounted in the right circuit breaker panel. A radio control is mounted in the aft fuselage. The remote control panel is located on the right console.

Functions and Locations of Controls

The controls for operating the UHF radio communication system are as follows:

UHF Radio Control Panel

Radio control panel, C-1015/ARC-27A, identified as UHF and located on the center console, provides the pilot with 20 preset channels, 1750 manual channels or the guard channel, all of which are selected from the 1750 frequency channels in the range of 225 to 400 megacycles. The channel selector (CHAN) provides selection of No. 1 through No. 20 preset channels, the guard channel (G) or the manual position (M). In the manual position (M), the three concentric dials (frequency selectors) on the right side of the panel, control the equipment frequency directly. The outer dial sets the first two digits of the frequency, the center dial sets the third digit and the inner dial sets the digit to the right of the decimal point. Other facilities provided are a volume control and vernier sensitivity control. The frequency of preset channels is normally set by maintenance personnel; however, the procedure is as follows:

1. Set the channel selector CHAN to the desired preset channel number.
2. Set the three concentric dials (frequency selectors) to the desired frequency.
3. Turn the set chan button (rotary push button) in the direction shown by the arrow until a stop is felt and then push the button into the panel until another stop is felt.

A standard function switch provides for mode of operation as follows:

SETTING	FUNCTION
"OFF"	Set inoperative
"T/R"	Transmitter and main receiver in operation. Guard receiver in standby. ADF in standby.
"T/R + G"	Transmitter and main receiver in operation. Guard receiver in operation. ADF in standby.
"ADF"	Transmitter in standby. Guard receiver in standby. ADF in operation through main receiver.

UHF Remote Channel Indicator

A UHF remote channel indicator is installed above the radar scope to allow the pilot to look forward while changing channels on the AN/ARC-27A.

Disconnect Assembly

The microphone and pilot's headset connections are provided as a part of the pilot's quick-disconnect assembly, located on the front edge of the ejection seat. The leads then are part of the oxygen hose assembly which mates with the pilot's mask.

COMMUNICATION AND ASSOCIATED ELECTRONIC EQUIPMENT

TYPE DESIGNATION	FUNCTION	RANGE	LOCATION AND CONTROL
Radar Altimeter AN APN-22	Indicates distance in feet from aircraft to ground	Land 0-10,000 feet Water 0-20,000 feet	Indicator on main instrument panel contains control and warning light. Warning light on AN/APG-51C indicator scope.
UHF Radio AN ARC-27A	AM radio telephone communication between aircraft and ship, aircraft and shore or between aircraft	Up to line of sight depending upon frequency and antenna coverage.	Control panel on the right console.
UHF Radio Auxiliary Receiver AN ARR-40	Auxiliary UHF communication receiver. Also gives bearing information when used in conjunction with the AN/ARA-25.	Same as the AN/ARC-27A.	Control panel on right console.
Direction Finder Group AN ARA-25	Indicates relative bearing of and homes on radio signal sources.	Frequency range of 225.0 to 399.9 megacycles 30-200 miles	AN/ARC-27 control panel on the right console. Indicator on main instrument panel.
Navagation Radio Set AN ARN-21	Indicates bearing and distance of a ground position equipped with radio set AN/URN-3 beacon. Determines identity of beacon and indicates dependability of beacon signal. Supplies fly left or right instruction for approaching a beacon.	Line of sight distances up to 195 miles. Range depends upon altitude.	Control panel on right console. Range indicator ID-310/ARN on main instrument panel. Course indicator ID-250/ARN on main instrument panel. Course indicator ID-387/ARN on main instrument panel.
IFF Radar AN APX-6B	Identifies aircraft as friend.	0-200 miles or line of sight	Control panel on the right console.
SIF AN APA-89	Provides specific identification of separate airplanes or of a single airplane within a group.	Same as IFF Radar.	SIF control panel on right console.
Radar Set AN APG-51C	Detects and tracks aerial targets; provides point-of-aim indication. Supplies range information to visual sight system. Provides surface search and beacon identification indications for navigational purposes.	Detection - 50,000 yards maximum Tracking - 150-30,000 yards Surface Search and Beacon 200 nautical miles (indicated range)	Control panel on left console. Indicator scope on main instrument panel.

Figure 4-5. Communication and Associated Electronic Equipment

Section IV NAVWEPS 01-245FCB-501

Antenna Switch

The antenna switch, installed in the throttle assembly (see figure 1-6), is used to actuate the coaxial cable switch which transfers radio communication from the upper broadband (fin) antenna to the lower broadband (left nose gear well door) antenna. Selection of the upper broadband antenna is made by placing the antenna switch in the UPR position while the LWR position selects the lower broadband antenna.

Microphone Button

Two microphone buttons are provided in the cockpit, one located on the throttle assembly and one on the radar antenna control handle. Depressing either of the microphone buttons makes transmission possible.

Operating Procedure

To place the UHF radio communication system in operation, proceed as follows:

1. Place the function switch on the control panel in T/R position. Allow an interval of one minute for the tubes to heat.
2. Select the frequency channel desired by means of the channel selector or by operation of the three band selector with the channel selector at M position. The frequency selected by means of the three band selector may be stored as a preset channel, if desired, by moving channel selector to a number and depressing the push-to-set-chan button.
3. Place the function switch in the T/R + G position. Reception is now possible on both the main and guard channel frequencies. Adjust the volume and sensitivity as desired.
4. Select reception or transmission on the upper or lower broadband antennas by selecting the UPR, or LWR position of the antenna switch.

DIRECTION FINDER

The direction finder is used in conjunction with the UHF radio communication system on a frequency band of 225-399.9 mcs. The direction-finding feature of the UHF receiver provides the pilot with a continuous indication of the relative bearing to the transmitting station. Operation of the direction finder is controlled by the function switch on the UHF radio control panel. Placing the function switch in the ADF position directs electrical input from the antenna, through the UHF receiver and direction-finder amplifier, to the single needle pointer of the radio magnetic indicator.

Radio Magnetic Indicator

The dial of the radio magnetic indicator is graduated every two degrees and 30 degree increments are marked with appropriate numerals. The indicator is equipped with two pointers. The single needle pointer

Figure 4-6. UHF Radio Control Panel

indicates the relative bearing from the aircraft to the UHF transmitting station. The double needle pointer indicates relative bearing to low frequency stations tuned in on the low frequency radio compass system.

FUNCTIONS AND LOCATIONS OF CONTROLS

The automatic direction finder is controlled from the UHF control panel. When the UHF radio is operating, the direction finder system is in stand-by. Placing the control in OFF position turns off both the UHF and ADF systems. The reception frequency is selected by the channel selector on the UHF control panel.

Direction Finding

1. Place the UHF control in the ADF position (allow three minutes warm-up if control was in OFF position).
2. Select the reception frequency by means of the UHF channel selector or the three band selector.
3. Observe the direction of signal arrival (relative bearing of source) as indicated by the arrow of the single bar pointer of the course indicator.

Note

The direction finding operation may be interrupted for short transmissions over the UHF radio by depressing either microphone button. The equipment will return to ADF operation automatically upon release of button.

Figure 4-7. Auxiliary Radio Receiver Control Panel

AUXILIARY RADIO RECEIVER AN/ARR-40

The primary purpose of the equipment as installed is that of an auxiliary receiver to the normal UHF Radio Set. The set can be used for all functions of the receiver section of the UHF communications system, and is interconnected with the UHF system in such a manner that one of the sets is tied to the ADF group at all times. In this manner, the auxiliary receiver, in conjunction with the ADF equipment, will furnish bearing information during receiving periods of two-way communications. The function of the auxiliary and main UHF receivers may be interchanged at any time by means of the function switches on the UHF and auxiliary receiver control panels, as described below. The set provides reception in the range of 265.0 to 284.9 megacycles. Electrical power is provided by the secondary d-c bus. All controls for the AN/ARR-40 receiver are located on a control panel which is mounted aft of the normal UHF control panel on the right console. Controls included are the function switch, channel selector switch, sensitivity control and volume control. The interchangeability of functions of the UHF-ADF and auxiliary receiver require certain control selections to be made on the UHF control panel; these are discussed below.

Function Switch

This rotary switch selects the desired type of operation for the set. The switch is marked AUX REC at the top, and MAIN T/R at the bottom of the panel. The control is so designed that selections made at the upper part of the switch for the auxiliary receiver have a counterselection at the bottom indicating the function that the normal UHF set should provide. The positions for the AUX REC portion of the switch are OFF, ADF, CMD and GRD. The counterselections for the UHF set are T/R, ADF and ADF.

Channel Selector

The rotary channel selector controls the frequency of the receiver, 20 preset channels are provided, and each channel position covers approximately 1 megacycle. A guard channel is provided, and is normally assigned a frequency of 243 mc.

Sensitivity Control

Rotating this control varies the gain in the amplifier stage of the system. The control is rotated until background hiss is heard, and then counter-rotated to eliminate the hiss. This insures maximum reception sensitivity without unnecessary background noise.

Volume Control

Volume is increased by rotating this control to the right, and decreased by rotating it to the left.

Operation of Auxiliary Receiver

For simultaneous reception of UHF audio transmissions and ADF bearing information the following panel control selections should be used:

1. UHF function switch (AN/ARC-27 control panel) - T/R
2. Function switch - ADF
3. Channel selector - SET
   Rotate control until desired channel appears in selector window.
4. Sensitivity control - ADJUST
   Vary this control for maximum sensitivity without background hiss.
5. Volume control - ADJUST
   Vary for desired audio level.

The above settings provide a transmission side tone, and provide ADF bearing information. They do not however, provide identification signals from the ADF. For such identification it is necessary to select CMD on the AN/ARR-40 function switch. After proper identification is made, return the function switch to ADF for continued bearing information. While the function switch is in the CMD position, no audio side tone is provided.

IFF

The AN/APX-6B radar identification set is used to automatically identify the airplane as friendly whenever it is properly challenged by suitably equipped friendly surface or airborne radar. The set has provisions for identifying itself as a specific friendly aircraft within a group and means for transmitting a special distress code. The control panel (see figure 4-8) for the IFF system is located on the right console. Power for operation of the set is obtained from the a-c monitored

Section IV

NAVWEPS 01-245FCB-501

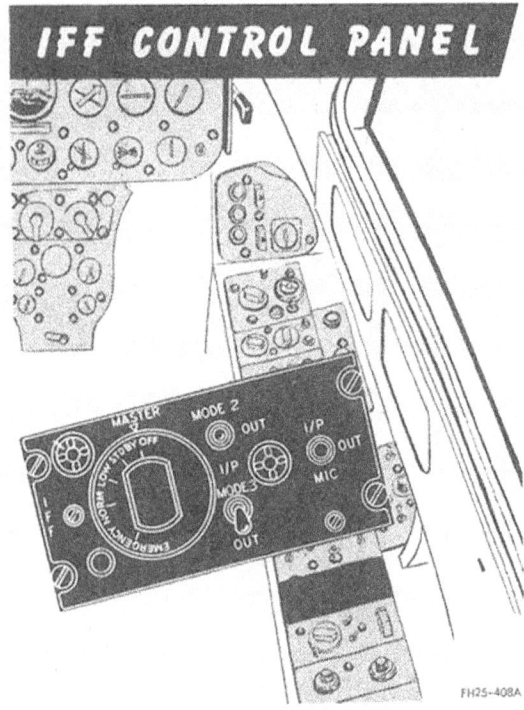

Figure 4-8. IFF Control Panel

a-c bus and 28 volt d-c power from the secondary d-c bus. This set is used in conjunction with the Coder Group, AN/APA-89. Refer to Section IV of the Confidential Supplement NAVWEPS 01-245FCB-501A for the operation of the coder group.

OPERATION OF IFF

1. Rotate master switch to NORM.
2. Rotate master switch to STDBY to maintain inoperative but ready for instant use.
3. Set mode 2 and mode 3 switches to OUT unless otherwise directed.
4. If in distress, press dial stop (red button) and rotate master switch to EMERGENCY position. Set will automatically transmit distress signals.
5. Rotate master switch to OFF to turn set off.

RADAR ALTIMETER SYSTEM

The radar altimeter system measures terrain clearance of the airplane by measuring the time elapsed between transmitting a frequency modulated signal and receiving the reflected signal. The system is designed to provide reliable operation over the ranges of 0 to 10,000 feet over land and 0 to 20,000 feet over water. The accuracy of indication is ± 2 feet from 0 to 40 feet and ± 5 percent of the indicated altitude from 40 feet to 20,000 feet.

Radar Altimeter

The radar altitude indicator (see figure 1-17), located on the main instrument panel, provides indication of the airplane's altitude on a single turn type dial, from 0 to 20,000 feet. "Drop-out" occurs when altitude limits of the system are exceeded. This disables the indicator and puts the needle behind a mask. An adjustable "bug" pointer at the outside of the calibrated scale on the indicator can be preset to desired altitudes and used as a reference in flying at fixed altitude. Two warning lights, one located below the radar altimeter and one on the outside edge of the ASC radar scope, will glow when the airplane is flying below the preset altitude. A tube and relay within the indicator operates these limit lights. Power for the radar altimeter system is supplied by the secondary d-c bus and the a-c monitored a-c bus.

FUNCTIONS AND LOCATIONS OF CONTROLS

On Limit Control

The on-limit control is the only operating control in the radar altimeter system. It is located in the lower left corner of the radar altitude indicator, on the main instrument panel. The control consists of a single knob that operates the system ON-OFF switch and is also used to select the limit altitude.

Starting the Radar Altimeter System

To start the equipment, turn on the on-limit control. The equipment will start operating approximately three minutes after the control is turned on.

Note

The indicator needle may be near 0 with the warning light on, and the switch OFF; therefore, always check switch position before flight, and never assume the set is operating.

CAUTION

Allow at least 12 minutes warm-up time after starting the equipment to insure final accuracy. If the temperature is below -40°C, 25 minutes should be allowed.

When the equipment is operating with the airplane resting on the ground, the indicator pointer will move to some point slightly above zero and will fluctuate two or three feet while taxiing. This is a normal condition. The indicator reading will drop back to zero when the aircraft assumes its normal flight attitude during take-off and meaningful readings will be obtained thereafter.

Limit Indicator System

Set the limit indicator preset "bug" to desired altitude by means of the on-limit control on the front of the in-

100

ANTENNA LOCATIONS

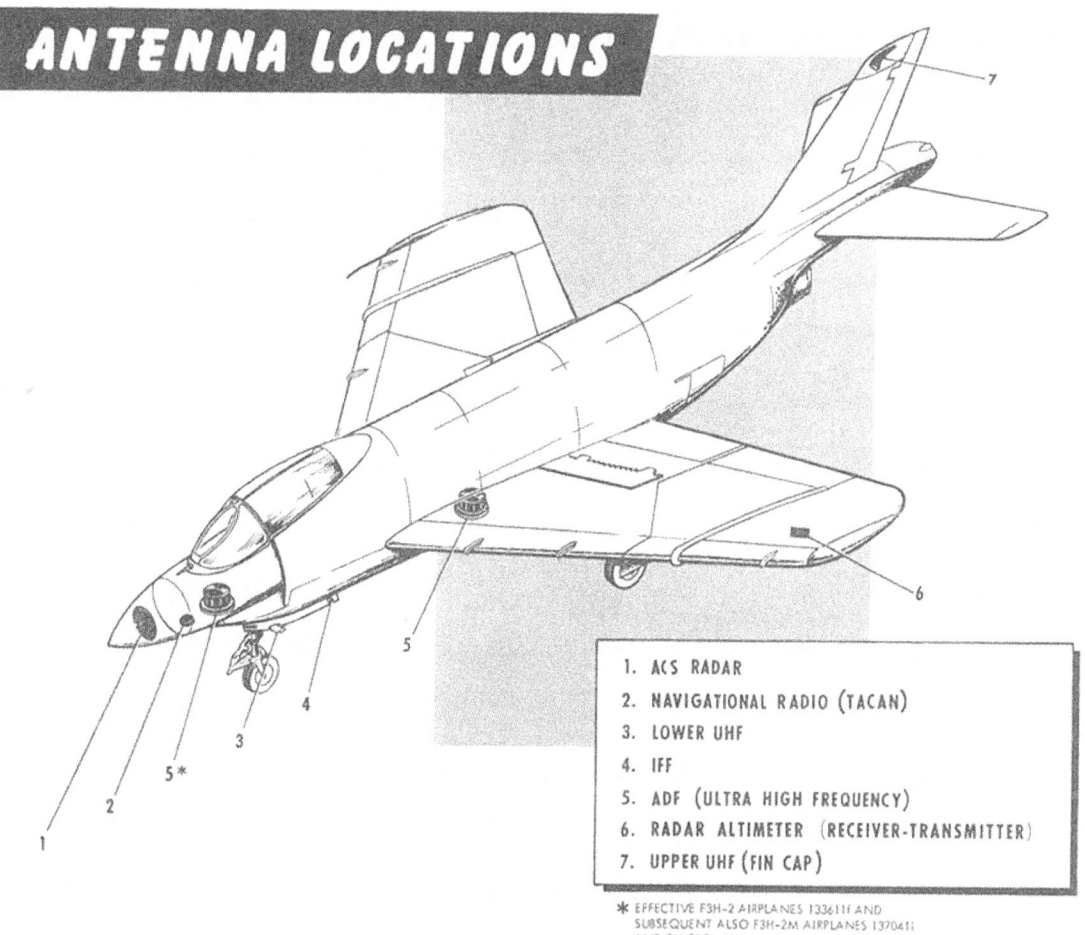

1. ACS RADAR
2. NAVIGATIONAL RADIO (TACAN)
3. LOWER UHF
4. IFF
5. ADF (ULTRA HIGH FREQUENCY)
6. RADAR ALTIMETER (RECEIVER-TRANSMITTER)
7. UPPER UHF (FIN CAP)

* EFFECTIVE F3H-2 AIRPLANES 133611 AND SUBSEQUENT ALSO F3H-2M AIRPLANES 137041 AND SUBSEQUENT.

Figure 4-9. Antenna Locations

dicator. At or below the preset altitude the red limit light on front of the indicator is illuminated. When flying above the preset altitude, the light will be turned off. The intensity of the limit light can be changed through the airplane's warning lights dimming system. To dim the warning lights, the instrument lights control knob located on the interior lights control panel, must be turned toward the BRT position to some position other than the OFF position. Flight at a preset altitude can easily be maintained by observing the position of the altitude pointer with respect to the limit preset "bug" without considering the actual scale calibrations when light conditions are encountered so the limit light cannot be readily seen.

Drop-Out

The radar altimeter system will stop indicating altitude when the reflected signal is too weak to override the system noise. "Drop-out" should not occur at altitudes below 10,000 feet over land or 20,000 over water. However, a climb, bank or dive of 60° or more will reduce "drop-out" altitude somewhat. Inverted flight will also cause "drop-out". When "drop-out" occurs, circuits within the system automatically disconnect the indicator synchro from the servo system and apply a fixed signal to it, which causes the pointer to assume a position behind the mask on the indicator dial between the 20,000 feet point and the 0 point. This fixed off scale position indicates to the pilot that the reading is meaningless.

Note

When "drop-out" occurs, it is necessary to reduce altitude to a point slightly below where "drop-out" occurred, or to level out from the maneuver which caused "drop-out". The return to normal operation following "drop-out" is indicated by the resumption of normal indicator operation.

Section IV

Stopping the Equipment

To stop the equipment, it is necessary to turn off the on-limit control on the indicator.

NAVIGATION RADIO (TACAN)

The ARN-21 (TACAN) is a short-range VHF navigational aid which converts radio signals received from a selected ground station into visual displays of azimuth and range. TACAN operates on 126 manually selected channels at altitudes below 50,000 feet. At altitudes above 50,000 feet an altitude limit switch cuts off power to the set. Power is supplied by the 28 volt d-c bus and the 115 volt single phase a-c bus. Azimuth information is broadcast continuously by the ground station. A beacon, which rotates at a constant rate, transmits a special pulse signal when it passes through the 090° radial. By measuring the length of time necessary for the beacon to rotate from this radial to the one on which the aircraft is located, azimuth can be determined. This information is displayed in terms of relative bearing, accurate to 1/4 degree, on the double-needle pointer of the ID-250 radio magnetic indicator, and in terms of course displacement on the vertical cross-pointer of the ID-249A course indicator. Unlike azimuth signals, distance signals are not broadcast continually. The airborne TACAN transmitter initiates a request for distance information. A pulse signal from the TACAN transmitter triggers a responding pulse signal from the ground station. The time lapse is translated into distance. Range information is displayed in nautical miles on the ID-310 range indicator. The maximum operating range of the TACAN distance function is 195 nautical miles, but bearing information is accurate beyond this range under most conditions. Ground equipment can respond to distance inquiries of more than 100 aircraft simultaneously without interference. A station identification signal, in morse code, is broadcast once every 75 seconds.

FUNCTIONS AND LOCATIONS OF CONTROLS AND INDICATORS

All of the ARN-21 indicators are located on the instrument panel. The TACAN control panel is located aft of the autopilot control panel on the right console and contains all of the controls.

Channel Selector Knobs

The desired channel is selected by means of a double knob. The large outer knob selects the first two digits of the desired channel, and the small inner knob the last digit. Any selection from 000 to 129 is possible, but only channels 01 to 126 are operative.

Do not select channels above 126 or below 01 as damage to the equipment will result.

Power Switch

The power switch has three positions: OFF, REC and T/R. In the OFF position, power to the set is shut off. In the REC position, the airborne transmitter which initiates requests for range information is inoperative, no pulse signals are transmitted and no range information is received. Bearing data only is obtained. The REC position is used when it is undesirable to emit signals from the aircraft, e.g., over enemy territory. Both range and bearing signals are received when the switch is in the T/R position.

Volume Control Knob

This control adjusts the volume of the station identification signal in the pilot's headset.

ID-249/ARN Course Indicator

The course indicator has a bearing selector knob, a bearing window, a to-from window, a bearing deviation (vertical) cross-pointer, a glide slope (horizontal) cross-pointer, and a heading needle. The horizontal cross-pointer is used only for ILS approaches and is inoperative in F3H-2, -2M airplanes. The magnetic course which the pilot desires to fly is set in the bearing window by turning the bearing selector knob. The display in the to-from window then indicates whether this course will carry the aircraft towards or away from the station. If flying the selected course will carry the aircraft towards the station, the word TO appears in the window. The deviation (vertical) cross-pointer shows the position of the aircraft (represented by the center dot) in relation to the desired course (represented by the vertical cross-pointer). If the cross-pointer is deflected to the right, the plane must be turned to the right in order to intercept the selected course. Each 1-dot deflection of the cross-pointer from the center indicates that the aircraft is 5° off course. When unreliable signals are received, a red OFF flag appears at the bottom of the vertical cross-pointer. The heading needle indicates the heading of the aircraft in relation to the selected course. When this needle is displaced at the same time the vertical cross-pointer is centered, the aircraft is crabbing to hold the selected course.

ID-250/ARN Radio Magnetic Indicator

The operation of this instrument is described in this section under the discussion of the ARN-6, TACAN information is supplied to the number 2 needle.

ID-310/ARN Range Indicator

The slant range distance from the aircraft to the transmitting station is displayed in the window of the range indicator. When the signal is unreliable, a horizontal red OFF flag drops down and partially covers the display. The error introduced by measuring slant rather than horizontal range is negligible, being only about 0.1 of a mile at the set's operating limits (50,000 feet altitude, 195 nautical miles from the station).

Figure 4-10. Tacan Control Panel

NORMAL OPERATION OF THE EQUIPMENT

Note

If reliable signals cannot be received, all of the indicators will "search" constantly.

1. Power switch - REC or T/R as desired. Allow approximately 90 seconds for warm-up.
2. Select the desired channel.
3. Volume - AS DESIRED
4. Observe the double needle indication on the ID-250 radio magnetic indicator.
5. Observe vertical cross-pointer deflection on the ID-249A course indicator.

Note

Check to see that the warning flag disappears completely.

6. Observe the range indication on the ID-310 range indicator.

Note

The power switch must be in the T/R position to make range information available.

7. Set the desired course in the bearing window of the ID-387. Fly heading to or from the station.

EMERGENCY OPERATION OF THE EQUIPMENT

There is no emergency procedure as such for TACAN. If difficulty is experienced the following checks are recommended. First determine that there is no obstruction between the ground station and the aircraft, for TACAN, like all VHF equipment, is subject to line-of-sight restrictions. If there are no obstructions, select a second station known to be within range. If operation is satisfactory on the second channel, switch back to the first station to determine whether the faulty operation was caused by a temporary pause in beacon transmission or an unknown obstruction between the beacon and the aircraft.

G-2 COMPASS SYSTEM

The G-2 compass system is utilized in F3H-2M airplanes 133623e thru 133638f and F3H-2 airplanes 133549d thru 133622f. It is a compass slaved directional gyro system consisting of a master direction indicator, adapter, and remote compass transmitter. The signals from the compass transmitter are routed to the adapter for amplification, and then are directed to the torque motor in the master direction indicator unit. This motor applies a precessional force to the gyro, which in turn causes the master direction indicator scale to follow the transmitter. In effect, the slowly responding gyro averages out the transmitter signals and provides a steady directional display on the indicator. A correspondence indicator is located in the center of the indicator face. This portion of the indicator provides a constant display of magnetic heading, since it is linked directly to the transmitter. Power to the system is provided by the primary a-c and primary d-c buses.

G-2 Compass Controls

A compass control switch, marked FREE DG, is installed on the pedestal panel. When in the FREE DG position, the slaved compass function is removed, and the instrument displays a directional gyro indication only. A spring-loaded knob is located adjacent to the indicator face. Depressing and rotating this knob resets the indicator card to any desired heading.

G-2 Compass Operation

The system will begin operating as soon as its a-c and d-c power requirements are met. However, accurate indications may not be relied upon until the gyro reaches its full operating speed. Under normal conditions, the gyro will be at speed in approximately three minutes, however, on extremely cold days, as long as fifteen minutes may be required. When sufficient time has elapsed to insure that the gyro is definitely at full speed, use the following procedure:

1. Select compass operation desired (FREE DG or COMP. CONT).
2. Depress reset knob firmly and rotate main dial to desired heading.
3. Keep knob fully depressed for at least two seconds.
4. Release knob straight out, avoid any twisting motion.

Note

If card heading is not manually changed at the time power is applied, and the system is in slaved operation, the new heading will eventually be slaved automatically. This may require some time however, since the precession rate is only about 3 to 4 degrees per minute.

Figure 4-11. Compass Control Panel

S-2 COMPASS SYSTEM

The S-2 compass system, as installed in F3H-2M airplanes 137033g thru 137095k and F3H-2 airplanes 136966g and subsequent is a directional gyro system which may be operated as a slaved or free directional gyro. In magnetically unreliable areas such as carrier decks and magnetic pole regions, it may be used as a free gyro. During slaved gyro operation, the magnetic direction sensing unit detects earth's magnetic lines of force and transmits positioning data to the directional gyro control via the compass amplifier. Thus the directional gyro always points to magnetic north. A synchro pickup in the directional gyro compass unit detects the gyro's heading and electrically positions the dial in the direction indicator (see figure 1-17) to provide the pilot with a stable magnetic compass indication of the aircraft's heading. With the system operating in the free gyro condition, the direction sensing unit is disconnected from the directional gyro control. The gyro then maintains any heading manually set by the pilot. The compass controller (see figure 4-11) is located on the right console. Electrical power to the system is provided by the primary a-c and the primary d-c buses.

S-2 Compass Operation

1. System is energized when power to primary a-c bus is applied.

Note

Upon initial application of power to the airplane, the S-2 compass switch must be in the SLAVED GYRO position, and the inverter circuit breaker must be in. If these controls are not in their proper positions upon application of d-c power, the fast-slaving feature of the S-2 compass will be lost.

2. Select SLAVED GYRO or FREE GYRO by mode selector switch.
3. Sync signal indicator will show error between heading detected by the directional sensing element and heading of the directional gyro. When not synchronized, pointer indicates the way the gyro must be turned to affect synchronization.
4. Turn the set heading control to direction indicated by the sync signal needle deflection. Gyro will precess in the direction desired. Turning the control to INC. slaves the gyro "up" scale, turning control to DEC. slaves the gyro "down" scale. When the sync signal indicator needle is within the width of the index mark (1/16 inch width), the system is synchronized within 1°.

LIGHTING EQUIPMENT

EXTERIOR LIGHTING

The exterior lighting consists of the position lights and fuselage lights. The exterior lights control panel, located near the aft end of the right console (see figure 4-12), contains all manual controls for the exterior lighting. The exterior lights are energized from the secondary d-c bus.

Figure 4-12. Exterior Lighting Control Panel

Navigation Lights

The navigation lights include the wing tip lights, and the tail light. The navigation lights are controlled by the master switch and the wing and tail lights switch. The master switch has positions of OFF, STEADY and FLASH. The wing and tail lights switch has positions of OFF, BRT and DIM. The master switch and wing and tail lights switch are located on the exterior lights control panel. When the master switch is placed in either the STEADY or FLASH position and the wing and tail lights switch is in the BRT position, the lights will be energized continuously at full brilliance. When the wing and tail lights switch is placed in the DIM position and the master switch is in either the STEADY or FLASH position, the lights will be energized continuously at reduced brilliance. When either the master switch or the wing and tail light switch is in the OFF position, the navigation lights will be de-energized.

Fuselage Lights

The fuselage lights include two light assemblies, one located on the top and one on the bottom of the fuselage. Each light assembly contains two lamps, one bright and the other dim. The fuselage lights are controlled by the master switch and the fuselage lights switch. The fuselage lights switch has positions of BRT, MAN and DIM. It is located on the exterior lights control panel. When the master switch is placed in the STEADY position and the fuselage lights switch is in the BRT position, the bright lights will be energized continuously. With the master switch in the FLASH position and the fuselage lights switch in the BRT position, the bright lights will flash at a rate of 80 times per minute. With the fuselage lights switch in the DIM position, the dim lights will be energized continuously or will flash, depending upon the position of the master switch. With the fuselage lights switch in the MAN position and the master switch in either the STEADY or FLASH position, the bright lights are energized for manual code flashing through the manual key, located on the exterior light control panel. An indicator light on the exterior light control panel, is energized at the same time as the fuselage lights when flashing code manually.

Formation Lights

In F3H-2M airplanes 133631f thru 137095k and F3H-2 airplanes 133581e and subsequent, amber colored formation lights have been added to the exterior of the airplane. One light is placed on each side of the fuselage forward of the intake ducts, and one light on the trailing edge of each wing tip. A three-position formation lights switch, marked BRT, DIM, and OFF, on the exterior lights control panel, control the operation of the lights. The master switch on the same control panel must be in either FLASH or STEADY position before the formation lights switch will operate. The formation lights will burn steady only, regardless of the position of the master switch. Power for the lights is provided by the secondary bus.

Figure 4-13. Interior Lighting Control Panel

Taxi Lights

Effective F3H-2 airplanes 143463o and subsequent, prior to incorporation of F3H ASC 155, a 50 watt taxi light is provided. Located on the nose landing gear above the approach lights, this light is controlled by a switch on the heat and vent control panel (figure 4-3), and by the approach light relay. The approach light relay function precludes the light remaining illuminated in the event its switch was left in the ON position after gear retraction. Power for the taxi light is provided by the primary d-c bus. Effective upon incorporation of ASC 155, a more powerful (450 watt) taxi light is provided for all F3H aircraft. Airplanes previously equipped with 50 watt lights have these units replaced, and the taxi light feature is added to the earlier aircraft not so equipped.

INTERIOR LIGHTING

The interior lights include instrument lights, console lights, console floodlights, instrument panel emergency floodlights, daylight floodlights, and high intensity instrument panel floodlights. The interior light control panel, located on the right console (see figure 4-13) contains most of the control switches for the lights. The interior lights are energized from the primary d-c bus.

Instrument Lights

The instrument lights consist of edge lights for illuminating most of the instruments on the main instrument panel and left forward console panel. The lights are controlled by the OFF to BRT instrument lights control switch located on the interior lights control panel.

Section IV

NAVWEPS 01-245FCB-501

The standby compass lights are also controlled by the OFF to BRT instrument light switch as well as OFF-ON standby compass switch located on the utility control panel. Emergency floodlights for the main instrument panel are controlled by the OFF-DIM-BRT instrument emergency floodlight switch located on the main instrument panel.

Console Lights

The console lights consist of edge lights for illuminating most console panels, sub-instrument panel and check lists, armament panel, and the warning lights fire test switch, included on the main instrument panel. These lights are controlled by the OFF to BRT console lights control switch, located on the interior lights control panel. The console floodlights are also controlled by the OFF to BRT console lights control switch as well as BRT-DIM-MED console floodlights switch also located on the interior lights control panel.

Daylight Floodlights

To provide additional cockpit brilliance as an aid to vision when flying on instruments, daylight floodlights are installed in the airplane, one at the aft end of each console. These lights provide general illumination of the entire cockpit area. The floodlights are controlled by the daylight flood switch, marked ON-OFF, located on the combination utility-heat and vent control panel of the right console.

Instrument Panel Floodlights

Upon incorporation of F3H ASC No. 156, high intensity instrument panel floodlights are provided for special missions. These high intensity white floodlights, located on each side of the cockpit are controlled by an on-off toggle switch mounted in the left floodlight assembly, immediately over the flap and slat switch. Power to these lights is provided by the primary d-c bus.

OXYGEN SYSTEM

The airplane is equipped with a high pressure diluter-demand oxygen system which consists of two oxygen cylinders, provision for an auxiliary cylinder, an oxygen regulator and the necessary lines, fittings, and check valves. The automatic positive pressure diluter-demand regulator located on the left console mixes varying ratio of cabin air and oxygen depending upon altitude and delivers the quantity demanded upon inhalation. The regulator incorporates an oxygen

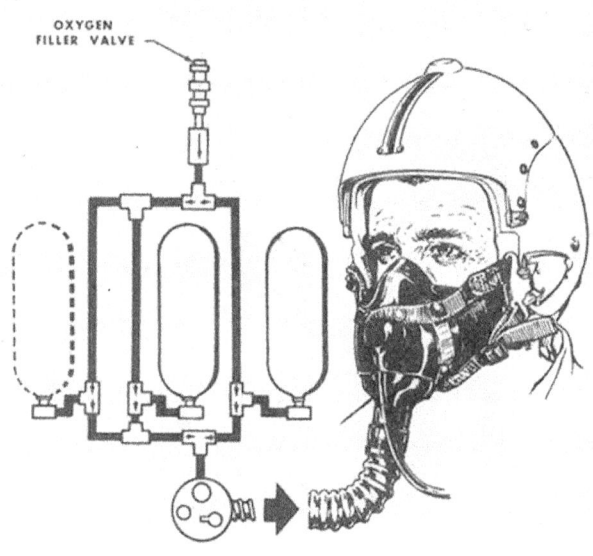

Figure 4-14. Oxygen System Schematic

cylinder pressure gage, a flow indicator, an air valve and a safety pressure valve. (See figure 4-15.)

Note

Only a pressure type breathing mask may be used with this regulator.

The operational limit of cabin altitude with this regulator is 43,000 feet. In emergencies, this limit may be exceeded by 2,000 feet for short periods of time. Sufficient pressure is automatically delivered for an emergency descent or if cabin pressurization is lost and cabin pressure is reduced to that of the surrounding air.

OXYGEN SELECTOR VALVE

The oxygen selector valve located on the face of the regulator has two positions: NORMAL OXYGEN and 100% OXYGEN. Under all normal operating conditions, the air valve is in the NORMAL OXYGEN position. Whenever carbon monoxide or other noxious gases are present, place the air valve in the 100% OXYGEN position regardless of altitude.

SAFETY PRESSURE

The safety pressure lever is located on the rim of the regulator face. The required positive pressures of oxygen are automatically supplied at 35,000 feet and above and the use of the manually operated safety pressure is unnecessary and may be uncomfortable. Routine use of safety pressure at lower altitudes is not recommended since the use of safety pressure reduces the effectiveness of air diluter and causes increased oxygen consumption. If symptoms occur suggestive of the onset of anoxia, immediately turn the safety pressure lever to the ON position.

PREFLIGHT CHECK

In order to properly check the oxygen equipment perform the following:

1. Turn oxygen supply valve ON at forward edge of regulator and check oxygen pressure gage. Pressure should be 1800 to 1850 psi when cylinders are fully charged.
2. Close oxygen supply valve, pressure indicated on regulator gage should not fall more than 300 psi in four minutes.
3. Place the quick-disconnect coupling of the breathing tube to the lips and blow gently into the open end. If there is no resistance to exhalation, leakage exists in the regulator or breathing tube.
4. Put on mask. To check mask fit, place thumb over disconnect at end of mask tube and inhale lightly. If there is no leakage, the mask adheres tightly to the face and a definite resistance to inhalation is encountered. If leakage is present, adjust mask.

WARNING

Do not use a mask that leaks.

5. Engage mating portions of disconnect coupling so mask is connected to oxygen system breathing tube. Turn on supply valve and check regulator operation by breathing several times at NORMAL OXYGEN and 100% OXYGEN. Observe flow indicator for blink verifying positive flow of oxygen.

NORMAL OPERATING PROCEDURES

Normal operation of the system is as follows:

1. Use oxygen for all daylight flights over 10,000 feet and all night flights.
2. Oxygen supply lever - ON
3. Oxygen selector valve - NORMAL OXYGEN
4. Safety pressure lever - OFF

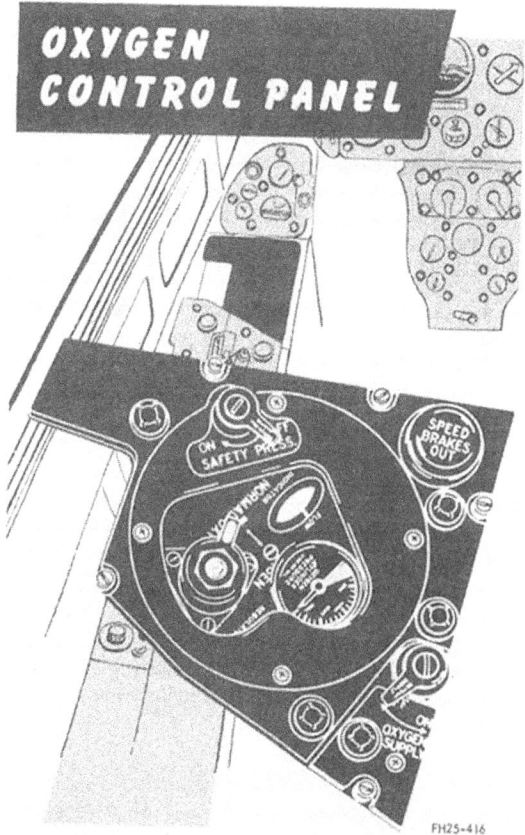

Figure 4-15. Oxygen Control Panel

5. When using oxygen, frequently check:
   a. Oxygen pressure gage. Do not exhaust supply below 300 psi except in emergency.
   b. Flow indicator to verify flow of oxygen through regulator. The flow indicator will remain open at approximately 41,000 feet. However, oxygen flow will be evident at the mask.
   c. Mask fit for leak tightness.
   d. Mask tube disconnect coupling for full emergency.
6. Upon completion of flight, oxygen supply lever - OFF.

EMERGENCY PROCEDURES

In an emergency condition, observe the following:

1. If symptoms occur which are suggestive of anoxia:
   a. Safety pressure lever - ON
2. If carbon monoxide or other noxious gases are present:
   a. Oxygen selector valve - 100% OXYGEN
3. If oxygen flow ceases:
   a. Oxygen system tube from mask tube - DISCONNECT
   b. Bail-out oxygen bottle - ACTUATE
   c. Descend to - 10,000 feet.

G-3H AUTOMATIC PILOT

The G-3H automatic pilot essentially is an electrical system designed to provide stable, accurate and automatic control of the aircraft in straight and level flight and to properly coordinate control surface movements during maneuvers. The autopilot will maintain any selected heading and will accommodate maneuvers in pitch and roll up to approximately ± 70 degrees. Incorporated into the system is a barometric device that makes possible flight at any selected barometric altitude. Synchronization devices in each axis of aircraft rotation allow engagement of the autopilot at any heading in 360° of azimuth or at any aircraft attitude within the ± 70 degree maneuvering limits in roll and pitch without an abrupt change in attitude. Undesirable yaw motions, and undesirable roll motions below 300 knots IAS are reduced to a minimum by the damper portion of the autopilot system. This damping phase of system operation may be used while the aircraft is under either manual or full autopilot control. For full autopilot operation, however, the damper system must be engaged. Aileron and rudder control surface motion during autopilot operation is not transmitted to either the manual control stick or to the rudder pedals. Stabilator motion, however, is accompanied by corresponding manual control stick motion in pitch. The stabilator feel trim system is automatically adjusted by the autopilot so that there is no necessity for a readjustment when changing over from autopilot to manual control.

Figure 4-16. Autopilot Control Panel

AUTOPILOT CONTROLS

The autopilot stick controller unit (see figure 4-16) on the right console contains all autopilot controls except the means for normal disengagement of the system. The manual trim switch on the manual control stick is used for this purpose.

Note

On airplanes with the G-2 compass system, the compass control switch on the sub-instrument panel should be placed in the COMP. CONT. (up) position before engagement of the autopilot. On aircraft with the S-2 compass system, the gyro switch on the compass control panel should be placed in the SLAVED position.

Damper Button

The damper button is depressed to engage the dampening system. Once depressed, the button will remain down until it is pulled up manually, power is removed from the system, or the emergency disconnect button is depressed. The damper button must be depressed prior to engaging the autopilot.

Engage Button

The engage button is used to place the autopilot system in full operation. This switch is not effective until the damper button has been actuated, and once depressed, it will remain down until the autopilot is taken out of the engaged mode. The autopilot can be engaged with the aircraft in any attitude within ±70° in pitch or roll and with the stick controller in detent. The attitude at time of engagement will be maintained until the aircraft is returned to level flight by depressing the level button.

Note

The engage button will not remain actuated until a two minute warm-up period has elapsed after power has been supplied to the aircraft.

Stick Controller

The stick controller enables the pilot to maneuver the aircraft, in both pitch and roll, while under autopilot control. With the stick controller in center detent, the aircraft maintains straight and level flight. By positioning the stick controller as he would the manual control stick, the pilot can induce into the autopilot signals that result in the desired maneuver. Maximum deflection in pitch will produce a climb or dive of 70° while maximum lateral deflection will produce a turn with a bank of 70°. Recovery from a climb, dive or turn can be made by returning the stick controller to detent.

Altitude Button

The altitude button is used to reference the autopilot to a selected barometric altitude. When depressed, this switch remains in the down position until it is disengaged by moving the stick controller out of detent in pitch or the autopilot is disengaged. With the altitude button actuated, the aircraft will maintain the barometric altitude, within close limits, at which the button was engaged. Prior to use of this button, the aircraft should be trimmed for straight and level flight. The altitude button should not be engaged while the aircraft is climbing or diving in excess of approximately 100 fpm. With the autopilot system operating and the altitude control button engaged (down), the limit airspeed is .90 indicated Mach number. At airspeeds above .90 Mach, with the altitude control engaged, a divergent pitch oscillation of 10 to 25 seconds per cycle will develop.

Note

Although the normal method of disengaging the altitude button is by means of the stick controller, the button also can be disengaged by disengaging the autopilot or by pulling the button up with enough force to overpower the solenoid. This latter method is recommended.

Hold Button

The hold button, atop the stick controller, is used to lock in desired aircraft attitudes. When used, this button must be pressed down when the desired attitude has been reached and must be held down until the stick has been returned to detent. Operation of this button is limited in banking maneuvers, however, in that a bank of less than approximately 15 degrees will not be held. The aircraft can be returned to level flight by operating the level button or by moving the stick controller slightly out of detent.

Level Button

The level button is used to return the aircraft to level flight, with stick controller in detent, from any attitude while under autopilot control.

Emergency Disengage Button

The emergency disconnect button is used to disengage the complete autopilot system. This button is not used for normal disengagement but only as an emergency means of cutting out the autopilot. After the emergency disconnect is released, a time delay of at least 140 seconds will occur before the full autopilot can be re-engaged. Twenty seconds elapses before the damper will engage and a 120 second delay follows damper operation before the autopilot will engage.

CAUTION

Use manual pitch trim switch on main stick to disengage autopilot. Use of emergency disconnect button with hands off primary stick can result in continued roll if disengagement is coincident with aileron servo displacement.

Pitch Trim

The pitch trim wheel section on the stick controller unit is used for minor adjustments in the aircraft's pitch attitude when under autopilot control. When initially in a neutral or zero position, this control provides a trim of 6 degrees nose down or 16 degrees nose-up. Although the amount of trim available in any direction will vary according to the initial trim, a total pitch trim range of approximately 22 degrees is available.

Note

The aircraft should be trimmed manually and the pitch trim wheel set to 5 degrees nose-up prior to full autopilot engagement.

Damper Selector Switch

Undesirable roll and yaw motions are reduced to a minimum by the damper portion of the autopilot system. A damper selector switch on the autopilot control panel is provided to give further damping selection during damper use without the autopilot engaged. The two-position toggle switch is marked YAW and YAW + ROLL. The pilot may desire high roll activity without damper effect, such as in a gunnery pass, and would select YAW damping only. However, during level flight the pilot may desire to restrict both yaw and

Section IV

roll tendencies by placing the switch in YAW + ROLL position. The roll dampening feature is "phased out" by the aneroid-operated gain control as 300 knots IAS is approached, and at that airspeed all roll dampening is effectively eliminated.

Note

Larger aileron movement will be resisted by the damper system when the damper selector switch is in the YAW + ROLL position.

Roll Potentiometer

The roll gyro trim potentiometer is a roll adjustment device used to compensate for a slight maintained bank that may exist while under autopilot control with the stick controller in detent. The potentiometer is covered by a cap. Rotation of the potentiometer inserts biases into the roll channels to correct roll attitudes.

Note

This is not a normal flight procedure and normally should not be accomplished without first attempting to check and adjust the system by ground test procedures. This adjustment should not be made unless requested by maintenance personnel.

Autopilot Circuit Breakers

Four autopilot circuit breakers, as well as amplifier and G-2 compass fuses, are located in the equipment compartment and are not accessible from the cockpit.

Note

Autopilot power requirements are such that failure of the aircraft's a-c or d-c power system will result in the automatic disengagement of the complete autopilot system.

PREFLIGHT CHECK

Prior to every flight on which the autopilot is to be used, it should be checked for proper operation. Since the full autopilot requires a 140 second warm-up period after the engine has been started, although the damper system can be engaged after only 20 seconds, it is advisable to perform this check after other preflight procedures have been completed. Also, since a number of autopilot functions depend upon flight and changes in aircraft attitude, this check will include only basic control maneuvers. Before engaging the autopilot, all control surfaces should be checked for freedom from obstructions and should be brought into a streamlined position by means of the rudder pedals and manual control stick. The stabilator should be kept in this position by holding the manual control stick until the autopilot has been engaged. After engagement,

any aileron motion can be observed from the cockpit while stabilator motion can be determined by observing action of the manual control stick. There will be no rudder motion during ground operation unless the aircraft is moved in azimuth. In this case, rudder deflection will be opposite to the direction of the turn. Upon initial engagement of the autopilot, the ailerons and rudder may move slightly. The stabilator, however, should not move. In checking aileron and stabilator movements under autopilot control, the stick controller should be moved to its limits in both pitch and roll. The ailerons should follow stick controller movement smoothly and at a constant rate regardless of how swiftly the stick controller is moved. At the same time, the stabilator leading edge should go down slightly. Aileron travel under autopilot will be only about one-fourth as extensive as under manual control. Movement of the stick controller in pitch should result in manual control stick motion in the appropriate direction. Overpowering of the autopilot in pitch can be accomplished by moving the manual control stick either fore or aft. This should require a pressure of about 20 pounds. Only slightly more than normal force should be required to manually move the ailerons while under autopilot control. The autopilot may be disengaged by actuating the manual trim switch on the manual control stick fore or aft by pulling up on the damper or engage buttons or by depressing the emergency disengage button. In the latter case, both the damper and engage button should pop up, while in the first case only the engage button should pop up.

OPERATION PROCEDURE

The autopilot can be engaged at any time while in level flight or while in a dive, climb, or bank of less than 70°. If desired, the autopilot can be engaged after take-off and while still climbing for altitude merely by depressing the damper and engage button. The stick controller, however, should be in detent at time of engagement. After the desired altitude has been attained, the aircraft can be leveled off either by depressing the level button or by disengaging the autopilot by means of the manual trim switch and manually returning or trimming to level flight. If the autopilot is disengaged, the aircraft should be trimmed for level flight before reengaging. If the level button is used, it may be necessary to adjust the autopilot pitch trim wheel for perfectly level flight. To maintain a constant altitude under autopilot control, the altitude button should be depressed after level flight if the desired altitude is attained. In no case should the altitude button be depressed while climbing or diving at a rate in excess of 100 fpm. Turns may be made with the altitude button engaged provided the stick controller is not moved out of detent in pitch. Any such movement will disengage the altitude control unit. To maneuver the aircraft while under autopilot control, manipulate the stick controller in a manner similar to normal use of the manual control stick. In making turns, however, it is not necessary to pull the stick controller back since the autopilot automatically provides "up" stabilator to prevent loss of altitude. Any turning maneuvers automatically cut out the gyro stabilized compass which

NAVWEPS 01-245FCB-501 Section IV

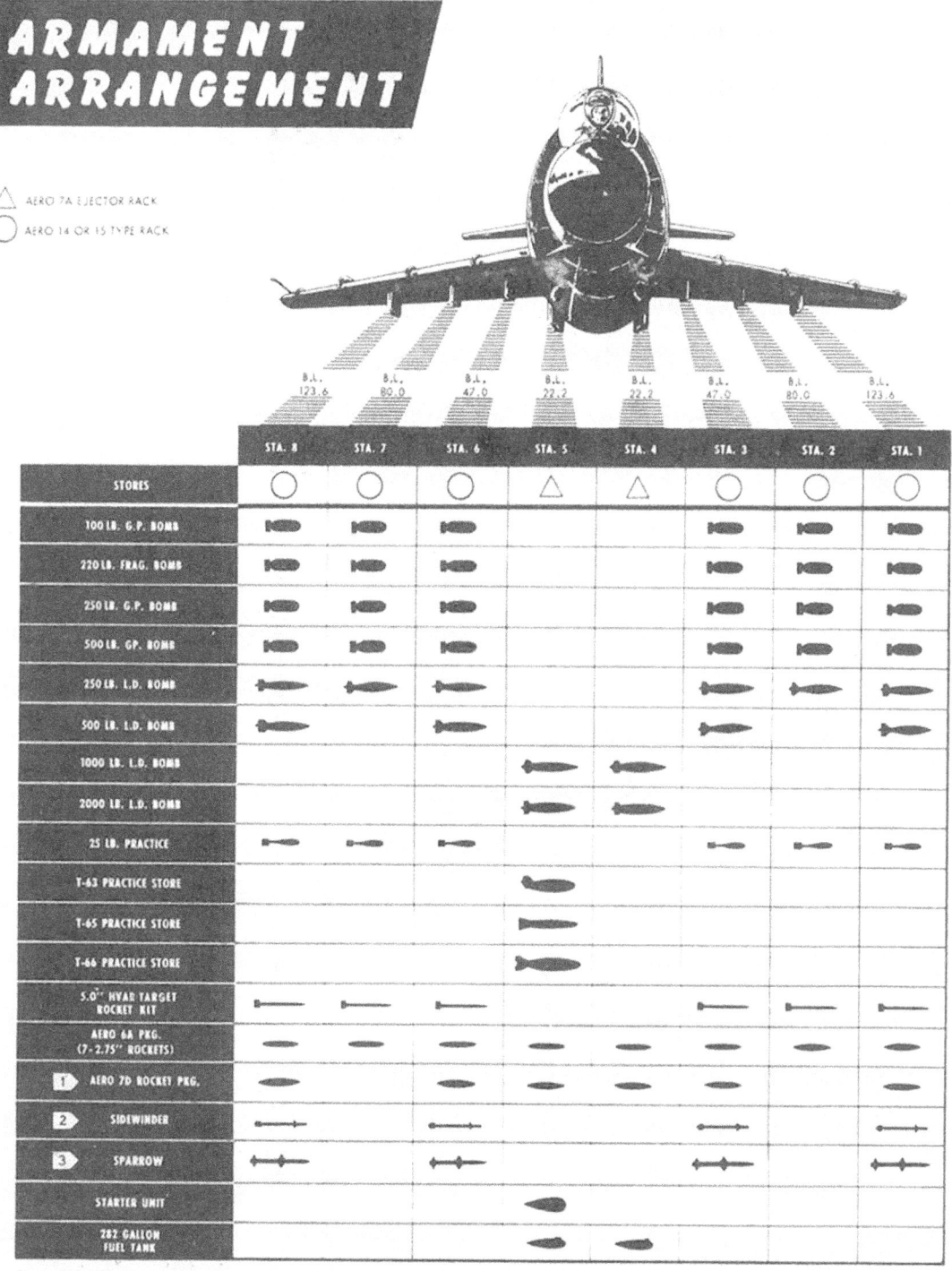

Figure 4-17. Armament Arrangement

Section IV

NAVWEPS 01-245FCB-501

provides directional headings for the autopilot. When the stick controller is returned to detent in roll, the compass is reconnected to the autopilot. In order to utilize this compass for directional control, the compass control switch on the sub-instrument panel should be in the COMP CONT (UP) position. In order to maintain any maneuver for an extended period without holding the stick controller in a deflected position, depress the hold button atop the stick controller and return the stick controller to detent. Then release the switch. This will maintain any maneuver within the range of the autopilot, except a bank of less than approximately 15°. To return to level flight, move the stick controller slightly out of detent or depress the level button. Overpowering the autopilot can be accomplished by conventional use of the manual controls. Since the aileron and rudder servos are integral parts of the manual control system, lateral movement of the manual control stick or rudder motion will move the servo units. Thus, the servos do not exert any force against stick or rudder pedal motion and overpowering will require no or only slightly more than normal force. If the servos are extended at the time of overpowering, however, there will be some loss of available control surface deflection. Also, with either the full autopilot or damper system only engaged, up to 1 1/2 inches of lateral manual control stick or one inch of rudder pedal motion may be required before there is an aileron or rudder response. This is due to servo screw jack extension in an effort to maintain a level aircraft attitude.

CAUTION

Although the stabilator, servo can be overpowered for brief periods, this should be done with caution and should not exceed a period of two seconds. If manual stick control becomes necessary, it is advisable to first disengage the autopilot by means of the manual trim switch.

To disengage the autopilot under normal conditions, actuate the manual trim switch fore or aft. This will allow manual control of the aircraft while retaining damper system operation. To disengage the damper system as well as the autopilot, pull up on the damper button, or in case of an emergency, depress the emergency disconnect button. Any of the solenoid type switches, damper, engage and altitude buttons, also can be disengaged by pulling the buttons up with enough force to overpower the solenoids. This is recommended.

Note

To avoid any possibility of control reversal at high airspeeds, it is advisable to disengage the autopilot at approximately the same airspeed as the changeover to spoiler control. These airspeeds are listed in tabular form in Section VI, figure 6-2, publication NAVWEPS 01-245FCB-501A.

ARMAMENT EQUIPMENT

Prior to incorporation of ASC 169, the airplane armament system consists of four fixed forward firing 20mm guns, six combination bomb racks and rocket launchers, with provisions for special Sidewinder and Sparrow III missile pylons. Upon incorporation of ASC 169, the two upper guns are removed. A sight unit which may be coupled with the radar system, is provided to enable the pilot to make the most effective use of the guns, rockets, missiles and bombs. The pilot is protected by armor plate located in the forward fuselage section, along the deck of the cockpit, and aft of the canopy. A gun camera is located in the lower nose section to record the results of gun and rocket firing.

GUNNERY EQUIPMENT

The MK 12 20mm guns are located in the lower outboard sides of the forward fuselage. Ammunition is supplied to the guns through flexible chutes from the four ammunition boxes located inboard of the guns. The ammunition boxes are mounted on an elevator assembly which is raised and lowered by a crank that is accessible in the nose wheel well. Each ammunition box is equipped with an electric booster motor to feed the ammunition to the guns. Spent cases and links are ducted overboard into the airstream beneath the aircraft. Armament controls are incorporated on the left outboard side of the main instrument panel (see figure 4-18). The gun trigger switch is integral with the control stick grip and operates the gun camera in addition to firing the guns.

Armament Master Switch

The armament master switch, located at the bottom of the armament control panel, is a two-position, ON and OFF, circuit breaker type toggle switch. The switch must be placed in the ON position before the guns can be charged or fired. Electrical power is supplied from the primary d-c bus.

Gun Control Switches

The two gun control switches, located on the armament control panel, are two-position toggle switches. The switch on the left controls the upper guns while the switch on the right controls the lower guns; this permits firing of the guns collectively or in pairs. The switches are normally retained in the SAFE position which charges and holds the bolt in the rear position. For operation, the switches are placed in the READY position which allows the bolt to be driven to the forward or battery position. The guns can then be electrically fired by depressing the trigger switch.

Gun Trigger Switch

A conventional trigger switch, integral with the control stick grip, energizes the gun-firing and gun camera circuits when depressed. The trigger has two detent positions. Depressing the trigger switch to the first detent energizes the gun camera and fully depressing the trigger energizes the gun-firing circuit.

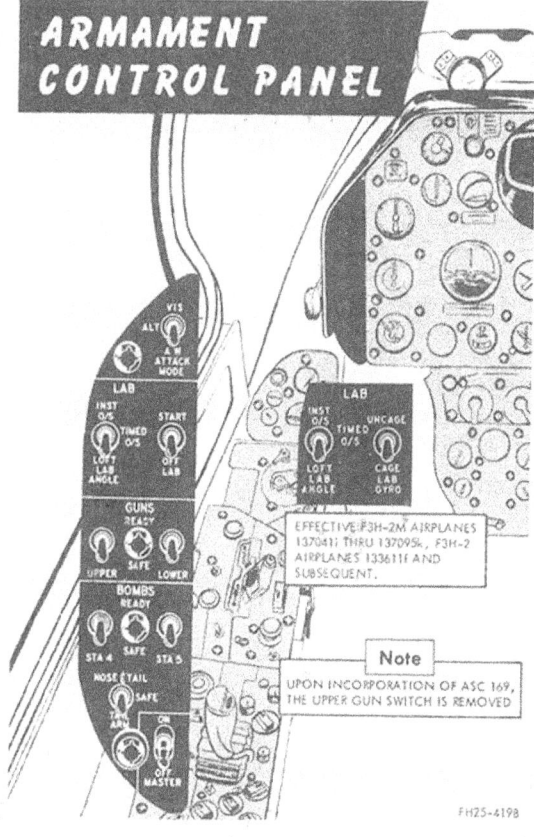

Figure 4-18. Armament Control Panel

Gun Camera

The gun camera is mounted on the bottom of the forward fuselage of the airplane. The camera works automatically when the armament master switch is ON and the trigger switch is depressed. The camera incorporates a built-in overrun device which allows it to operate from one to five seconds after the trigger switch is released. A heater and a receptacle for a lens heater is built into the camera and is operated by the camera controls. The camera may be operated without firing the guns by placing the armament master switch in the ON position, weapon selection switch to GUNS position, the guns switches to SAFE position and squeezing the trigger switch on the control stick. (See figure 1-14.)

SIGHT UNIT

The MK 11 Mod 3 sight unit, conventionally located to reflect reticle images on the center section of the windshield, is a component part of the aircraft's fire control system. A fixed reticle image is projected on the reflector plate by light directed through the fixed reticle and a series of lenses and mirrors so that the image appears on the windshield. A gyro reticle image or "pipper" is also projected on the reflector plate by light passing through a small aperture onto a fixed mirror which reflects it to the gyro mirror via a series of lenses and a gyro reticle. The range coils which restrain the sight gyro are controlled by the Mark 86 computer which in turn receives range information from the radar. Precession of the sight gyro during tracking causes the gyro mirror to position the "pipper" on the reflector plate and indicate to the pilot the computed lead for the target. The "pipper" appears centered on the target when the lead angle is correct. Electrical power for the sight unit is supplied from the a-c/d-c monitored d-c bus.

Sight Controls

(See figure 4-19.)

Gyro Switch

The gyro switch, mounted on the gun sight control panel is a three-position toggle switch with OFF as the mid position. Placing the gyro switch to either side of OFF position energizes the lead computing gyro and one of the filaments of the dual filament gyro reticle lamp.

Fixed Switch

The reticle lamp switch, mounted on the gun sight control panel, is a three-position toggle switch with OFF as the mid position. Placing the reticle lamp switch to either side of OFF position energizes one of the filaments of the dual filament fixed reticle lamp.

Dimmer-Bright Rheostat

The sight dimmer rheostat, located on the gun sight control panel, adjusts the illumination intensity of the reticle images. To increase reticle image to desired brilliancy, rotate clockwise from DIMMER position toward BRIGHT.

Fixed Range Selector Dial

The fixed range selector dial, mounted on the gun sight control panel, is graduated in hundreds of feet by calibrated markings from 6 to 60. When range between target and attacking aircraft has closed to that selected on the fixed range dial, a "within range" tone can be heard by the pilot in his headset. When attacking aircraft reaches minimum allowable range, the tone ceases, indicating to the pilot a pull-out should be initiated.

Range Volume Control

The range volume control, located on the gun sight control panel, regulates the volume of the "within range" tone. To increase volume, rotate the range volume control clockwise toward HIGH.

Gyro Uncage Switch

The gyro uncage switch is located in the throttle grip. The grip is spring-loaded to the caged position and must be rotated counterclockwise to uncage the gunsight gyro and the all-weather components of the fire control system. The grip must be placed in the uncaged position when tracking targets in either the visual or the all-weather mode in order for the fire control system to generate the correct lead.

BOMB AND ROCKET EQUIPMENT

The airplane is provided with six Aero 14 type combination bomb racks and rocket launchers, conventionally located on the underside of the wings, and two fuselage pylons provided with Douglas ejector type racks. The Aero 14 type racks are designed to carry rockets and/or up to 500 pound bombs. The two fuselage pylons, with the Douglas ejector type rack installed are designed to carry stores weighing up to 3,600 pounds, auxiliary fuel tanks or an A.P.U.. The bombs and rockets are released electrically by power supplied from the primary d-c bus and controlled by the pilot. Provisions are made for jettisoning the stores in an emergency.

Bomb and Rocket Controls

Controls necessary for selecting, arming and launching rockets, or releasing bombs, are located on the armament control panel and weapon selection panel (see figures 4-18 and 1-18). The armament master switch and the bombs switches (ready-safe switches for STA 4 and STA 5 and the arming switch) are located on the armament control panel while the weapon selector and station selector are located on the pedestal panel.

Stations 4 and 5 Ready-Safe Switches

The ready-safe switches for STA 4 and STA 5 are provided so that stores may be released in sequence, by using the station selector, or individually. With the switches in SAFE position, stores will be retained on stations 4 and 5 without interrupting the firing sequence.

Bomb Arming Switch

The bomb arming switch is provided to arm the bombs prior to releasing. The switch has three positions; NOSE & TAIL to arm the nose and tail of bombs; TAIL to arm only the tail of bombs; and SAFE to permit releasing "duds" or unarmed bombs.

Weapon Selector

Two different weapon selection panels are used in the F3H-2 airplane. These panels will be changed at local option to satisfy the armament mode required. In the "BOMB and ROCKETS" mode, a selector panel marked BOMBS, GUNS, RKTS, SPRW, SDWR and TEST is used.

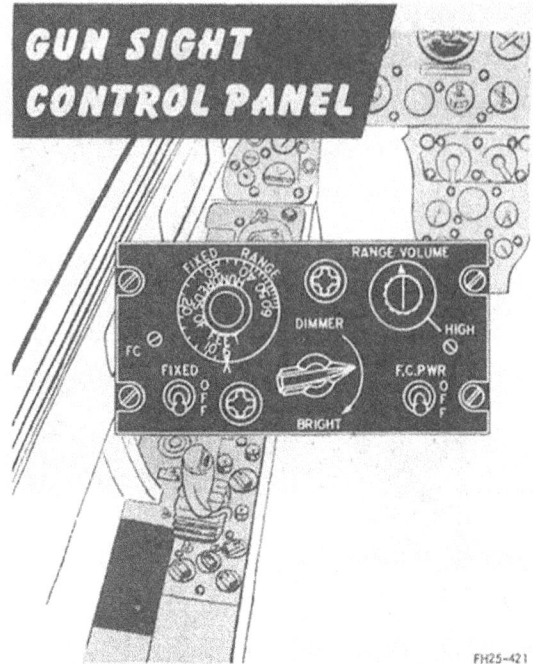

Figure 4-19. Gun Sight Control Panel

For the "MISSILES" mode, the F3H-2 airplane utilizes the missile control panel. This panel provides toggle switch station selection and a rotary weapon selector marked SPW III, SIDEWDR, GUNS and TEST.

Station Selector

The station selector is a rotary type switch provided for the pilot to select a desired station or stations from which a bomb, rocket or missile is to be launched. Selections, marked on the dial, are SINGLES, PAIRS, SALVO and stations 1-8-2-7. Turning to the No. 1 position on the dial under the sector marked SINGLES, the launching sequence will be 1, 7, 3, 5, 8, 2, 6, and 4. With No. 1 position on the dial under the sector marked PAIRS, the launching sequence will be: 1 & 8, 2 & 7, 3 & 6 and 4 & 5. The selector is so constructed and wired that each time the bomb button is depressed it will advance one notch clockwise on the dial. With the selector placed in the sector marked 1-8-2-7, bombs or rockets on these stations will be launched simultaneously, automatically advancing the selector to SALVO so that the remaining load may be launched in a like manner. With the selector placed in the sector marked SALVO, bombs or rockets on all stations can be launched simultaneously.

Bomb Button

The bomb button is located to the left of the trim switch on the control stick grip (see figure 1-18). This button, when depressed, will release bombs and launch rockets or missiles, provided that the proper mode has been selected on the weapon selector and the proper station location or firing sequence selected on the station selector (see figure 1-18). Depressing the bomb button also energizes the gun camera circuit.

Note

The gun camera will run only while the bomb button is depressed, plus approximately five seconds of automatic overrun. If full camera coverage of a rocket or missile strike is desired, the bomb button must be held down through the entire strike.

IN-FLIGHT REFUELING SYSTEM

To increase the effective striking range of the aircraft, provisions are made for the installation of an in-flight refueling kit. With the ability to refuel while airborne, the fuel load can be reduced to enable take-offs with maximum payloads.

IN-FLIGHT REFUELING PROBE

The hydraulically actuated probe is mounted on the upper right hand side of the fuselage just aft of the cockpit. In the retracted position, the probe tube nests in the fairing with the nozzle protruding forward. In the extended position, the probe nozzle is 54 inches outboard of the fuselage at approximately the 2 o'clock position. Refueling is completely automatic, requiring minimum pilot effort for the operation. Refer to Section VII of this publication for In-Flight Refueling Procedure.

Note

Prior to in-flight refueling, if the pilot has used the purge & dump switch, and the switch has not been replaced in the NORMAL position, the wing fuel transfer valve will have been closed and the wing tanks will not receive fuel. The external tanks will retain pressurization causing slow refueling of the tanks. The pilot may utilize this factor if there is known damage or malfunctioning within the wing cells. The remaining tanks will refuel normally.

ANTI-G SUIT PROVISIONS

An anti-"g" suit control valve is located on the aft section of the left console. The valve receives air from the low pressure air system and meters it to the pilot's anti-"g" suit when a force of approximately 1.75 "g's" is applied to the aircraft. A HI and LO control allows for adjustment of rate of inflation of the anti-"g" suit. In the LO range, the valve opens at 1.75 "g" and allows 1 psi of air pressure to pass to the suit for every increase of 1 "g" force thereafter. In the HI range, the valve opens at 1.75 "g" but delivers 1.5 psi per "g" force thereafter. A button on top of the valve may be manually depressed to test the anti-"g" equipment on the ground or in straight and level flight. Prior to flight with engine running, depress the manual cap to test operation of the system. On long flights, this feature makes it possible for the pilot to occasionally inflate the suit for body massage to lessen fatigue. The suit is connected to the anti-"g" system at the pilot's gear quick-disconnect assembly beneath the seat.

MISCELLANEOUS EQUIPMENT

DATA CASE

The data case is located in the aft outboard portion of the right console.

CHECK LISTS

The landing and take-off check lists are located on the main instrument panel.

SPARE LIGHTS

Spare lights for the console panels are provided the pilot. The lights are located aft of the data case on the right console.

MOORING FITTINGS

The mooring fittings are located aft of each main gear well in the nose gear retracting linkage, and at the catapult holdback hook.

COVERS AND GUARDS

The following covers and guards are provided for the airplane: engine air duct cover, pitot tube cover, cockpit canopy cover, forward compartment inlet duct cover, wing butt cover, angle-of-attack probe cover, engine afterburner cover, air inlet and exhaust duct cover, engine inlet duct guard, wing static boom cover and angle of yaw probe cover.

TOW TARGET EQUIPMENT

A tow target release mechanism is mounted to the left of the tail skid and is operated through a cable linkage from the arresting gear. To jettison the towline and target, the arresting gear is lowered which opens the latch of the release mechanism through the cable linkage.

This page intentionally left blank

Section V
Operating Limitations

SEE PUBLICATION
NAVWEPS 01-245FCB-501A
OPERATING DATA
FOR NAVY MODEL
F3H-2 AIRCRAFT

This page intentionally left blank

SECTION VI
FLIGHT CHARACTERISTICS

STALLS

In the landing configuration the airplane does not stall in the sense of older aircraft, that is, the nose or wing does not drop abruptly nor is there a sharp build-up in stall buffeting and associated loss of control effectiveness in the normal flight region. Rather, the airplane merely begins to "mush" as the speed is reduced below 125 knots. The controls remain positive down to very low speeds and the airplane can be rotated easily at low speeds. However, accurate control of airplane sinking speed is not possible below 125 knots IAS (minimum safe speed) at landing gross weight. A full stall with accompanying buffet occurs only after decelerating through the "mush" range.

WARNING

SPEEDS LOWER THAN 125 KNOTS IAS AT LANDING GROSS WEIGHT SHOULD NOT BE USED IN THE LANDING PATTERN

There is no buffet warning as the minimum safe speed (125 knots IAS) is approached nor is there any appreciable stall buffet until the "mush" speed range is reached. This condition exists with flaps and slats extended. With flaps and slats retracted (gear extended), buffet warning exists; the minimum safe speed is approximately 140 knots IAS at landing gross weight. It is therefore necessary for the pilot to carefully observe airspeed and attitude when approaching the minimum safe speed. A stall warning vibrator or "stick shaker" acting in conjunction with the angle-of-attack indicator, warns the pilot of an approaching stall condition in the landing configuration. However, a sufficient margin exists to allow the pilot to return to a proper flight attitude by normal reaction to the warning. Refer to Stall Warning Vibration and Angle-Of-Attack Indicator in Section I.

CAUTION

- Slats should be used at slow speeds. Slat selection is made in conjunction with flaps; however, the slats can be extended by the emergency pneumatic system for emergency slow flight or landing situations. Refer to Section III, Landing Emergencies.

- With full external fuel tanks installed and approach power removed, the nose will begin to drop at approximately 130 knots IAS.

WARNING

The pilot must avoid speeds below 125 knots IAS in the landing configuration at altitudes lower than 2000 feet since excessive rates of descent are easily developed. Recovery from excessive rates of descent should be effected in a similar manner to a normal stall recovery together with prompt application of power.

ACCELERATED STALLS

Reaching a full stall in accelerated flight is improbable due to the heavy buffet and maneuvering instability preceding the accelerated stall. Buffet begins as an airplane tremor and develops into progressively heavier buffet as the normal load factor (g) is increased. Because of buffet amplitude, the airplane becomes unstable as a tactical gun platform prior to developing the full stall. For this reason and because of the very heavy buffet preceding the stall, there will rarely be occasion to fully stall the airplane in accelerated flight.

Section VI

SPINS

Intentionally spinning the aircraft is prohibited. However, flight tests have shown the following characteristics: The airplane is spin-resistant; it must be stalled, then forced to sideslip into the roll-off. Neutralizing stabilator prior to roll-off will stop the spin entry, upright or inverted. Maintaining near zero sideslip angle will prevent any spin. This spin resistance is more pronounced on left spins, due to the gyroscopic effect of engine rotation. Once established, spins are quite oscillatory, early turns being characterized by wallowing and hesitations. Inverted spins are somewhat smoother, but exhibit the same characteristics if allowed to develop for several turns. It is usually necessary to hold against-the-spin aileron in order to fully develop a spin.

SPIN RECOVERY

Upright spins are characterized by hesitations in rotation; recovery can usually be effected by neutralization of control during such hesitations, and may nearly always be effected by use of with-the-spin aileron. Recoveries from upright spins are characterized by a very rapid cessation of rotation, whereas inverted spin recoveries normally exhibit a slower cessation of rotation and a steepening attitude, ending up in a vertical roll. The airplane can be flown out at all recovery altitudes once rotation has ceased. Care should be exercised during all recoveries to avoid entering an accelerated stall, and it should be kept in mind that at least 10,000 feet is necessary to complete recovery from a fully developed spin. The following procedures have been found most effective for spin recovery:

Upright Spin Recovery

1. Apply one-half (1/2) aileron deflection in direction of spin.
2. Apply full or partial opposite rudder.
3. Maintain partial back stick while rotation is ceasing.
4. When rotation has almost ceased, neutralize all controls.
5. Fly airplane out of dive.

WARNING

If aileron is held opposite to the direction of rotation during upright spins, the spin characteristics will be steady and nonoscillatory. Recovery from a steady-state spin will require positive use of the recovery technique listed above.

Inverted Spin Recovery

1. Hold stick as far forward of neutral as possible.
2. Apply rudder opposite to direction of rotation.
3. Apply one-half (1/2) aileron opposite to direction of spin (same side of cockpit as rudder), and opposite to direction of turn needle deflection.
4. When rotation has almost ceased and airplane attitude becomes very steep, neutralize all controls.
5. Fly airplane out of dive.

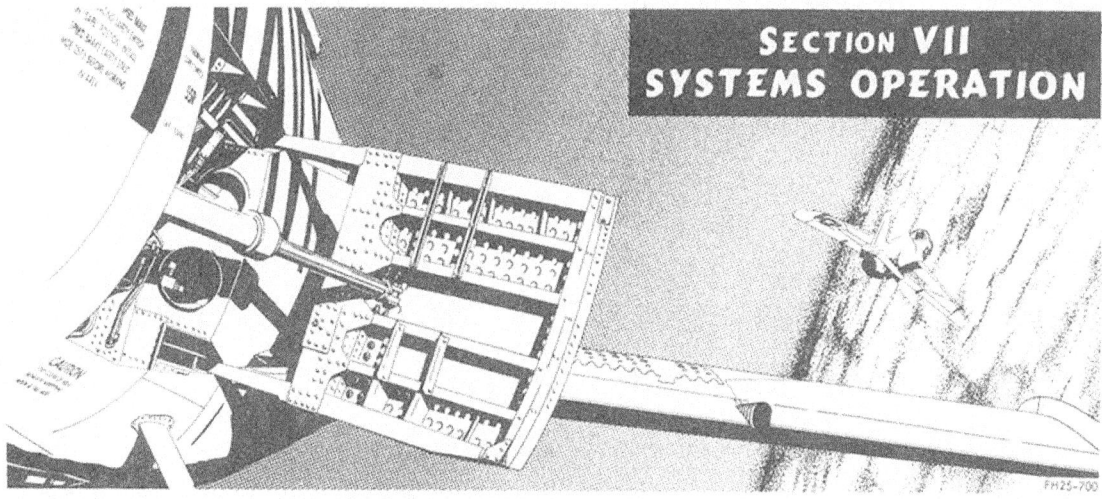

SECTION VII
SYSTEMS OPERATION

FLIGHT CONTROLS

LATERAL CONTROL SYSTEM

Lateral stick movements are transferred to the control end of the aileron hydraulic cylinders through a conventional series of push rods and bell cranks. Actually this mechanical linkage connects to the autopilot servo unit which is located forward of each hydraulic cylinder. This autopilot servo acts as a damper when the autopilot is not being used. The aileron cylinders are tandem units, each section containing an independent cylinder, one of which obtains hydraulic fluid under pressure from the power hydraulic system and the other receives pressure from utility hydraulic system. Normal operation is by both systems, however, the ailerons may be operated by either system in event of failure of the other. At high speeds, deflection of ailerons on one hydraulic system will be limited, but at low speeds, control response is the same as with normal operation. Flow of hydraulic fluid to the aileron hydraulic cylinders from both the power and utility systems is controlled by internal servo valves located in the cylinder assembly. When the stick is held stationary in any position, the servo valve traps hydraulic oil on both sides of each piston. In effect, this locks the piston hydraulically until the stick is moved again. Air loads cannot move the aileron, nor will these loads be felt at the control stick. The fact that air loads cannot move the surface is a very important feature since it reduces any flutter tendency. To reduce high-speed aerodynamic loading of the outer wing panels, and to increase roll rate, a unique lateral control system has been incorporated. In this system aileron control functions exactly as in the conventional system up to a predetermined airspeed, at which point a shift is made to a spoiler system which assumes lateral control until the airplane again enters the lower speed range.

Spoiler Control System

At predetermined airspeeds (see figure 6-2, Section VI) an airspeed switch acting on a solenoid hydraulic selector valve causes hydraulic pressure to be directed to a hydromechanical shift mechanism which transfers lateral stick movements mechanically to the spoiler actuators. During spoiler operations, ailerons revert to the neutral position. The spoilers are actuated by dual hydraulic cylinders with integral servo valves. The actuators work simultaneously, but independent of one another, one being operated by power control system pressure, and the other by utility system pressure. In the event of failure of one hydraulic system, the other actuator will still function. As an added safety feature, the shift mechanism is spring-loaded to the aileron control condition. In the event of failure of the power control hydraulic system, system pressure bleeds off through a restrictor allowing a time interval of about 5 minutes before spring pressure begins to regain the aileron condition.

CAUTION

Pilots should be aware that if a-c or d-c power is interrupted to the autopilot even momentarily the aileron servos will lock in that position, regardless of the deflection (up of 15° total authority) at the time power was interrupted. Re-engaging the autopilot or roll damper momentarily will eliminate this trapped signal condition. The roll damper should always be engaged momentarily prior to flight to ascertain that the aileron servos are in the neutral position.

Note

No provisions are made for autopilot control of the spoilers. However, when engaged the auto-

LATERAL CONTROL SYSTEM

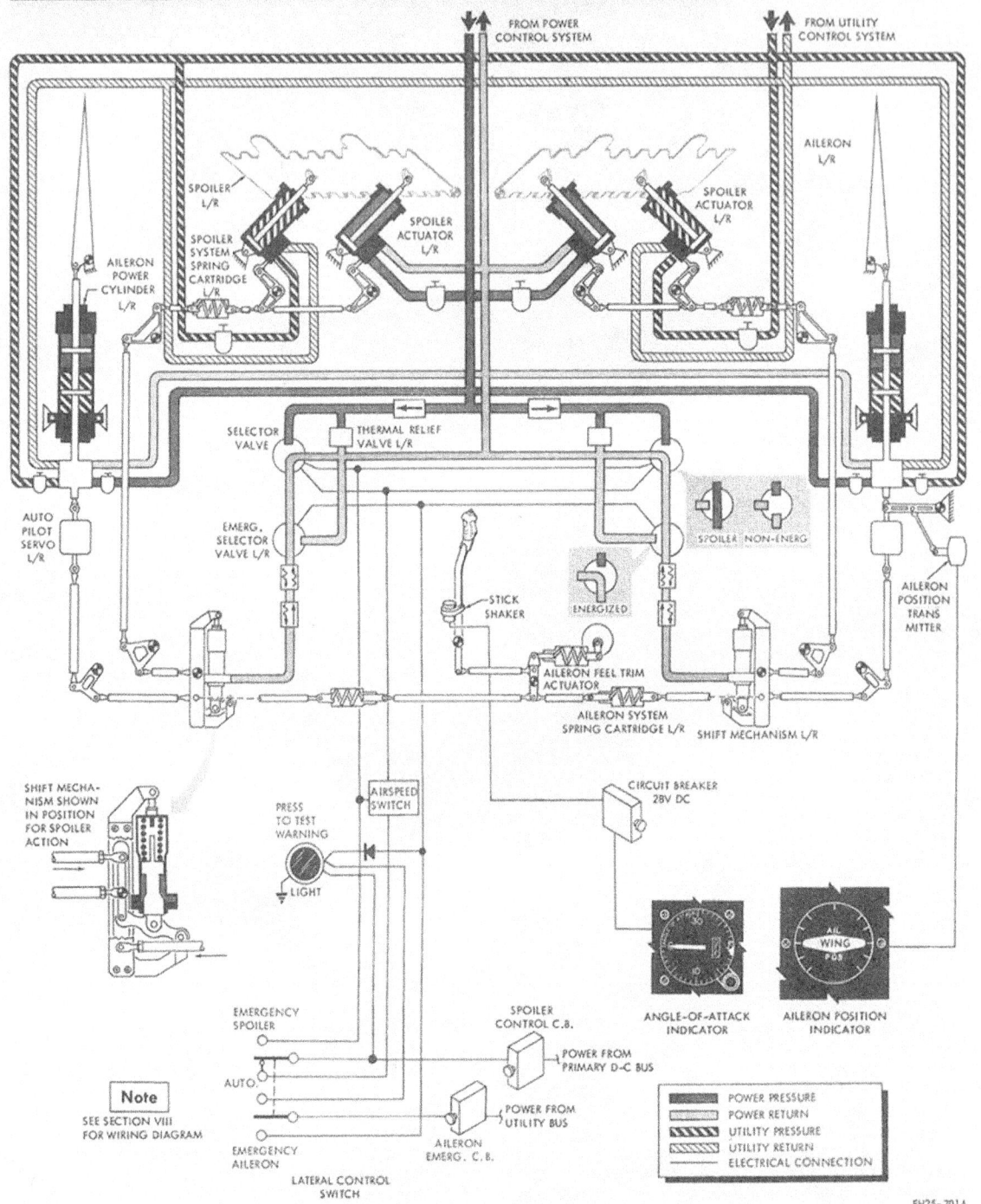

Figure 7-1. Lateral Control System

pilot continues to deflect the ailerons, even though they are neutralized during spoiler operation. Since autopilot aileron correction will oppose spoiler movement, there is a possibility of control reversal, and a definite reduction in control effectiveness. It is recommended, therefore that the autopilot is disengaged above spoiler switchover airspeeds (see figure 6-2, Section VI, Confidential Supplement to this handbook).

Lateral Control Switch

A guarded three-position switch, marked EMERG SPOILERS, AUTO., and EMERG AILERON is located on the inboard, left hand side of the glare shield. The purpose of this switch is threefold. In the EMERG AILERON position the switch transfers lateral control of the aircraft back to the ailerons in the event of electrical power failure. In the AUTOMATIC position the lateral control system functions normally, the spoilers being actuated by the airspeed switch at predetermined airspeeds. A guard has been provided which centers the switch toggle to prevent inadvertently moving the switch out of the automatic position. The EMERG SPOILERS position has been provided for ground test of the spoilers. This position overrides the airspeed switch allowing the spoilers to be operated while the airplane is on the ground. Electrical power to the EMERG SPOILER position of the lateral control switch is provided by the primary d-c bus, power to the EMERG AILERON position is from the utility d-c bus, and AUTO. is an open position receiving power from the airspeed switch. A light located above the switch illuminates when the switch is in any other position than AUTO. Electrical power to this light is supplied by the utility d-c bus.

Lateral Control Feel System

Due to the irreversibility of the aileron hydraulic cylinders, there is no stick force in a power control system except that necessary to overcome system friction and cylinder valve force. To provide you with a "feel" or stick force, it is necessary to simulate the force by artificial means. In the aileron system, this is accomplished by a double-acting spring cartridge so arranged that the spring is compressed when the stick is moved in either direction from neutral. The spring cartridge will return the control stick to neutral when the stick is displaced and then released. Stick force is constant for a given degree of aileron deflection regardless of airspeed. To enable you to trim the airplane laterally, one end of the feel system spring cartridge is connected to an electric actuator. The actuator is controlled from the trim switch on the control stick, and it positions the spring cartridge to maintain any desired lateral stick position required for trimming. Due to the placement of the spoiler control shift mechanism within this aileron control system linkage, the simulated feel and trim systems accomplished in the aileron linkage also function identically in the spoiler control system. As an added safety feature, the push rod system includes another spring cartridge in each wing which acts as a push rod during normal operation. If any jamming occurs in the aileron or linkage, the spring may be compressed by pilot effort. This prevents the stick from becoming locked and allows operation of one aileron, should the other aileron become jammed due to battle damage. The breakout force of this spring is 17 pounds and to fully compress it (full aileron deflection) requires 35 pounds so the pilot can expect an additional stick force of from 17 to 35 pounds if one aileron should jam.

STABILATOR CONTROL SYSTEM

The stabilator is a movable, one piece, longitudinal control surface, commonly referred to as a "slabtail". Pilot control is by normal fore and aft stick movements through a series of push rods and bell cranks acting on a dual hydraulic cylinder. Normal operation is by means of both power and utility system hydraulic pressure. The stabilator can also be operated by either hydraulic system upon the failure of the other, but the maximum obtainable stabilator deflection will be somewhat less at high speeds. Normal aerodynamic forces acting on the stabilator are not transmitted to the irreversible type dual power cylinder.

Stabilator Feel System

The stabilator "feel" system is designed to give stick forces that are proportional to airspeed. This is accomplished by three units: The bellows, the balance springs, and the trim bell crank. The bellows contain a diaphragm, one side of which is subjected to ram air pressure with the other side exposed to static pressure. The resulting differential produces a force that is transmitted to the trim bell crank and balanced against the balance springs. The trim bell crank and attendent linkage is so designed that any longitudinal stick movement will upset this balanced condition and produce a resistance or stick force. Changes in airspeed will also upset this balance of bellows and spring forces, resulting in a nose up or nose down stick force. To permit retrimming to zero stick force, an actuator is provided within the trim bell crank which, when operated by the control stick trim switch, positions a portion of the trim bell crank with respect to its pivot point, to again balance the bellows and spring forces. This action may be compared with a common see-saw; that is, if a heavy weight is to be balanced by a lighter weight, the heavy weight must be moved closer to the fulcrum. The push rods in the feel system have override springs to enable the pilot to manually override the feel system in the nose down direction in the event of a runaway trim actuator. A viscous damper is used in the stabilator feel system linkage which increases the stick forces for rapid movements of the stick. This feature tends to prevent exceeding the structural limitations of the airplane inadvertently. A "bob" weight is attached to the control stick to produce additional stick force as "g's" are applied.

Section VII
NAVWEPS 01-245FCB-501

STABILATOR CONTROL SYSTEM

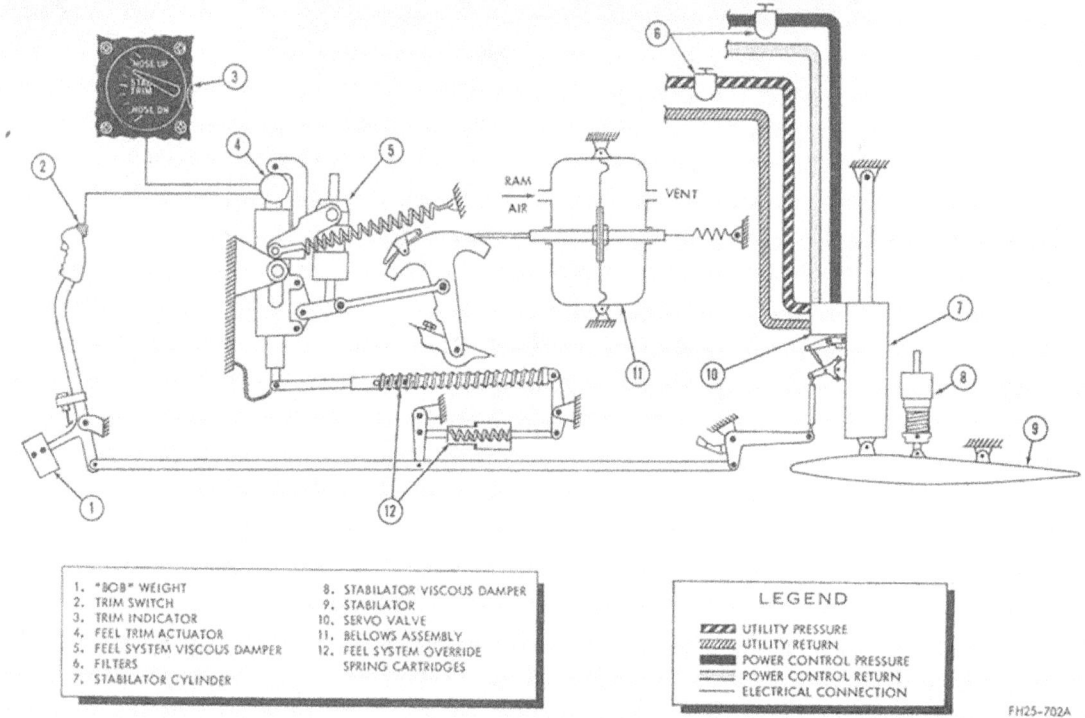

1. "BOB" WEIGHT
2. TRIM SWITCH
3. TRIM INDICATOR
4. FEEL TRIM ACTUATOR
5. FEEL SYSTEM VISCOUS DAMPER
6. FILTERS
7. STABILATOR CYLINDER
8. STABILATOR VISCOUS DAMPER
9. STABILATOR
10. SERVO VALVE
11. BELLOWS ASSEMBLY
12. FEEL SYSTEM OVERRIDE SPRING CARTRIDGES

LEGEND
- UTILITY PRESSURE
- UTILITY RETURN
- POWER CONTROL PRESSURE
- POWER CONTROL RETURN
- ELECTRICAL CONNECTION

FH25-702A

Figure 7-2. Stabilator Control System

RUDDER CONTROL SYSTEM

The rudder control system employs standard rudder pedals, a push rod system, a hydraulic cylinder, the rudder and feel system. Pedal movement is transferred by push rod system to the autopilot servo forward of the rudder irreversible control cylinder. Aerodynamic forces are not transmitted to the rudder pedals and an artificial feel system is employed to simulate these forces. The rudder operates on the utility hydraulic system only. In the event pressure is lost in this system, an internal by-pass valve opens in the rudder hydraulic cylinder. The cylinder then acts as another link in the rudder system and the rudder can be moved manually by the pilot. A viscous damper is coupled directly to the rudder to prevent flutter during certain critical flight conditions.

Rudder Feel System

The rudder feel system consists of a double-acting spring cartridge, and a single-acting hydraulic cylinder. Below 225 knots, the feel forces are supplied entirely by the spring cartridge. Above 225 knots, the airspeed switch turns on utility hydraulic pressure to the single-acting cylinder.

Note

Pressure in this cylinder requires greater pilot effort to move the rudder pedals. An electric trim actuator is connected to one end of the spring cartridge. Trimming of the rudder system is accomplished by operation of this actuator which lengthens or shortens the coupling between the feel system and the rudder push rod system. The actuator is controlled electrically from the cockpit.

TRIMMING THE AIRPLANE

There are no trim tabs on the airplane. This is possible because with irreversible controls, air loads are balanced by the hydraulic cylinders and are not felt at the stick. Trimming the plane is accomplished by positioning the entire control surface. The aileron and stabilator trim switch is located on the stick grip and the rudder trim is aft and slightly outboard of the throttle. The stabilator has a feel trim indicator located on the left hand sub-panel. Rudder and aileron position indicators are located on the left-hand subpanel and should be trimmed to zero deflection prior to take-off.

124

WING FOLD

The outer wing panel fold and spread operation is accomplished from the pin pull lockpin handle at the wing fold line underside. This door operates the linkage to the lockpin. The three-position wing fold switch is mounted above the door and when positioned in the FOLD position, the pin pull selector valve directs pressure to the pin pull actuating cylinder, retracting the wing pins and closing the pin pull limit switch, which energizes wing fold selector valve to direct pressure to extend the wing fold actuating cylinder and fold the wing. When positioned in the SPREAD position, the wing fold selector valve directs pressure to compress the wing fold actuating cylinder and spread the wing panel. Upon reaching the SPREAD position, the down limit switch is closed, energizing the pin pull selector pin pull actuation cylinder inserting wing pins. Closing the pin pull lockpin handle inserts the lockpin in the forward wing pin. When folding or spreading the outer panels, observe the following precautions:

1. Jury struts - REMOVED
2. Do not fold or spread wings broadside to the blast of an aircraft's engines.
3. Do not fold or spread wings in winds over 45 knots.
4. Doors 65, 66 and 93 - INSTALLED
5. Flaps and slats - RETRACTED

FOLD WINGS

To fold wings, proceed as follows:

1. Pin pull lockpin handle - OPEN
2. Wing fold switch - FOLD
3. Return the switch to the STOP position after folding the panel.
4. Repeat steps 1, 2 and 3 to fold the opposite panel.

Note

● Install jury struts after folding wings.

● Wings cannot be folded with slats extended nor can the slats be extended with wings folded, except by the emergency pneumatic system.

SPREAD WINGS

To spread wings, proceed as follows:

1. Wing fold switch - SPREAD
2. After panel has spread and pins have extended close the pin pull lockpin handle.
3. Repeat steps 1 and 2 to spread opposite panel.

Note

Red warning posts, which are attached to the pinlocks, will be flush with wing skin if pinlocks are fully inserted. The posts will extend above the wing surface inboard of the wing fold line when pinlocks are not inserted.

CAUTION

● Ashore. Whenever aircraft are parked or towed with wings folded, jury struts will be installed. Taxiing with wings folded and jury strut not installed will be held to a minimum.

● Afloat. Jury struts will be installed at all times wings are folded except immediately prior to spreading wings before launching.

ENGINE STARTER COMPRESSOR UNIT

The engine is equipped with a pneumatic type starter which requires an external compressed air source for operation. The engine starter compressor unit is used to furnish the compressed air source. This unit is a portable, self-contained "power package". It consists of a centrifugal gas turbine compressor, generator-recharging battery power system, and a fuel supply system, all contained within a streamlined pod which can be mounted on station 5 beneath the fuselage. Also, the unit may be used as portable ground equipment by extending its three stowable wheels. Engine starting may be accomplished without removing the unit from the station 5 pylon by connecting the compressed air line which is stowed in two sections in the aft end of the pod. The completed line and an electrical line from the pod are connected to the airplane through fuselage door 33 beneath the left wing. The other end of the air line connects to the compressor unit via an elbow adapter which is stowed in the pod tail cone when not in use. Starting procedure normally requires assistance of a ground crew member to connect and start the compressor and indicate to the pilot when the compressor is developing the proper air load. Pilot control is over ingress of air to the starter air control valve (refer to Engine Start Switch) and starter by manipulation of the engine start switch. In the event that the A.P.U. is to be used for air pressure only, i.e., without the electrical lines being connected, a ground crewman must actuate the air bleed and shutoff valve on the A.P.U. (the starter button will be inoperative). The pilot must signal to the crewman that the engine rotor has reached self-sustaining speed, and that the valve should be closed. The standard signal for this is a closed hand waved over the head. The signal should be made when the engine speed is approximately 36% rpm. Operating instructions on the compressor unit are located inside the left hand access door of the unit. After the engine has been started (refer to Section II) the air line adapter elbow and electrical line may be disconnected from the airplane and pod and stowed in the pod.

CAUTION

Failure of the engine starter button to "pop up" automatically or failure of the ground crewman to close the air bleed and shutoff valve at the proper time (36 to 40% engine rpm) may result in overspeeding the starter with a possibility of disintegration or seizure of the starter turbine.

Section VII NAVWEPS 01-245FCB-501

Figure 7-3. Air Starter Pod

CAUTION

Make sure the tail cone of the compressor unit is open prior to starting and closed after stowing the compressed air line. The proper compressor unit to use is MDE25235-5 or -7. If an alternate starting air source is used, the temperature must not exceed 355 degrees Fahrenheit and pressure must not exceed 64 psi.

WARNING

Areas adjacent to the compressor unit exhaust exit and the airplane starter exhaust exit are hot.

ENGINE OPERATION

COMPRESSOR STALL

Compressor stall can be induced during ground or flight operations by an engine control system malfunction, faulty operating technique, or an engine malfunction. Compressor stall can be contributed to or caused by flying in or crossing through the jet wake of a leading aircraft. The resultant increase in compressor inlet temperature appreciably affects the engine stall margin. Compressor stall results in a very rapid increase in exhaust gas temperature, a decrease in engine speed, and engine vibration; flight reports have indicated that it may also be associated with explosive reports from the engine. If compressor stall should occur, immediately retard the throttle to IDLE to break the stall and reduce turbine outlet temperature. If this is unsuccessful, retard the throttle to OFF to eliminate the stall, then make a normal ground or air start.

Note

Initiation of afterburner will not break a surge or stall.

WARNING

After clearing a weather area, shift de-ice switch to AUTO. Stall tendency is increased when the engine de-ice system is operating and may be critical in combination with rapid power changes.

STALLS DURING STARTING

Compressor stall may occur during engine starting, especially on hot days, if the starting air pressure, temperature, or a combination of the two, is too low. The air supply under any of these conditions does not contain the energy required by the engine pneumatic starter to assist the engine in accelerating from "light-off" rpm to self-sustaining or idle rpm. The result is insufficient airflow through the compressor and compressor stall with an accompanying surge, which is recognized by lack of increase in rpm, abnormal increase in turbine outlet temperature and engine roughness. If the proper starting unit is used, starting stall should not occur (refer to ENGINE STARTER COMPRESSOR UNIT). However, should stalling begin to occur during starting the corrective action is to manipulate the throttle between IDLE and OFF, being careful not to move completely to the OFF position at any time. Engine rpm should be observed, and at 41 percent the starter button manually PULLED up (if it has not "popped-up" automatically) to shut off the air supply to the starter. If the throttle is inadvertently moved into OFF position and the engine "flames-out" the start should be aborted and the engine allowed to drain off residual fuel prior to the next starting attempt. If turbine outlet temperature is dropping rapidly below 550° at 50% rpm, compressor stall is not likely to occur. However, if turbine outlet temperature is holding at 550° or higher, a compressor stall is probable. Stall may be prevented by modulating throttle between 45% and 50% rpm to start temperature down.

IN-FLIGHT REFUELING PROCEDURES

1. Approach tanker plane from the rear and slightly below the refueling drogue.
2. Maintain a position approximately 100 feet aft, 50 feet below and a little to the left of the drogue until airplane is trimmed and formation speed is determined.
3. Extend probe by placing the fuel selector switch to AIR-REFUEL.

4. Before engaging drogue, turn OFF the following items:
    a. Radar system
    b. Fire control system
    c. Direction finder group
    d. Radio compass system
    e. IFF system
5. Maintaining a moderate to slow rate of closure, fly the probe nozzle into the drogue cone.

Note

- Rapid rate of closure will move drogue forward too fast for proper reel-in, thus causing slack in the hose and resulting in a violent whipping action which may damage the probe or drogue.

- The recommended airspeeds for drogue engagement are 250 to 300 knots IAS.

6. After contact is made, slowly fly drogue forward approximately ten feet to initiate refueling operation. Green light on tanker indicates refueling is in progress.

Note

With increased weight due to additional fuel, a constant power increase is necessary to maintain a formation position with tanker.

7. When tanks are full, reduce speed slightly to disengage probe from drogue coupling.
8. Retract probe by moving fuel selector switch out of the AIR-REFUEL position.

Note

Prior to in-flight refueling, if the pilot has used the purge and dump switch, and the switch has not been replaced in the NORMAL position, the wing fuel transfer valve will have been closed and the wing tanks will not receive fuel. The external tanks will retain pressurization causing slow refueling of the tanks. The pilot may utilize this factor if there is known damage or malfunctioning within the wing cells. The remaining tanks will refuel normally.

EMERGENCY SYSTEMS CHECK-OUT PROCEDURES

EMERGENCY LANDING GEAR CHECK (AIRBORNE)

1. Pull landing gear circuit breaker.
2. Pull the landing gear handle to the EMERGENCY position (approximately 1 inch) gear will extend.

To return the system to normal operation:

3. Push handle forward to the gear down position; wait approximately 30 seconds to allow high pressure air to vent from the emergency lines.

4. With handle remaining in the gear down position, close landing gear circuit breaker. Note that pneumatic pressure is building up before retracting landing gear.

Note

Erratic gear operation during the initial up cycle will occur if the gear up position is selected instead of gear down prior to closing the circuit breaker. This is due to not repositioning the emergency shuttle valve in the system.

5. Landing gear system is now ready for normal operation.
6. Ground charge pneumatic system to 3000 psi if airplane system has not replenished loss in flight.

WARNING

If this procedure is not followed, an extreme high pressure condition may develop as a result of having hydraulic and pneumatic pressures in the system simultaneously, or by air compressor recovery with air pressure trapped in the cylinders. This extreme pressure may rupture the hydraulic reservoir, filter or heat exchanger, with the resultant loss of the hydraulic system, and the added fire hazard of having hydraulic fluid free to run into the engine section.

FUEL BOOST PUMP CHECK

With the engine running and fuel tanks full, pull a-c and d-c boost pump circuit breakers and check fuel boost pressure for readings between 15 and 19 psi. This indicates pressure supplied by the negative "g" boost pump. (Obviously low fuel in the feed tank will uncover the negative "g" pump, therefore, no pressure will be supplied.) Push the a-c boost pump circuit breaker in and recheck the pressure gage for pressures between 20 and 30 psi. Pushing the d-c boost pump circuit breaker in may result in a 1 to 5 psi increase in boost pump pressure. It is important to check the pumps in the order indicated because the d-c pump will normally supply full pressure without the a-c and/or negative "g" boost pumps.

FUEL LOW LEVEL / FUSELAGE TRANSFER CHECK

1. After take-off, leave the fuel selector in the FUS position until 1000 pounds of fuel has been consumed.
2. Momentarily switch to WING position and check the fuel transfer light OUT. Return to the FUS position.
3. Check the fuselage fuel quantity when the fuel low warning light illuminates. The fuselage fuel quantity should be 1500 ± 100 pounds.

4. Switch the fuel selector to the WING position and transfer all wing fuel.
5. Return to FUS position.

Note

If the aft tank flapper valve is stuck open or the aft fuel transfer pump is inoperative, the fuel low warning light will illuminate at approximately 2800 pounds of fuselage fuel.

EMERGENCY SLATS CHECK (AIRBORNE)

1. Flap and slats circuit breaker - PULL
2. Slats control switch - EXTEND
3. Actuate emergency handle.

To restore system to normal operation:

4. Raise emergency handle; wait 30 seconds for air to bleed from system.
5. Reset circuit breaker.
6. Flap and slats switch - RETRACT

WARNING

If the above check sequence is not followed, loss of hydraulic system may occur.

WHEEL BRAKE OPERATION

The power boosted brake cylinders do not exhibit a great amount of resistance, or pedal pressure consequently, violent or forceful application of toe pressure may "bottom out" the brake cylinder pistons. A check valve is built into the cylinder to relieve the excess hydraulic pressures encountered during these full-pedal brake applications. The opening of this check valve is accompanied by a sudden drop in the foot pressure required. This may lead the pilot to believe that he has lost his brake pressure, however, he is actually applying the maximum brake pressure available. Care should be exercised in brake application as they are extremely powerful, and can be locked quite easily. A fully locked wheel usually offers LESS retardation than very light normal braking. If one wheel is locked during application of the brakes, there is a very definite tendency for the airplane to turn away from that wheel and further application of brake pressure will offer no corrective action. This produces a rapidly decreasing coefficient of friction between the skidding tire and the runway, while the coefficient of friction between the other tire and the runway remains near optimum for braking effectiveness. It is therefore, apparent that a wheel once locked will never free itself until brake pressure to that wheel is reduced sufficiently to permit the wheel to rotate. It has been found that optimum braking occurs when the wheel is in a slight skid. The wheel continues to rotate, but at a speed of approximately 80 to 85 percent of its normal free rolling rotational speed. Increasing the rolling skid above approximately 15 to 20 percent will only decrease the braking effectiveness. Since no anti-skid system is fitted, recognition of maximum braking force is strictly a matter of pilot sensitivity. As with other examples of operating "on the limit", the only sure way of determining maximum braking effort is to exceed it. Since this is seldom a desirable technique, the pilot should attempt to mentally catalogue his body response to normal braking, in order to more readily recognize the maximum, if an emergency should require it. For all conditions, normal and emergency, the most desirable braking technique is a single, smooth application of the brakes with a constantly increasing pedal pressure (to just below the skid point) as the airplane decelerates. In the event of a reduction in retardation being felt while exercising maximum braking, pedal force must be fully released in order to allow the skidding wheels to regain full rolling speed before further application of brakes.

CAUTION

Do not pump the brakes at any time, since this action will only reduce the amount of constant pressure available at the brakes and will tend to store heat energy within the brake assembly.

If it is suspected that the brakes have been used excessively, and are in a heated condition, the airplane should not be taxied into a crowded parking area. Peak temperatures occur in the wheel brake assembly from 5 to 15 minutes after maximum braking and is further transferred to the tire. To prevent brake fire and possible tire explosion, the specified procedures for cooling brakes should be followed. It is recommended that a minimum of 15 minutes elapse between landings where the landing gear remains extended in the slipstream, and a minimum of 30 minutes between landings where the landing gear has been retracted to allow sufficient time for cooling between brake applications. Additional time should be allowed for cooling if brakes are used for steering, crosswind taxiing operation, or a series of landings.

Section VIII
CREW DUTIES (Not Applicable)

SECTION IX
ALL WEATHER OPERATION

ALL WEATHER FLIGHT

Aircraft covered by this handbook have all weather capability only when water traps (ASC 143 Rev. b) and J71-A-2E engines are installed. Otherwise, the aircraft are restricted from flight in clouds with ambient temperatures below freezing. Such flight involves the hazard of engine seizure as a result of moisture ingestion. However, flight tests show that the modified aircraft are capable of ingesting rain, freezing rain, ice, and hail under the most severe condition and without seizure or damage to the engine.

Note

If conditions permit, flight through severe weather conditions should be accomplished in the MIL range to eliminate the possibility of rpm droop while in afterburner. 95% is recommended; see IN THE STORM, SECTION IX.

INSTRUMENT FLIGHT

WARM UP AND GROUND CHECK

1. Gyro on SLAVE position and synchronized (S-2 Compass)
   a. Gyro on COMP. CONT. position and reset to correspond with inner card (G-2 Compass).

WARNING

Gyro compass and Attitude Gyro must have a 3 minute warm up period after both d-c and a-c power are applied before indications are reliable.

2. Align Attitude Pitch indicator for proper attitude (7 1/2° NOSE UP)

3. Determine that UHF channels are pre-set for tower control, departure control, FAA frequencies, etc.
4. Check radio navigation gear for proper operation.

TAKE-OFF

1. Visually line up aircraft with runway. Allow aircraft to roll forward a few feet to align nose-wheel.
2. Check runway heading with Radio Magnetic indicator.
3. Pitot heat ON if precipitation or flight through clouds is anticipated.
4. Engine De-ice switch to MANUAL if icing or freezing precipitation conditions exist.
5. Check instruments.
6. Hold brakes and advance throttle to MIL power.
7. Release brakes; maintain heading with brakes until rudder becomes effective (approx. 50 knots).
8. When airborne, establish a safe rate of climb.
9. Retract wheels.
10. When safe airspeed and altitude are attained retract flaps and slats (170 knots).

CLIMB

1. Trim for climb.
2. Avoid prolonged climbs thru areas where precipitation or icing are known or suspected to exist.
3. Avoid if possible angles of bank in excess of 30°.

CAUTION

A nose down trim condition may result during flight through icing conditions. This is caused by icing of the ram air pick up line of the stabilator feel trim system.

131

Section IX　　　　　　NAVWEPS 01-245FCB-501

Note

When climbing through freezing precipitation, and afterburner operation is mandatory it may be initiated with de-ice switch in MANUAL provided that restrictions in Section V, page 27, are observed.

CRUISE

1. Align Attitude Indicator for level flight.
2. Pitot heat OFF and Engine anti-icing system to AUTO position if cruising in clear air.

RADIO AND NAVIGATION EQUIPMENT

The VHF and UHF equipment will give reliable and static free operation under the most severe weather conditions.

HOLDING

1. Upon arriving at holding fix, assume maximum endurance power setting and airspeed for airplane weight, configuration and altitude.

DESCENT

1. Manual heat control lever to the full DEFROST position.
2. Pitot heat ON if precipitation or flight through clouds is anticipated.
3. Engine De-Ice switch to MANUAL if icing or freezing precipitation conditions exist.
4. Speed brakes OUT.
5. IDLE power (88% if precipitation or icing conditions are encountered).
6. Best penetration airspeed.
7. In descending turns, limit the angle of bank to 30°. Constant rates of descent are increasingly difficult to maintain as angles of bank increase over 30°.
8. Pitot heat OFF and Engine De-Ice switch to AUTO upon reaching clear air, or if time does not permit, after landing.

Note

- Missions to be flown under instrument conditions may require an extra margin of time and fuel and should be planned accordingly.

- EGT temperatures as low as 135°C may be encountered during a descent with IDLE power.

NIGHT FLYING

The following checks and information are in addition to those given for normal instrument flight.

ON ENTERING AIRPLANE

1. Interior lighting - CHECK
2. Navigation lights and exterior lights - CHECK

3. Flashlight - CHECK
4. Interior lighting - ADJUST
5. Oxygen supply - CHECK

DURING FLIGHT

Adjust interior and instrument lights to desired brilliance.

APPROACH

If remaining oxygen supply permits, use 100% prior to traffic pattern.

COLD WEATHER OPERATION

Normal operating procedures as outlined in Section II should be adhered to with the following additions and exceptions:

1. Check entire airplane for freedom from frost, snow and ice; see that all light snow, ice or frost is removed.

Note

Do not chip or scrape away ice as damage to airplane may result.

WARNING

Snow, ice and frost collections in the airplane surface are a major flight hazard. The result of this condition is loss of lift and increased stall speeds.

2. Shock struts and actuating cylinders free of ice and dirt.
3. Fuel drain cocks free of ice and drain condensate.
4. Pitot tube, fuel vents, all ice or dirt removed.
5. All exterior covers removed.

WARM UP AND GROUND CHECK

Turn cockpit air-conditioning system ON as soon as possible after starting.

WARNING

- Be sure all instruments are allowed adequate warm-up period and are operating normally before take-off.

- If any abnormal sounds or noises are present during starting, discontinue starting and apply intake duct preheating for 10 to 15 minutes.

TAXIING

1. Avoid taxiing in deep or rutted snow since frozen brakes will likely result.
2. Increase space between airplanes while taxiing at sub-freezing temperatures, to insure safe stopping distance and to prevent icing of airplane surfaces by melted snow and ice from the jet blast of a preceding airplane.

BEFORE TAKE-OFF

1. Make normal power run-up.

Note

The thrust developed by the engine in low temperature is noticeably greater and brake demands will be greater to hold position.

CAUTION

If engine icing conditions are encountered, place the engine de-ice switch in the MANUAL position. A slight momentary EGT rise (5° to 10°C) may be noted, which insures that the de-icing air valve is functioning properly.

2. Pitot heat switch - ON

LANDING

If snow and ice tires are installed, use brakes intermittently and carefully to keep tread from filling and glazing.

Note

Hard braking on ice or wet runways can result in dangerous skidding or fishtailing.

AFTER LANDING

1. Pitot heat - OFF

BEFORE LEAVING AIRPLANE

1. Leave canopy partly open, unless weather prevents to permit circulation. This helps prevent canopy cracking from differential cooling and decreases windshield and canopy frosting.
2. Check all protective covers installed.

HOT WEATHER OPERATION

Normal operating procedures as outlined in Section II should be adhered to with the following additions and exceptions:

Note

If outside temperature is above 100°F, the turbine out temperature will read RED LINE before the throttle is in the full MIL position on the quadrant.

WARNING

When entering clear high ambient air temperatures, check to insure the de-ice switch is in the AUTO position. Engine surge tendency is increased when the de-ice system is operating, and may be critical in combination with rapid power changes.

CAUTION

Do not attempt take-off or engine operating in a sand storm or dust storm if avoidable. Park aircraft crosswind and shut down engine to prevent sand or dirt from damaging engine.

TAKE-OFF

The required take-off distances are increased by temperature increase. Check required take-off distances vs temperature charts, figures A-9 and A-10.

APPROACH AND LANDING

Ground roll will be considerably greater at high temperatures. Check landing distance chart, figure A-127.

BEFORE LEAVING AIRPLANE

1. Leave canopy open to permit circulation.
2. Check all protective covers installed.

TURBULENT AIR AND THUNDERSTORM FLYING

Sometime in the course of a pilot's career he is required to fly through a thunderstorm because of the importance of a mission or when there is no alternate route available. It is essential therefore, that a pilot understand and employ the proper technique for a safe flight through a thunderstorm. Passage through some storms is rough, the rain heavy brilliant lightning, turbulence is usually moderate to severe, and the hazards of ice and hail can be expected. These conditions plus the possibility of structural failure within the aircraft, resulting from overcontrolling by the pilot and engine droop tendency, demand constant alertness. Proper technique and procedure, however, will minimize or eliminate these dangers. Throttle setting and pitch attitude are the keys to this technique.

APPROACHING THE STORM

A straight course through the storm will expose the aircraft to precipitation and turbulence for the shortest period of time. In storms associated with frontal activity a course perpendicular to the squall line is desirable for the most rapid penetration. Power setting and flight attitude required for desired penetration airspeed should be established well before reaching

133

the storm. This power setting and flight attitude should be maintained throughout the storm. This is the best means of maintaining a constant speed and flight path through the storm. Fluctuations in barometric pressure and wind gust conditions will cause the pressure instruments to vary to such an extent as to be unreliable. Pitot icing may cause the airspeed indicator to indicate an airspeed considerably below the actual airspeed. In severe thunderstorms, the actual altitude may vary several thousand feet due to extremely strong up-and-down drafts. Before storm entry perform the following:

1. Pitot heat - ON
2. De-ice switch - MANUAL
   A slight momentary EGT rise (5° to 10° C) may be noted as the de-ice switch is placed in MANUAL insuring that de-icing air valve is functioning properly. This EGT rise may be more apparent on a ground de-ice system check.
3. Autopilot - OFF
4. Harness - SECURE AND LOCKED
5. Turn off radio equipment rendered useless by static.
6. Daylight floodlights - ON
7. At night, turn interior lighting to brilliance to minimize lightning effects.

IN THE STORM

1. Maintain pitch attitude and if very heavy precipitation is encountered, use 95% rpm until clear of the heavy precipitation area. Refer to Section III for rpm droop and recovery in heavy precipitation.

   #### Note
   The best airspeed is a compromise between controllability, stress and engine droop. At high airspeeds, controllability is better, but greater stress and engine droop tendency is imposed. At lower speeds, structural stress upon the aircraft and engine droop tendency is less but controllability is somewhat sacrificed. Refer to Section V for recommended airspeed range for flight in severe turbulence.

2. Devote attention to flying and be aware that engine droop may occur in areas of heavy precipitation.
3. Maintain heading. Do not make turns unless necessary.
4. Use as little longitudinal control as possible to maintain desired attitude.
5. The artificial horizon will give the best indications of relative flight path for pitch and bank corrections.

GCA PATTERN

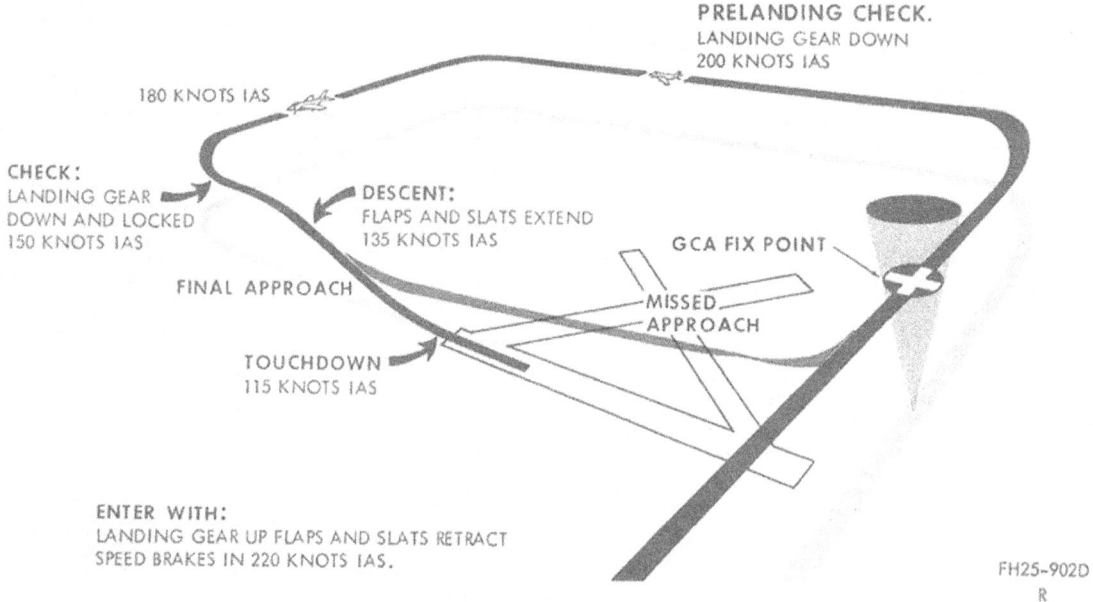

Figure 9-1. GCA Pattern

PRECIPITATION

Prior to entering precipitation conditions where freezing conditions exist, switch pitot heat ON and de-ice to MANUAL. F3H-2 airplanes 145232q and subsequent, and all airplanes in which ASC 143B have been accomplished, have a water-removal system. This system collects and removes from the walls of the engine air inlet ducts some of the water entering the ducts. The actuation of the pitot-heat switch starts a jet pump which assists in the extraction of collected water at low airspeeds (below 250 knots). When the de-ice switch is actuated, a slight turbine outlet temperature rise (5° to 10°C) should be noted indicating that the de-icing air valve is functioning properly. The turbine outlet temperature may rise above the engine red-line temperature momentarily (2 to 3 seconds) until the amplifier responds and opens the exhaust nozzle to reduce the temperature to redline.

Note

The possibility of rpm droop will be considerably reduced if flight through precipitation is made in the MIL range. 95% is recommended; see IN THE STORM.

Flight tests have shown that sufficiently heavy precipitation while in afterburner can result in considerable rpm reduction and possibly cause the afterburner to blow out, even with an operative de-ice system. This drop in rpm is basically caused by (a) fuel control pressure-sensing aneroid blockage by ice which decreases the fuel available to the engine, and (b) increased mass flow and engine cooling due to ice and/or water which increases the fuel required to run at stabilized rpm. Greater precipitation and indicated airspeeds tend to promote droop. A full rpm droop is characterized by a rapid (5 to 20 seconds) decrease in rpm to about 83 to 85% where the inlet guide vanes close, exhaust nozzle opens and the turbine outlet temperature will drop to 520° to 600°C. The result is a cycling condition in which the inlet guide vanes and exhaust nozzle oscillate, accompanied by a very small rpm change (approximately ±1%). A less critical rpm droop is characterized by a rapid reduction of 1 to 3% as the fuel control pressure-sensing probe becomes blocked. At this point the rpm may either stabilize or continue to decrease very slowly. In either case, once the rpm decreases below the fuel control-governor break point (95 to 96%) droop will continue rapidly to approximately 85%. Under still less critical conditions, droop may never extend below 96 to 98% rpm. However, the pilot should be aware that full droop is possible. Recovery from a full rpm droop to 85% should be effected by moving the throttle from afterburner to a position slightly below full military. This will result in quicker recovery and a higher stabilized rpm than that obtainable at full Military. The rpm will increase during droop recovery and stabilize between 96 and 98% within 30 seconds until the fuel control pressure-sensing probes become unblocked, at which time the rpm will recover fully. Although the F3H has all-weather capability as demonstrated in actual severe weather flight tests, prudence dictates that areas of very heavy precipitation be avoided. If droop is encountered, the proper recovery procedures will restore almost full engine power. Departure from the area of precipitation will then promote normal engine operation, at which time maximum power may safely be resumed.

WARNING

Do not retard throttle to OFF on a mistaken assumption that the engine has flamed out. If engine flame-out has occurred, engine rpm will fail to respond to throttle movement and the turbine outlet temperature will quickly drop to approximately 300°C and continue to decrease.

CAUTION

- When hail is encountered, it may be going up, suspended by drafts, or falling, so change of altitude is not logical. The course should not be changed, but a reduction in airspeed should be made to reduce danger of structural damage.

- If icing is encountered, determine what type and if glare or glaze icing, climb to higher altitude, maintaining normal climb by advancing power. Pilot should be aware that engine rpm droop is possible.

- When in freezing precipitation, descent should be conducted at an RPM above 88% to ensure that the inlet guide vanes are open and that sufficient hot bleed air is available to de-ice these vanes.

This page intentionally left blank

Appendix I
OPERATING DATA CHARTS

SEE PUBLICATION
NAVWEPS 01-245FCB-501A
OPERATING DATA
FOR NAVY MODEL
F3H-2 AIRCRAFT

This page intentionally left blank

ALPHABETICAL INDEX

Asterisk (*) denotes chart or illustration

A

A-C Power Supply System. 19
    generator 19
    generator warning light 36*
    selector switch. 19
Accelerometer. 31
Access to Cockpit. 49, 52*
Afterburner 1, 10, 11
Aileron Control System 22, 121
    artificial feel. 24, 123
    trim. 24, 123
Air Conditioning, Cabin. 91
Airplane Description 1
Air Ducts 8
Airspeed and Mach Indicator 30, 32*
Air Start Procedure 67
Air Starter Pod 126
All-Weather Operations. 131
    cold weather procedures 132
    flight in turbulence or thunderstorms 133
    hot weather procedures 133
    instrument flight 131
    night flying 132
Altimeter 30, 32*
Angle-of-Attack Indicator 31, 32*
Antenna Locations. 101*
Antenna Switch. 98
Anti-G Suit 115
Anti-Icing System 95
Approach and Landing. 62, 63*
Approach Light System 29
Armament Arrangement. 111*
Armament Equipment 112
Armament Control Panel 113*
Arresting Gear. 29
Arresting Gear Control 29*
Automatic-Opening Safety Belt 40
Automatic Pilot, G-3H 108
    altitude button 109
    circuit breakers 110
    control panel 108*
    damper button 108
    damper selector switch 109
    description 109
    disengaging. 109
    disengaging button, emergency. 109
    engage button. 108
    engaging procedures 109
    operation 110
    pitch trimming wheel. 109
    preflight check 110
    return to level flight 109
    stick controller. 109

B

Before Entering Cockpit. 49
Before Leaving Airplane 64

Before Starting Engine 55
Bellows Failure. 88
    complete 88
    partial 88
Block Letters 4*
Bomb and Rocket Equipment 114
Brakes. 29, 128
Brake Failure 73
Brakes, Speed 27
    switch. 27

C

Cabin Pressurization and Air Conditioning . . . 91
    defrosting procedure. 94
    emergency ventilation 93
    heating procedure 94
    pressurization procedure 94
    control switch 91
    temperature 93
    control switch and rheostat. 94*
    ventilation 93
Canopy. 34
    emergency handle 34
    emergency operation 34
    external emergency handle. 38
    external switch 37
    internal switch 34
Catapult Holdback Handle 7
Catapult Launch 64
Check List. 49
    approach 62, 63*
    before starting engine 55
    before take-off 60
    before taxiing. 58
    climb. 62
    engine air start. 63
    engine shutdown 64
    exterior inspection. 50*, 51*, 52*
    interior check 53
    landing 62
    night take-off. 61
    stopping engine. 64
    take-off 60
    wave-off 63*, 66
Climb 62
Clock .32*, 33*
Cockpit
    access 52*
    lights 108
Cold Weather Procedures. 132
Control Stick 25
Control Stick Grip. 26*
Cooling
    afterburner. 9
    engine 9
    oil 11

D

Danger Areas	56
Data Case	115
D-C Generator Failure	84
Defrosting	94
Descent	62
Description of Airplane	1
Direction Finder	98
Disengaging Autopilot	109
Ditching	76
Ditching versus Ejection	84

E

Ejection Seat	38, 39*, 40, 41, 42*, 43*, 44, 45, 46*, 47*
Martin Baker seat inspection points	54*
Ejection Limitations, Martin-Baker Seat	83*
Ejection Procedures	77, 78*, 79*, 80*, 81*
Ejection Sequence	80*, 81*
Electrical Fire During Flight	72
Electrical Power Supply	18
a-c power supply	19
d-c power supply	18
Electrical System Schematic	16*, 17*
Emergency Afterburner Modulation	70
Emergency Hydraulic Power	22, 86
Emergency Hydraulic Pump Handle	22*
Emergency Jettisoning	89
Emergency Landing Gear Operation	86
Emergency Opening of Canopy	76*
Emergency Slat Operation	86
Emergency Systems Checkouts	127
Emergency Ventilation	93
Engaging Autopilot	112
Engine	1
air start	67
anti-icing system	95
de-ice system check	96
ducting system	8
failure	67
after take-off	68
after take-off	68
during take-off run	68
fire detection system	34
fire during flight	72
ground run-up and checks	58, 59, 60
starting procedures	57
Entering Cockpit	53
Escape Procedure	77
Exhaust Nozzle	8, 70
Exterior Inspection	50*, 51*, 52*
Exterior Lighting	104
control panel	104*
External Canopy Switch	37

F

Face Curtain Pull Handle	40, 44
Failure of Bellows	88
Failure of Electrical Power	84
Failure of Engine	67
Failure of Generators	84
Failure of Stabilator Trim	88

Fire	71
detection system	34
during flight	72
warning light	34*
while starting	72
Flaps	26
Flaps and Slats Control Switch	26*
Flap Position Indicator	26, 28*
Flight Characteristics	62
Flight Control System	22, 121
lateral control schematic	122*
lateral control system	22, 121
lateral control feel system	24, 123
rudder control system	25, 124
stabilator control schematic	124*
stabilator control system	25, 123
stabilator feel system	25, 123
Flight in Turbulence and Thunderstorms	133
Folding Wings	124
Forced Landing	73, 74*
Fuel Low Level/Fuselage Transfer Check	128
Fuel System	
afterburner system	10
airplane system	11*, 12
control panel	14*
engine system	2, 6*
fuel boost system	13
fuel transfer system	13
fuel quantity data table	13*
fuel quantity gage	18
schematic	12
Fuselage Fuel Vent	15
Fuselage Lights	105

G

G-2 Compass System	103
GCA Pattern	134*
General Arrangement	2*
Generator Failure	84
Generator Switch, A-C	19
Generator Warning Lights	34*
Gun Sight Unit	113
Gun Sight Control Panel	114*
Gunnery Equipment	112

H

Heat and Vent Control Panel	95*
Heat, Ventilation and Pressurization Schematic	92*
Heating, Cabin	94
Hot Weather Operation	133
Hydraulic System	12, 21
equipment operated	21
pressure indicator	21
schematic	20*

I

Icing	132
IFF Control Panel	100*
IFF Radar	99
Ignition System	9
Inertia Reel	45
In-Flight Refueling System	115
procedure	127

Instruments 8, 32*, 33*
   accelerometer 31
   airspeed 30
   altimeter 30
   angle-of-attack 31
   attitude indicator 31
   flap position indicator 28*
   fuel quantity indicator 18
   hydraulic pressure indicator 21
   inlet fuel pressure gage 8
   landing gear indicator 28*
   radar altimeter 100
   radio compass 102
   rate-of-climb 30
   S-2 compass 104
   tachometer 8
   turbine outlet temperature 8
   turn-and-slip 30
Instrument Lights 105
Interior Lighting 105
Interior Lights Control Panel 105*

L

Landing 62
   flat tire 75
   forced landing 73
   normal 62
   under spoiler control 75
Landing Gear System 27
   emergency lowering 28, 86
   landing gear control 27*
   main gear 27
   nose gear 27
   position indicator 28
Landing Pattern 62, 63*
Lateral Control System Schematic 122
Lateral Control System 23, 123
Left Console 36
Left Subpanel 38
Lighting Equipment 104
   console 106
   daylight floodlights 106
   exterior 105
   formation lights 105
   fuselage 105
   instrument 105
   interior 105
   navigation 105
   taxi lights 105

M

Main Difference Table 3*
Main Instrument Panel 32*, 33*
Main Landing Gear 27
Maximum Glide Distance 72*
Microphone Button 98
Mirror Landing Approach 65
Miscellaneous Equipment 115
   anti-G suit 115
   check lists 115
   covers and guards 115
   data case 115
   mooring fittings 115
   spare lights 115
   tow target equipment 115

N

Navigation Radio System (TACAN) 102
Night Flight 132
Normal Landing 62
Normal Procedures 49
Nose Gear 27

O

Oil System 11
Operating Procedures
   all-weather 131
   emergency 67
   normal 49
Operating of Communications Equipment . . . 96
Oxygen System 106
   control panel 107*
   emergency procedure 108
   normal checks 107
   preflight checks 107
   safety pressure 107
   schematic and duration chart 106*
   selector valve 107

P

Partial Stabilator Feel Bellows Failure 88
Pedestal Panel 33
Pilot's Ejection Seat 38, 39*, 40, 41, 42*,
   . . . . . 43*, 44*, 45*, 46*, 47*
Pitot-Static System 30
Pneumatic System 22
   pneumatically operated equipment 22
   pneumatic system schematic 24*
   pressure indicator 23
Power Control Panel 5*
Preflight Exterior Checks 50*, 51*, 52*
Pressurization, Cabin 91
Pressurization Schedule 93*

R

Radar Altimeter 100
Rate-of-Climb Indicator 30
Right Console 37
Right Subpanel 18*
Rocket Equipment, Bomb and 114
RPM Droop in Heavy Precipitation 69, 135
   recovery procedure 69, 135
Runaway Feel Trim 88

S

S-2 Compass System 104
Safety Belt, Automatic-Opening 40
Seat Adjustment Switch 39
Servicing Diagram 48*
Shipboard Operating Procedure 64
Slats 27
Smoke Elimination 73
Speed Brakes 27
Spins 120
Spoilers 23, 121
Spreading Wings 125
Stabilator Control System Schematic 124*

Alphabetical Index

Stabilator Failure
    bellows 88
    trim 89
Stalls 119
Stall Warning Vibrator 26
Stalls During Starting 127
Starter Compressor Unit 125
Starting Procedure 56, 57
Starting System 10
Stopping Engine 64
Systems
    cabin pressurization, air conditioning 93
    electrical 18
    fuel 2, 10, 12
    hydraulic 21*, 12
    in-flight refueling 115
    landing gear 27
    oil 11
    oxygen 106
    pneumatic 22

T

Table of Communication and Associated
  Electronic Equipment 97
Tachometer 8
Take-Off 60
Taxi Lights 105

Throttle 7*
Thrust and Nozzle Position Indicator 8
Trim Position Indicator 60*
Turbine Outlet Temperature Gage 8
Turn-and-Slip Indicator 30

U

UHF Radio 96
UHF Remote Channel Indicator 96
UHF Control Panel 98

V

Variable Area Exhaust Nozzle 8
Variable Nozzle Control Failure 70
Ventilating Control Panel 95*
Ventilation, Cabin 91

W

Warning Lights 34
Wave-Off 66
Windshield Defrosting 94
Wing Flaps and Slats 26
Wing Folding and Spreading 125

©2009 Periscope Film LLC
All Rights Reserved
ISBN #978-1-935327-73-8   1-935327-73-9

Aircraft At War DVD Series

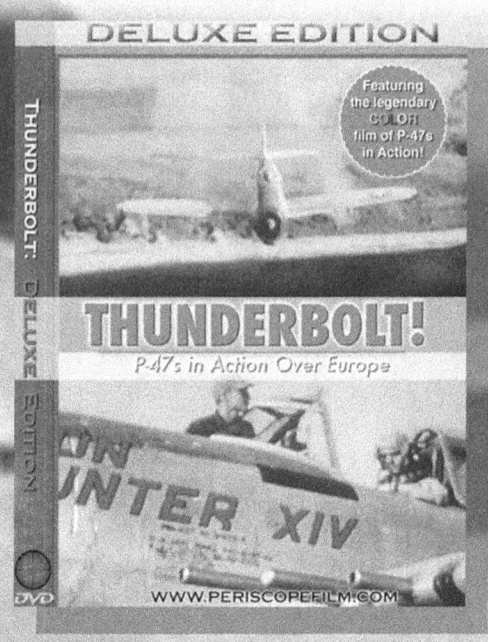
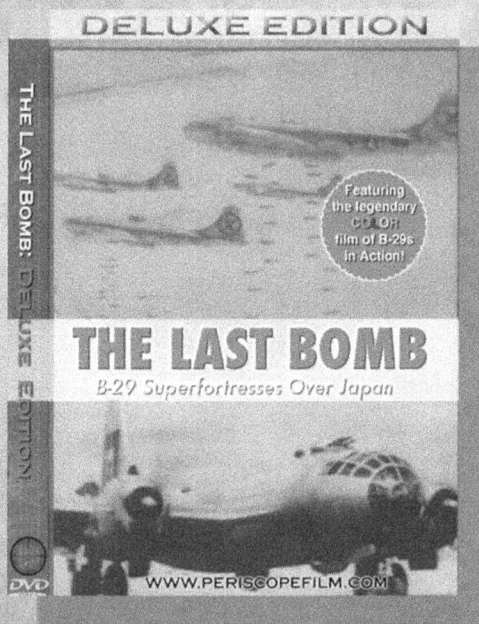

Now Available!

Epic Battles of WWII

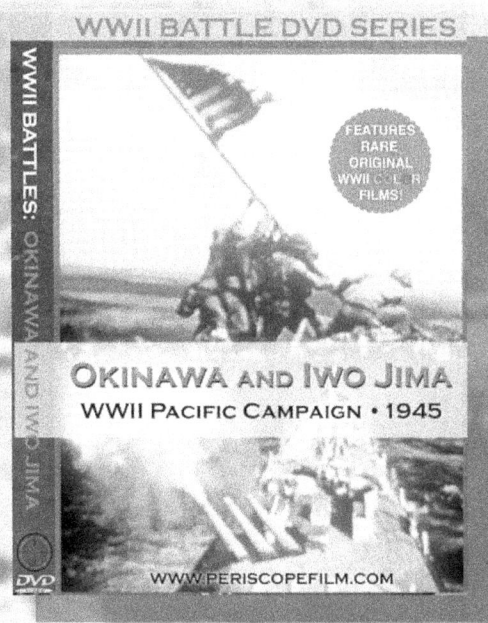

Now Available on DVD!

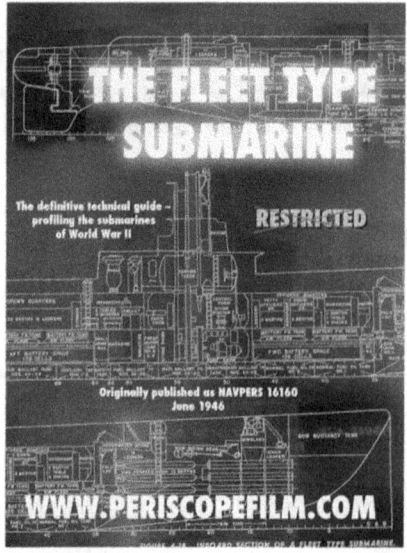
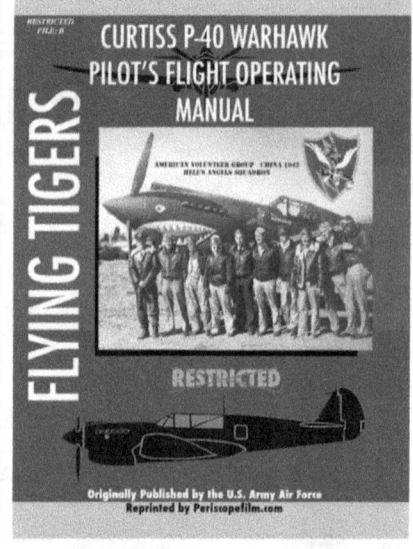

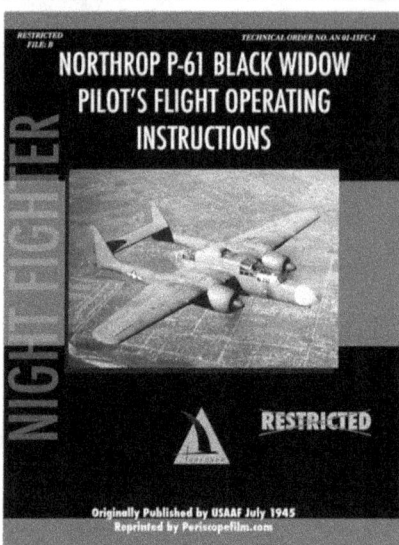

ALSO NOW AVAILABLE
FROM PERISCOPEFILM.COM

www.ingramcontent.com/pod-product-compliance
Lightning Source LLC
Chambersburg PA
CBHW080511110426
42742CB00017B/3076